THE WORLD OF
WILLIAM
SHENSTONE

William Shenstone by Edward Alcock.

THE WORLD OF
WILLIAM
SHENSTONE

Audrey Duggan

BREWIN BOOKS

First published by
Brewin Books Ltd, 56 Alcester Road,
Studley, Warwickshire B80 7LG in 2004
www.brewinbooks.com

ISBN 1 85858 251 2

A Cataloguing in Publication Record
for this title is available from the British Library

Typeset in Times
Printed in Great Britain by
Cromwell Press

CONTENTS

Acknowledgements   vii

Preface   viii

Introduction   ix

Chapter 1   School Days and Early Influences   1

Chapter 2   Oxford and Friendship   5

Chapter 3   Early Poetry   12

Chapter 4   Harborough and Mickleton   15

Chapter 5   Settling In: 1736 – 1740   19

Chapter 6   Man about Town   22

Chapter 7   The Schoolmistress   26

Chapter 8   Mary Arnold and Mary Cutler   32

Chapter 9   Cheltenham and the Pastoral Ballad   38
             – A Chapter Ends: 1743-1745

Chapter 10   The Luxborough Letters   44

Chapter 11   A Garden of Poetry and Emblem   60

Chapter 12   Songs, Ballads and Elegies   75

Chapter 13   The Pensées   83

Chapter 14   Friends and Family: 1745 – 1755   86

Chapter 15   "People in our Parish"   96

Chapter 16   New Horizons and the Miscellanies   100

Chapter 17   'Cleone' and Dodsley's 'Select Fables'   109

Chapter 18   Percy, the "Reliques" and the Mulberry Tree Plot   116

Chapter 19   Thomas Hull and the Final Curtain   122

Chapter 20   The Will   130

Chapter 21   Conclusion   132

Bibliography   134

Personalia   138

References   143

List of Illustrations   151

Appendices   154

Index   165

To the memory of William Shenstone Esq in whose verses were all the natural graces and in whose manners was all the amiable simplicity of pastoral poetry with the sweet tenderness of the elegiac.

(Anon)

By kind permission of Lord and Lady Cobham.

ACKNOWLEDGEMENTS

I would like to thank so many of my friends and colleagues for their help including: Jean Holland and Denis McCready who were always ready with advice when there were problems with the computer; David Temperley who allowed me access to his library; David and Valerie Shepherd for the loan of an early edition of Johnson's Dictionary; Norman and Jean Price for reading and offering advice on the text and to Lynn Barber my helpful proof reader. To this list must also be added; Howard Moore and other members of the Classics Department of Solihull School; Dennis Tomlin, the school archivist, and Lorraine Johnson, the school secretary, all of whom have contributed to making my path easier. Neither must I forget to thank Andy Barton of Jessop's Group in Solihull.

I would also like thank Lord and Lady Cobham of Hagley Hall and his secretary, Joyce Purnell who have kindly allowed me photographs of the Hall, the First Lord Lyttelton and the "gothic" castle. Thanks are due to Mr and Mrs Paul Johnson of Mickleton Manor for granting my husband permission to photograph their home; to Peter Russell of the Somers Sports and Social Club for a photograph of The Grange and to Alan Vernon for supplying me with a colour portrait of Virgil's Grove.

My thanks are due to the Rector of Halesowen Parish Church for permission to photograph; similarly to the Rectors of Snitterfield and Harbury and St Lawrence's Church at Mickleton; and to the numerous and enthusiastic church wardens who kindly directed me to where I needed to go.

The following also deserve an appreciative mention; staff of The British Library, the National Portrait Gallery and Carol McDonnel of the Office of National Statistics; Bath and North East Somerset Customer Service; Patrick Baird and staff of The Local Studies and History Department and Nicky Rathbone and staff of Arts, Language and Literature at Birmingham Central Library; Birmingham City Archives Department; Christine Penny and her staff of Birmingham University Library's Special Collections; Dianne Barre of Birmingham University who passed on to me so much relevant literature; staff of the Dudley Archives and Local History Service; Halesowen Public Library; Kidderminster Library; the William Salt Library, Stafford; the Shakespeare Birthplace Trust Records Office, Stratford-upon-Avon; Shropshire Archives Department; Solihull Central Library; Warwickshire County Records Office and Worcester Records Office.

Finally I want to say "thank-you" to Alan Brewin, my publisher, who has never been too busy to respond with alacrity to my queries: and to Horace R Wilson for allowing me access to many of his own illustrations of local interest. Then there is my husband, Geoffrey, without whose active and constant support I should not have been able to bring this undertaking to a conclusion.

PREFACE

Having lived with William Shenstone for over two years, I have become fond of the man and my aim is to introduce him to others so that they, too, may come to appreciate his wit, learning and compassion.

Like all of us he had faults. He was pernickety as well as kind; he had his foibles as well as generosity of spirit: and he could be downright mean. But ultimately the balance sheet totals in his favour and his letters and prose works, as well as the poetry and his skills at landscape gardening, make him very well worth getting to know.

Whenever possible I allow Shenstone to speak for himself and have kept the original spelling which today's readers will soon get used to. But for the sake of clarity I have changed the eighteenth century form of 's'. "Suppose" makes more sense to us than "fuppofe". I have also aimed for clarity in the way the text is organised and one of the advantages of this book is that it does not have to be read chronologically. There is the section on The Leasowes garden, or the Luxborough Letters, or the poetry or the prose which can be "dipped" into at will – each complete in itself.

Finally there is the question of money. For in order to make sense of Shenstone's constant shortage of funds it is helpful to have some idea of what a pound was worth in his day. Very approximately, one pound in 1750 would have been the equivalent of one hundred and eight pounds today, which means that his inherited income of three hundred pounds a year would have been worth in the region of thirty-two thousand pounds. If this is compared with the five thousand pounds that Lady Fane paid for her "grotto", which would have cost in twenty-first century terms, well over half a million, it becomes clear that what Shenstone achieved at The Leasowes on his limited income was little short of a miracle. It is an achievement which together with his other accomplishments bids us to turn the page and allow Shenstone, the man, to emerge from comparative obscurity to take his place alongside his peers.

INTRODUCTION

Shenstone was a poet, a man of learning, wit and letters. He was also a substantial critic and editor – and – if that were not sufficient, one of the leading landscape gardeners of his age. He was born in 1714 into "a land of hamlets and villages": a Worcestershire[1] countryside that in its then isolation was as different a world from ours today, as diamonds are from coal. It was a time when extremes were a fact of life. When the brutality of public executions and the squalor of abject poverty co-existed with a perception by the more fortunate of taste, elegance and genteel luxury.

One of Shenstone's contemporaries was Horace Walpole; the politician, novelist and gossip who lived in a mock gothic castle called Strawberry Hill at Twickenham. It was from here in 1764, that he wrote *"The Castle of Otranto"*, a gothic novel, and the precursor of a genre which has survived up until today in films like *Dracula* and *Dr Hammer's House of Horror*. It was a time when people were seeking the new and the strange, a search which was to facilitate the rise of the novel which in Shenstone's day quickly became popular in the works of Samuel Richardson and Henry Fielding. Shenstone read *Pamela, Clarissa* and *Tom Jones* as they emerged from the press and his critical comments concerning them are as lively as they are entertaining.

This was the age of the coffee-house: of Garrick and the great Dr Johnson who strode the London literary scene like a colossus. Shenstone knew them both and as a younger man was, like them, a frequenter of coffee-houses when he visited the capital where they were centres for the dissemination of views and gossip.

In his letters Shenstone reflects the news of his day. He writes of the second Jacobite Rebellion and of a Battalion of Horse, marching through Birmingham on its way up north to confront the rebels. Or with pleasure of Handel's *Messiah* enjoyed on a visit to the local Three Choirs Festival. But whatever his subject, whether it be political or domestic, it is the way he presents his material that makes it so enjoyable. For it is spiced with wit and the discernment of a lively mind: fashioned with the precision of a master craftsman.

Shenstone was a master, too, in the art of garden design. People flocked to see his imaginative innovations in his garden at The Leasowes, and it was not long before many of the landed gentry who wished to re-model their estates in the new fashion, were to seek his advice. It was in his garden that Shenstone "posted" his inscriptions; poems affixed to root houses or alcoves or "Gothick" seats for the general enjoyment and instruction of his guests: poems that, today, have been discredited with faint praise. His songs and ballads have been misunderstood: their simplicity mistaken for banality in much the same way as the *Letters* which conform to eighteenth century rules have been taken at face value and not as the "game" which everybody else at the time was busy playing.

There is also the problem of language change which seems to matter more when the concern is with letters and pensées. Shenstone's Pensées, a collection of his thoughts on various topics of his day, and of course his letters, are more personal than the novel – more revealing of the author than the play is of the playwright or the poem of the poet. Shenstone has been branded as snobbish. But when he writes of "my good friends the vulgar", there is little pejorative intent. For he is writing of the public, as distinct from the gentry, a group with which he frequently, although not always, seems to have had excellent rapport. There are many other words which over the years have changed their meaning. Shenstone's "complaisant" friends are being complimented, for they are anxious to please. In the eighteenth century, our modern understanding of the alternative word 'complacent', as smug or self-satisfied would have been unknown.

There is another reason which may account for Shenstone's neglect and it is to be found in Dr Johnson's *Lives of the Poets* which does little to enhance and much to harm the poet's reputation. For Johnson disapproved of the choices Shenstone made: his love of gardening and his decision to live away from London. The Doctor's wit is barbed:

> *Whether to plant a walk in undulating curves, and to place a bench at every turn where there there is an object to catch the view; to make water run where it will be heard, and to stagnate where it will be seen; to leave intervals where the eye will be pleased, and to thicken the plantation where there is something to be hidden, demands any great powers of mind, I will not enquire.*[2]

However, in spite of the Doctor's disapproval it is clear that Shenstone had multifarious talents and was actively involved in two of the eighteenth century's most important literary events. With his publisher and great friend, Robert Dodsley, he was to edit and collate much of the poetry that found its way into volumes IV and V of those famous *Miscellanies*: and later in the same capacity he was to become involved with Bishop Percy and his *Reliques of Ancient Poetry*. Both were to become vastly popular in their day and both, later, were to be subject to savage criticism. But such criticism is to superimpose modern attitudes upon the way that men and women thought over two hundred and fifty years ago. Both the *Miscellanies* and the *Reliques* mark a watershed in the way that people were to think about poetry and whatever their failures, they had considerable strengths too.

Shenstone's sudden death at the age of forty-eight, when he was about to be honoured with a pension for his services to literature, was cruel. But death in the seventeen hundreds was an ever present enemy and one which many were obliged to confront too soon. Yet the poems, the pensées and the letters live on: especially the letters which provide a bravura rendition of life as it was – a "keyhole" version of events and his thoughts concerning them that are as fresh to read and enjoy now as they were then. With Shenstone we are able to re-enter a world that is past – join with him and his coterie of exceptional friends in a rapport which is at the same time entirely personal and hugely entertaining. Shenstone's world – a world which deserves to be neglected no longer.

Chapter 1

SCHOOL DAYS AND EARLY INFLUENCES

William Shenstone was born on 18th November 1714. A precociously bright child he was the son of Thomas, a yeoman farmer of The Leasowes, or "Lezzers" as it was known locally in Shropshire, and Ann Penn, one of the Penns from Harborough Hall. The Penns were gentry in the way that the Shenstones were not and the children of this marriage, William, and eight years later Joseph, were to straddle a class divide in an age when class consciousness was a fact of life and the gentry and aristocracy were virtual rulers.

William learnt to read early and pestered his parents for books. As a very little boy of three or so he would cry if his father did not return on market days with a "packet" and sometimes on winter evenings his parents were obliged to resort to subterfuge. To ensure a quiet night the child would be given a "parcel" which in the dark contented him until the morning, although what would have happened then is open to speculation!

In their way the parents were enlightened. It was soon to be clear that they had an exceptional son and they responded by first sending him to Sarah Lloyd who ran a thriving dame school in Halesowen. Little did she know it but later both she and her school were to become immortalised in Shenstone's burlesque poem *The Schoolmistress,* in which he paints an affectionate portrait of the little world over which she presided. It was a world in which discipline was maintained by means of her cane – her "little birchen tree" which never failed to introduce a tingle of apprehension when it was produced. But Sarah Lloyd was kindly enough in her way. She would not hesitate after a caning to offer the unfortunate child a sweetmeat as recompense. Shenstone was to publish his poem in 1742, many years after the events which he describes took place. But his memory is evergreen and it is clear that those early school days are remembered with more joy than pain. Indeed it is with nostalgia that he writes to his friend Jago in that same year "Of my old school dame Sarah Lloyd", and points out that now her son Thomas "Reigneth in her stead!" Humorous words with a subtext that carries a frisson of fear as well as affection.

After the little dame school in Halesowen and when it was clear that William would benefit from an academic education, his parents had to decide where he should go next. There would have been a number of schools to choose from and Halesowen Grammar School on their doorstep, which Dr Johnson tells us he attended briefly, was one of them. But in spite of this they were to settle eventually upon an establishment some distance away – Solihull School on the south side of Birmingham. With hindsight, the reason for their choice becomes clear. For it was a school which not only offered an excellent grounding in the Classics which were to provide a springboard into the world of academe, but also a comprehensive introduction to English literature as well. At this time the teaching of English alongside classical literature was both unusual and innovative and such a curriculum was more comprehensive than that offered by other schools.

So it was that young William became a boarder at Solihull School in Warwickshire. It was an establishment run by another strict disciplinarian, the Reverend William Crumpton, who at the early age of twenty-one had previously held the post of headmaster at Dudley Grammar School. This was a man whose foresight was the main reason for Solihull meriting its fine reputation. He was a mathematician of some note and it is likely that he was the author of a textbook on the teaching of decimals and music: *A Plain and Comprehensive Treatise of Decimals and Mensuration... and...an Introduction to Practical Music, etc.* So it is unsurprising that his approach to education, which offered a wider curriculum, was one which enjoyed the patronage of a number of local gentry.

In Shenstone's time the school was situated in what today is Park Road – in a large house on the borders of Malvern Park where the child would have been one of a select group of boarders. These were the children who, together with day boys, were subject to a regime which was, by modern standards, harsh. The school day was long, running from seven until eleven in the morning; and from one until five in the afternoon. During term time work stopped on Thursdays at three o'clock which was the only midweek respite that the boys enjoyed. Saturdays, too, were half days, but only Sundays and holy days were entirely free. School holidays were much shorter than those we enjoy today, for an eight week vacation in the summer was unheard of. It was stipulated that holidays should run from:

> *The Wednesday noone before each Easter and Whit-Sunday 'till the Monday seven-night following, and such hours a day before and after Christmas as are usually excepted in other schools.[1]*

Solihull was to be of great importance to Shenstone, not only for the thorough grounding in Latin that he was to receive and from which he developed his lifelong admiration for Virgil; not only for his introduction to the delights of English literature and especially Spencer, who in later years was to become the inspiration for his own masterpiece, *The Schoolmistress*, but also for a particular friendship that he would strike up with Richard Jago, the son of the rector of Beaudesert in Henley-in-Arden. For even at an early age Shenstone was to demonstrate his capacity for making and, more importantly, keeping close friends; and this friendship was one which would last for life. The two boys had much in common. Both were academically bright and enjoyed Shakespeare, Spencer and Dryden. Both were destined for a place, even though in Jago's case a minor one, in the echelons of English Letters. Jago's poem, *The Blackbirds* still gives pleasure today and in his longer and autobiographical *Edgehill* we glimpse what the return to school after the Christmas holidays is like:

Hail Solihull! respectful I salute
Thy walls;...when from the sweets
Of festive freedom and domestic ease,
With throbbing heart to the stern discipline
Of pedagogue morose I had returned.[2]

For young William, who had already endured the rigours of Sarah Lloyd's dame school, the return might have been less traumatic; but no doubt even he would have felt some qualms as he left the friendly and less formal portals of home.

Even so they were, on the whole, happy days for the two children and Jago recalls the times that they spent together. He writes of their long country rambles in the holidays when Shenstone was a welcome guest at his father's vicarage – of two young boys whose heads were full of Virgil and of Shakespeare and who, as they wandered together by the banks of the Avon, were acutely aware that they were treading in the footsteps of that great Warwickshire bard. For there they would:

... range in solitary shades
And scoop rude grottoes in the shelving banks – [3]

Where even the mudpies they fashioned as children were hallowed by Shakespeare's memory!

It was while he was at Solihull School that Shenstone was to meet William Somervile of Edstone Hall. Somervile was a neighbour of the Jago family and already a poet of some repute. So the meeting at the vicarage is likely to have made a considerable impression, as it is probable that Shenstone was already penning his verses and an introduction to an established poet would have provided welcome encouragement. And after a fashion the two became friendly; although Somervile, the archetypal "huntin' and shootin'" English squire and the considerably younger Shenstone who loathed the idea of hunting and who never really conquered the skills of horsemanship, were never intimates.

Somervile hunted every day and the "thrill" of the chase was not only one to which he looked forward every morning but one that is graphically described in his poem of the same name. *The Chase* was written in 1719 when he was thirty-six. It is his best known poem, the one with which he made his name; and in it he tells of how an unfortunate and exhausted young hart sinks down to become "To the relentless crowd a bleeding prey". How before she is dead, the huntsman removes "Her reeking entrails and yet quivering heart" to throw them to the pack as a prize for "...all their toils".

This same huntsman, John Hoitt, has an eye-catching memorial tablet in St Peter's Church, Wootton Wawen where he is buried:

Here Hoitt, all his sports and labours past
Joins his loved master Somervile at last

The inscription ends with a truism redolent of *Hamlet*:

> *Servant and Lord, when once we yield our breath*
> *Huntsman and poet are alike in death*
>
> *(Anon)*

As the lines make clear, Sir William is also buried in St Peter's Church in a tomb that is as memorable as befits his status. He was a magistrate and Master of Fox Hounds whose memory reflects a tradition which exemplified the care of horse and hound but negated the hunt's unfortunate victim as a nameless prey.

But all this is to take us away from two young boys at Solihull School in the seventeen twenties - who were unconcernedly working at their studies, enjoying their school days and preparing for where they would lead – Oxford, when new heights would be scaled and new friends garnered. Oxford which is where the narrative continues.

Chapter 2

OXFORD AND FRIENDSHIP

1724 was the year that the ten year old William lost his father. The family's loss did not interfere with his visits home, but it must have been unsettling for the child even though he had the stability of school to support him and the security of the Jago vicarage where he was welcomed as a surrogate member of the family.

In fact neither of Shenstone's parents was to live to old age and in 1732 when his mother died aged only 39, her two sons, William who was eighteen and Joseph who was eight years younger, were parentless. What happened next is uncertain. According to Dr Johnson the two boys went to live with their maternal grandmother, but if this were the case it was only for a short time; for very soon after, William and Joseph were welcomed into the Dolman family at Broom.

Thomas Dolman, the rector of Broom or Brome as it was frequently spelt, was the boys' uncle by marriage. His wife was Ann Shenstone's sister and their two surviving children, Thomas and Maria were to be amusing companions who would figure a good deal in the future. At this time the Reverend Dolman presided over a little church with its bell in a tree. On Sundays and for all other important occasions, this was rung by the parish clerk and when the latter died the young Shenstone celebrated his bell ringing in an early unpublished poem;

> *Certes[1] there are that hum a tune*
> *And sing a song right well;*
> *Yet sure no song was like my psalm,*
> *No music like my bell.[2]*

It was from Broom and under the guidance of his uncle, that Shenstone was to take the next big step in his life with the decision that same year of 1732, to enter Pembroke College, Oxford, as a commoner. At first there was talk of eventual ordination and the hope that William might one day become the next incumbent of Broom. Nothing came of it however, for at Pembroke College, Johnson's "nest of singing birds" where the roll-call of eminent students was long, Shenstone's religious views developed in a way that would make it impossible for him to accept the confines of eighteenth century Anglicanism. This and his inherited income which was to make the necessity of finding work less pressing meant that the idea was quietly dropped. In the meantime Methodism was in the making, and Shenstone up at Pembroke would have been introduced to its eloquent preachers and fervent outdoor gatherings. He would have known George

Whitfield whose sermons drew large crowds and yet in spite of all the excitement he was to remain uninvolved.

Shenstone did not go up to Oxford alone. With him went Richard Jago, but to University College as a servitor. In modern terms this meant that the latter had to work his way through college - a necessary measure because his father was unwilling or unable to pay tuition fees. Jago would instead, perform menial tasks for both staff and fee paying students in return for free lectures. A similar system was also in operation at Cambridge where the "fizzer" was the equivalent of Oxford's servitor. It was an arrangement which enabled Jago to obtain his degree and pursue his career as a country parson; but it was seen as demeaning. Dr Johnson was reputedly horrified that the son of a Warwickshire rector should have been subjected to such treatment and blamed the son's father for not making alternative arrangements. For the implications of the system were far reaching. In theory, commoners who paid for their tuition were not expected to fraternise with servitors who did not, which was a way of perpetuating the class divide – or in Jago's case, promoting it.

But in fact the two friends did continue to meet, although not openly, and their friendship is to be seen as a triumph in the face of what, today, would be regarded as snobbery. And Jago's future as both poet and parson was to be an interesting one, not least for a frivolous reason; his experiences with the supernatural. For whereas the mature Shenstone was to regard ghost stories as nonsense, a view made clear in his Pensées: "The cause of superstition has lost ground" he was to write, "The notion of ghosts has been altogether exploded"; there is evidence that Jago's attitude was to be more open to compromise. Perhaps this had something to do with his Cornish ancestry: to a great great grandfather, the Reverend Robert Jago, who in the sixteenth century had a considerable reputation as a ghost layer and who reputedly horse whipped the ghost of a Jew who had hanged himself in front of the house of his mortal enemy in order to inflict supernatural vengeance. Or perhaps not. But at any rate, Jago's poem, *Peto's Ghost* tells of an apparition which appeared to him late one night when, as a young parish priest, he was returning home from a political meeting in Warwick:

> *...thro the dark and lonesome shade*
> *Shone forth a sudden light:*
> *And soon distinct a human form*
> *Engaged my wondering sight.*[3]

It would seem that this "ghost" had an express purpose. For having requested where Jago's political sympathies lay and registered its approval, it conveniently disappeared: and although it is easy to see in this poem a desire to impress and to further the poet's career, a second encounter was to be different. It was to occur years later in 1755 and concerned his own parishioners of Harbury who were frightened by nightly sightings of a ghost in the churchyard there, and who requested help and advice from their vicar. By now a well-loved and conscientious parish priest, Jago was to take the matter seriously enough to preach an admonitory sermon with its theme of "extraordinary warnings"; was pleased enough with the contents to publish them in a pamphlet which he sent to anyone who was interested!

But to return to Oxford and to Shenstone in his first year as an undergraduate; for it is now time to take stock of this young man. What did he look like? What kind of person was he? Physically he was large and raw boned. Graves, his first biographer, describes him as ungainly – but he had not yet started to run to fat. He was quick of wit and when interested and at ease his expression was one of sparkling animation. When the opposite was true he would become wooden, retire behind a façade which portrayed him as awkward and gauche. He held strong likes and dislikes and was already very much an individualist, a trait which was demonstrated in the way he dressed. It was the age of the wig – everybody wore one: "Black, white brown or grizzle as – fancy suggested". But Shenstone would have none of it. Instead he wore his own hair, thick and coarse, tied back with a ribbon. It was an act of defiance which was to cost him dear. He was to be alternatively laughed at and whispered about but he was not to be moved. He disliked artificiality and the wig was nothing if not artificial. And he had a passion for simplicity. The same simplicity for which he was to strive later on in his poetry and in his garden at The Leasowes, where formality was eschewed for the more casual and less artificial attire of nature, herself. Even so, the shouted comments of his "enemies at the gate" offended him as he made his way into All Souls to see his new friend, Richard Graves.

Years later, Graves was to pen his *Recollections* as a refutation of Dr Johnson's unkind portrayal of Shenstone in his *Lives of the Poets* and the Memoir describes what Oxford, in the seventeen thirties, was like. In it he tells of how he met the poet, and of the social choices available to undergraduates at that time. Most exclusive of all were "the bucks of the first head", whose meetings were lively affairs and whose preferences were for "port wine and arrack punch" poured down their throats in large quantities. From lower down the social scale came the beer drinkers; "The West Country Set" who smoked and sang bacchanalian songs, one of which opened their meetings with sentiments that might still appeal today:

Lets be jovial, fill our glasses
Madness 'tis for us to think
How the world is ruled by asses
And the wisest swayed by drink![4]

He writes of a third and far more sober group. Young men who met to read Greek and who punctuated their endeavours with sips of water, a drink that would not have seemed so tame as it might today. For recently, spa towns like Bath and Cheltenham had taken to bottling and transporting their water and the drinking of it had become something of a novelty. It was a novelty fuelled by Dr George Cheyne who in his popular *Essay on Health and Long Life*, published in 1728, had proved himself an ardent exponent of the benefits of spa waters. Benefits, no doubt, in which these young water bibbers were hoping to share.

It was at the first two of these three groups that Shenstone was to meet a couple of young men; Anthony Whistler and Richard Graves who, like Jago, would become friends for life. It was at a time when all three were experimenting with the port wine and beer drinking sets which offered limited appeal; and although for a complex of reasons Shenstone was a shy young man it was he, on this occasion, who took the initiative. He was quick to perceive that both Whistler and Graves, like himself, were ill at ease and so one evening he invited them both to breakfast with him at his rooms on the following day.

Of the two it was Whistler, whose family had been Lords of the Manor at Whitchurch near Pangbourne; Whistler the old Etonian with a ready wit and the easy self confidence of his class; the author of an admired poem, *The Shuttlecock,* who was never to fulfil his early promise. As a young man he was able, well read and charming but lacked discipline and determination. However, he was to prove a loyal friend and his early death was to cause Shenstone much sadness; so was the destruction of the poet's letters by the Whistler family. For these, together with his correspondence to Richard Graves and Jago, would have proved an important addition to the cache of Shenstone's letters that have survived.

Richard (Dick) Graves, on the other hand was altogether different. He was destined for scholarship and to become, a not inconsiderable, novelist: his *Columella* is a gentle and affectionate satire upon Shenstone's reclusive life at The Leasowes. He would later decide upon ordination and as a man of honour, the choices which he would be obliged to make deserve a mention. Graves was also gentry, but as a younger son would be obliged to earn his living. After graduating in 1736 and by means of a series of rapid promotions: from Dean of the Faculty of Arts at his college, to the Rectorship of Theology and Natural Philosophy, and in 1745, to the bursarship of his college, his future in academe seemed assured. His first novel, *The Spiritual Quixote*, a gentle parody upon the rise of Methodism had also achieved success so his star was rising. But an event in his private life was to change all that and this is what happened.

To augment his income, Richard Graves had secured a curacy at Aldsworth, a village within easy reach of Oxford; and in order to carry out these additional duties he rented rooms with a respectable yeoman family at Dumouth Farmhouse which still exists today. The problem was Lucy, the fifteen year old daughter of the house; or to be more precise – Lucy and Richard. For this lively and attractive young girl was given the task of looking after the presentable young curate and the inevitable happened. What is of interest is the way that Graves responded to the pregnancy; for after much soul searching he determined upon marriage – with a girl from a different class and one who was little more than a child herself. Indeed, by today's standards he would have been in deep trouble. As it was, and in spite of opposition from his family they were married, clandestinely, in London. Then after the birth of their child, Lucy was sent away to a boarding school for young ladies in order to learn the social graces that she would later require as the wife of a clergyman.

In his charming little poem, *The Parting*, Graves tells of how they both felt. First from Lucy's point of view:

> *But oh! The feted hour has come*
> *That forced me from my dear;*
> *My Lucy that through grief was dumb.*
> *Or spake but by a tear.*

Then from his own perspective:

> *Nay life itself is tasteless grown*
> *From Lucy whilst I stray;*
> *Sick of the world I muse alone*
> *And sigh the live long day.*[5]

Verses which, in spite of the cliché in the final line, express genuine emotion, and set the scene for an experiment that worked. The marriage was entirely happy and when Lucy died aged only forty-six, Graves was inconsolable.

These, then, were the two young men who Shenstone on that auspicious evening invited for breakfast. Young men who with Jago, unable to be present because of his status as servitor, were to form the nucleus of the Warwickshire Coterie. A group which was to derive its name from where its members were frequently entertained at Lady Luxborough's Warwickshire home; whose letters shed an interesting light upon life in the provinces during the eighteenth century.

Shenstone's invitation was for a "working breakfast" rather as today we talk of a "working lunch" – and there were rules laid down. As a framework for discussion each was to bring along his own literary text and the choices tell something of the character of all three. The host's preference was for Charles Cotton's *Virgil Travestie*, a burlesque written in 1664 and now popular at a time when both imitation and satire were much admired. Shenstone was passionate about Virgil. He was an excellent Latin scholar and his letters are frequently peppered with classical quotations. He also had a lively sense of humour and before long was to write his *The Schoolmistress*, a masterpiece which began as a burlesque of another of his favourite poets, Edmund Spencer. So on both counts he would have been equipped to orchestrate a spirited and lively debate.

The text which Richard Graves was to bring was very different. His choice was Johannes Eckhard's *Causes of the Contempt of the Clergy* and at a time when Methodism was on the rise, this would have been seen as relevant. For the medieval Eckhard, the leader of a popular religious movement in the Germany of his day, had parallels with John Wesley and there would have been much in his text to excite discussion.

The third of the trio, Anthony Whistler, chose to bring along a poem, Alexander Pope's *The Rape of the Lock* which has the distinction of being one of the few literary texts that is as well known today as it was then. *The Rape* was written in 1714, the year of Shenstone's birth and its theme, the excesses of the affluent upper class, is satirised in the theft of a young woman's lock of hair. The poem is as funny as it is wicked and meaningful; for Whistler its content would have had a special relevance and provide enough material to keep the three young men busy for a long time to come.

How long the first "breakfast" continued is not recorded: but an intelligent guess must be that the young men would have had sufficient material to have lasted them indefinitely. So it is no surprise to learn that they decided to meet frequently and in turn in each other's rooms; and that to the accompaniment of "Florentine Wine" organised a series of wide ranging discussions. They read philosophy together: and plays and poetry – especially poetry which by now was Shenstone's chief delight, for he was already writing his own verses. Looking back he was to describe these times and to link the enjoyment of poetry with the bond of friendship.

> *... that sweetly vacant scene*
> *When, all beneath the poplar bough*
> *My spirits light, my soul serene*
> *I breathed in verse on cordial vow*
> *That nothing should my soul inspire*
> *But friendship warm and love entire.*[6]

Later he was to recall Oxford again; when disenchantment with his own literary efforts was uppermost in his mind:

> *I saw my friends in ev'ning circles meet;*
> *I took my vocal reed and tun'd my lay*
> *I heard them say my vocal reed was sweet;*
> *Oh fool! To credit what I heard them say.*[7]

But for the present, there was only Shenstone's detestation of dancing and card-playing which limited his chances of making friends - only his "character" of Graves written while waiting for the latter in his rooms. For this was to give rise to rumour and speculation. It was left lying about and an anonymous student briefed others that the three friends were meeting in order to dissect the character of every single freshman in their year! It caused hostility; but no matter. For Shenstone it was the genuine affection of his friends: Graves, Whistler and Jago, which far outweighed (for him) the doubtful gain of a wider acquaintance. He enjoyed the facilities that the university had to offer and was soon wining and dining in some style. Indeed the Oxford Battels Books record his weekly expenses as being surprisingly high. At around approximately eleven shillings a week they outrun Graves by as much as four shillings. And a decade later, Johnson's at eight shillings and four pence per week were much more modest.

This liberal spending while at Pembroke was to have resonances for the future. For by the time Oxford was no more than a delightful memory, and Shenstone had chosen to settle at The Leasowes in rural seclusion, he was constantly to bewail his lack of funds – even on occasion borrowing money from his own servants! Then, his inherited income of £300 per annum was to seem decidedly paltry, even when set against the annual stipend of a typical country parson of one hundred and forty pounds. For Shenstone's eyes were elsewhere, fastened upon the almost limitless assets of his aristocratic friends. Poverty and wealth, then as now, was comparative.

By comparison his friend, Graves, was both thrifty and hard working. A fact which makes it arguable that Shenstone's patrimony was to prove a mixed blessing, removing as it did, the urgency of courting success. But it could not remove the companionship of his friends. The reading, the rambles, the discussions and the poetry. Above all the poetry which served during those Oxford years, to fire him with the inclination to become a poet.

Chapter 3

EARLY POETRY

Shenstone came down from Oxford without a degree in 1732. It was the year of his majority which meant that he came into his inheritance and The Leasowes, the family farmstead, was now officially his. At the time the farm was tenanted by John Shenstone, a relative, and so the young man was presented with a choice. Until the lease expired he could move in and share his home which he did eventually decide to do, or he could settle briefly at Harborough, the home of his mother's family for over two hundred years, and an estate in which he also had a share.

To begin with Shenstone chose Harborough, a timbered Elizabethan manor house which he had known since childhood. It harboured many treasured memories and he was extremely fond of the place. In one of his best known elegies (number XV) he was to write of the way of life that such houses and the families that lived in them used to represent. Like some today, he felt that there was change in the air and that it was not always for the better. He writes of the surrounding countryside: of the little church nearby with its ivy crowned tower and pealing bell: of the shaded pool in the grounds with its fringe of ancient elms and the rooks that nested there.

During these early years in the seventeen thirties, Shenstone continued to retain strong links with his old Oxford college. His name was not finally erased from its Books until 1741 and during this period he was to spend two quite lengthy summer breaks back at Pembroke – in 1737 and again in 1739. On both occasions he was joined by his friend, Anthony Whistler, and how successful the two young men were in reincarnating the joys of their undergraduate days who can tell?

The first visit is by far the more important. Shenstone had been busy at Harborough writing his poetry and in 1737 the main reason for his return to the university was to oversee the publication of his first Collection of verse, *Poems on Several Occasions*. It was to be a slim volume and its importance was to lie in the fact that it contained the first known draft of *The Schoolmistress*, Shenstone's masterpiece which later was to be expanded from the twelve verse version here into the thirty-six stanzas we can read today.

In later years the poet was to go to great lengths to seek out and destroy these early poems, for with the lengthening perspective of age he came to see the contents as irrevocably flawed. Nonetheless, the Collection included a number of poems of interest and one of them is *The Snuff Box*. This "tea cup" epic written in imitation of Pope's *Rape of the Lock* is a re-working of an earlier poem *The Diamond* which has an interesting history. Written in 1734, a copy was to resurface years later in 1774. It was enclosed in a letter to the actor and playwright Thomas Hull which tells of the pleasure that Mrs M – has received upon reading Shenstone's name "respectfully and publicly revived" in the playwright's Dedication to his play, *The Tragedy of Rosamond*: and she points out that the poem which she has held since Shenstone's death, is "a small" token of the esteem in which she holds both the man and his work.

In a second letter this same lady goes further. She not only believes *The Diamond* to be similar to the *Rape of the Lock* but preferable because of its "greater delicacy of sentiment"! Preferable it is not; but perhaps Shenstone's own verdict, written in his maturity and pencilled on the manuscript, is too harsh:

> *This was written before the Snuff Box at the time I lived at Harborough... and has*
> *A more simple plan than the other; but... little or nothing to recommend it besides.*

But whatever one's view, it is a fact that this unknown lady's sentiments are representative of the popularity and esteem in which Shenstone was held in the decades after his death and before influences such as that exerted by Dr Johnson began to erode his reputation.

Another poem which works well is *Colimira*, a mock pastoral: for this "shepherdess" is a slatternly kitchen maid whose "charms" are such as the rest of us would prefer to forget. The setting for *Colimira* is the kitchen of a large establishment. There, sprawling by the fire is the girl's admirer and as she carries out her mundane tasks all that she does is reflected through the lens of her lover's eye. So that even the way she sweats in the heat of the kitchen is given a romantic gloss!

> *... In pearly rills*
> *Adown her goodly cheeks the sweat distils.*

Her ragged dress is satirised in the same way:

> *Whilst rags... from my fair one's gown*
> *In russet pomp and greasy pride hang down.*[1]

So are we encouraged to picture her blowing life "with full blown cheeks" into the dying fire: or swearing at the dogs, "those lazy devils" who lie in the warmth of the hearth. It is an amusing piece and not without merit.

Not only are a number of these early poems fun; but they are important for what they tell us about the way that Shenstone's work was to develop in the future. In *Verses to a Lady* he first expresses what later was to become a central theme: condemnation of city life with its "dress and pomp" and praise for its opposite "The sweets of tranquil life and rural ease". Far from being unique, it was a way of thinking much met with in eighteenth century literature: but usually, as in Fielding's *Joseph Andrews*, it was the adaptation of a convention, whereas in Shenstone's case it was genuine. For him it had a special resonance. For he did turn his back on London; he did settle in the country;

and when later, as in the great poem of his maturity, *Rural Elegance*, he extols the virtues of a simple life, it is from the heart.

A number of the poems, and especially *Love and Music*[2] demonstrate that Shenstone is already adept at the elegantly turned compliment. Both love and music, he argues, have power to stir the emotions and in the final stanza of this brief and charming poem they are brought together in an amusing accolade to Selinda:

> *Thus love or sound affect the mind*
> *But where their various pow'rs are joined*
> *Fly, daring mortal, fly!*
> *For when Selinda's charms appear*
> *And I her tuneful accents hear –*
> *I burn, I faint, I die.*

It is sad that these early works are virtually impossible to obtain - that Shenstone tried so hard and with such success to prevent their circulation. For in their way they are invaluable. They demonstrate how seriously the young man took to heart the advice of Horace, one of the greatest of classical poets, who maintained that ability must be reinforced by means of hard work: that reading and imitating the achievements of those already successful was an important way forward. They show also that Shenstone's way was clear. He was to become a poet. So what went wrong? Why the later disillusion and unhappiness? The lethargy which, on occasion, was to stifle his endeavours? Few lives are simple and fewer answers are straightforward, but as the map of his life is charted a number of possible responses become clear.

Chapter 4

HARBOROUGH AND MICKLETON

It was during the time that Shenstone was living at Harborough that Richard Graves came on a month long visit. In his *Reminiscences* the latter describes how they spent their time, in ways that were reminiscent of their undergraduate days, still vivid and remembered with nostalgia. They rambled, they read and they discussed; and time passed deliciously without the pressure of work or the exertion of socialising beyond the confines of the estate. Shenstone also wrote "several little pieces of poetry" which Graves believed to be excellent but which are now, sadly, lost.

But it was not all a country idyll, for the two had disagreements – one of which was to result in Shenstone retreating behind a wall of silence. It was a sulk which lasted for two whole days, and one only has to imagine the absence of a morning greeting or the interminably long and silent meals to empathise with poor Dick Graves for whom the whole sorry and rather "childish" business was to become "a pain and grief".

So it was in desperation that the latter determined to effect a remedy. The "offending" comment had been made in jest and he set about making this clear. If Shenstone would not listen, he could at least be encouraged to see a message left in a likely place. On the wall of the summer house which the two would pass each day on their walks, he wrote a single line in chalk: "I will be witty", a comment which he hoped would meet with sufficient approval to elicit some response. That he was successful was soon clear. For within a short time Shenstone replied with:

> *Matchless on earth I thee proclaim*
> *Whose will and power I find the same.*[1]

This, too, called for an answer and it was not long before the wall was "scribbled" from top to bottom and a cordial reconciliation effected, much to the relief of both.

Graves' anecdote, although trivial, is of interest for the light it throws upon Shenstone's character. It demonstrates how easily, even in those early days, his mood could change, how his propensity for taking umbrage was one which could involve even his close friends. However once the storm clouds had passed, the two young men continued to spend their time in "agreeable loiter" and both took care that a single incident should not be allowed to poison the whole.

During the next few years, Shenstone was to owe a considerable debt to Graves and his family. On many occasions he was invited to their home at Mickleton where Morgan

Graves who had inherited the rambling but comfortable old manor house from his father in 1729, was to make him welcome. The father had been:

> *A most worthy and virtuous gentleman, a most excellent scholar, antiquary,*
> *and man of great modesty...(was) a great friend to his tenants and to the poor.[2]*

The elder son, however, was not cast in the same mould. For upon coming into his inheritance he had embarked upon the sale of his father's vast collection of rare books; and this, wrote the Oxford antiquary, Thomas Hearn, in a comment which has resonances for today, was no doubt due to the influence of "some illiterate fine sparks" who considered reading to be a "dry and unprofitable study". It was one of life's ironies that the younger son, Richard, an acclaimed scholar with a bright future, should have been denied access to a library which he would have treasured and from which he would have benefited. A fact not lost upon a number of self-educated, local men of the time like I.A.Ballard, the Chipping Campden tailor and antiquary who recorded that: "The younger son hath a genius to things of this nature, and in all probability... will often wish that all had been preserved". Even so there is little evidence that Richard Graves felt any hostility towards his brother and surprisingly, Shenstone seems to have enjoyed Morgan Graves' company although they had little in common except an all important love of gardening and garden design. For it was the elder brother, at this time engaged in redeveloping his estate along the lines of those adopted by Philip Southcote, a relation of his at Woburn, who was the first to encourage Shenstone to think in terms of attempting something similar at The Leasowes.

At Mickleton Shenstone was warmly welcomed into the menage of the manor house where he was first to be introduced to the delights of female companionship. There he met Mary Graves, Richard's sister, and fell a little in love; Graves tells us that he was "insensibly captivated", sending her verses upon arriving back home in October 1736. In the poem which was accompanied by a coloured drawing of flowers, he compares her beauty with theirs, "which languish when applied to you". He explains how the lines had come to be written. It was "when I had not great flow of spirits, namely when I had just left Mickleton and you...". And he paints the gaiety that he has just left behind, the "constant sound of delight" unlikely to be met with anywhere else.

For the Mickleton household was a lively one and constantly filled with young guests, including as a matter of course, friends such as Whistler and Jago. There was dancing in the evening and card-playing and although Shenstone was voluble in his dislike of both, he seems, on these occasions, to have put up with such diversions with a good grace. Later he was to pen a couple of delightful, short poems illustrative of how he felt. One describes a girl dancing, who from the sidelines of the dance floor is a joy to watch. For she:

> ... dost not only dance in *time*
> But streaks like *time* along.[3]

The other is to Utrecia Smith, a young girl who has chosen to sit out the dance and, instead, converse with him. It is a poem in which Shenstone compares the gyrations of the dance floor with the activities of a "busy restless world": one in which he signals instead, his preferences for the quiet of an interesting conversation. The poem is brief and worth quoting in full:

I

Whilst round in wild rotation hurled
These glittering forms I view,
Methinks the busy restless world
Is pictured in a few.

II

So may the busy world advance
Since thus the fates decree:
It still may have its busy dance,
Whilst I retire with thee.[4]

The story of Utrecia Smith is both sad and interesting; and one which Graves recounts in his *Recollections* with imaginative insight. She was the daughter of the local curate, the Reverend William Smith and his wife who managed to bring up four children, two sons and two daughters on a limited income derived from three sources:

A small living of about fifty pounds a year, a curacy of thirty
Pounds a year and a life-hold estate of about the same value.[5]

But his total income which, at most, would have amounted to one hundred and sixty pounds per annum, was one which he put to good use. With it he managed not only to acquire a substantial library and live in a "genteel" fashion, but also to move in social circles which, on occasion, would include the Graves' family and other local gentry. Neither is it surprising to learn that the gallant old man lived on to become a nonagenarian!

But in spite of all this, Utrecia's life was to be blighted and so much promise sacrificed. For she was a young woman of exceptional talent: was so well read and expressed herself on paper so expertly that even the university educated Richard Graves would forbear from offering his opinion on literary matters until she had voiced hers. The two were to become romantically involved in an understanding which lasted for four years; one which made it seem that her future was assured. But sadly it was not; for Graves after some agonising, decided to end the relationship in order that he might concentrate on furthering his career. It was a decision that he was to regret and to feel guilty about in the future. Utrecia was heartbroken and quite soon after became ill, whether or not as the result of her distress cannot be known: but within a matter of months the poor girl was dead. And one thing is clear: Graves believed himself responsible for what had happened; in expiation raised a commemorative urn to Utrecia in Mickleton Church, where it is still to be seen, extolling her unusual gifts.

Shenstone was also fond of the girl and badly shaken by her death. The parallels with Shakespeare's Ophelia were obvious and his heartfelt little poem, *Ophelia's Urn*, poses the question to which all and especially her parents, would have wanted an answer.

> *Why has such worth, without distinction dy'd.*
> *Why like the desert's lilly, bloomed to fade?*[6]

But no one, and especially the young, will grieve for ever; and a few years later another girl, Fanny Fletcher, to whom he also was to send his poetry, describes amusingly the effect of his departure upon the Mickleton household:

> *With you fled all life and spirit ...; a total eclipse succeeded you and*
> *the sun will shine no more 'till your bright influence dispels the cloud...*[7]

It is comment which, even allowing for the hyperbole of the time, makes clear that the poet's wit and sparkling conversation made him good company and a popular guest.

So it was that the Mickleton visits continued, bringing Shenstone welcome respite from his solitary hours at home. He kept in touch with Mary, for in the early months of 1740, when Graves was taken seriously ill at Oxford, she writes to Shenstone informing him of her brother's recovery. In a letter that contains no hint of romance and from which it is clear that the poet's earlier advances have met with little success, she tells of events that by now have "determined (Dick) to leave Physick and turn Friar". It was a decision that was to have repercussions for the remainder of his life.

Mickleton was always to be there for Shenstone; but after Graves' marriage and after the poet had moved from Harborough to take up residence at The Leasowes, it was to feature less in his letters and his life. Mary was to marry although not to a man who would please her family; and the crowd of young people who had thronged the old house melted away as the future with its shackles and responsibilities beckoned. But Morgan Graves remained and Shenstone in his maturity writes of visiting his family, but now only briefly, and on his way to somewhere else. By the middle of the seventeen forties, the enjoyable, rumbustious houseparties of those early Mickleton days – like Oxford – had become a memory.

Chapter 5

SETTLING IN: 1736 – 1740

It was in the summer of 1736 that Shenstone decided to vacate Harborough and live with his tenant at The Leasowes. What the arrangements were is not known but it is clear that the locals all knew about the new owner and it was not to be long before Sir George Lyttelton, Shenstone's most influential neighbour and heir to the Hagley Estate, rode over with his brother-in-law, William Pitt, to introduce himself.

These were two powerful men. At the time of their first meeting Sir George was already Member of Parliament for Oakhampton in Somerset and was destined for high political office. Years later he was to become Chancellor of the Exchequer, "Strangely bewildered in his figures" records Horace Walpole gleefully. Pitt, too, was to wield the reins of power, becoming in 1756 the most influential man in Britain when, known as "the Great Commoner", he subsequently served as Prime Minister in coalition governments.

The effect of their arrival upon Shenstone can but be imagined. Always eager to cultivate the influential and the well-born, as indeed was everybody at that time, the visit would have seemed propitious as he contemplated a future plucked from relative obscurity. It is a pity that no record of the meeting exists and that we only hear third hand from Graves that it ever took place, for it was an event that was to prove memorable. Shenstone and Lyttelton, both of a similar age, had much in common. In spite of the disparity in their backgrounds, both were poets and both were to develop a keen interest in garden design. And although, on rare occasions, Shenstone was unable to quell a spark of jealousy, "the pompous piles of Hagley" were, nonetheless, to become for him a place of welcome and a focus for some of his best known social poetry. Both men were to benefit from the encounter. Shenstone from the influence of his important neighbour who would often bring his house guests round to admire The Leasowes and Sir George who was delighted to gain as a friend, a man of learning and letters who would entertain the guests at his table with both poetry and amusing conversation.

Later the two were to become targets for criticism. Shenstone was to be censured by Johnson for settling in the country and by Thomas Gray, of *Elegy in a Country Churchyard* fame, for not being sufficiently innovative in his poetry. Sir George, in spite of his family connections was to fare even worse. He was later to fall foul of Lord Hervey by means of a poem written as a young man with the latter in mind.

> *Let prudence guide you but let honour bind,*
> *In show, in manners, act the courtier's part,*
> *But be a country gentleman at heart.*[1]

These lines were to provoke a response in the great man's *Memoirs*, memorable not so much for accuracy as for malice. First he is moved to describe his "friend's" appearance.

> *Mr Lyttelton was in his figure extremely tall and thin; his face was so ugly, his person so ill made, and his carriage so awkward, that every feature was a blemish, every limb an encumbrance and every motion a disgrace...[2]*

He then turns his attention to the delivery of Sir George's parliamentary speeches which had "little meaning" were "ill put together" and delivered in a "lulling monotony". Once, Sir George Lyttelton had sincerely believed this man to be his friend.

The Lyttelton brothers, George, Richard and William were liberal patrons of the arts. It was Sir George who befriended James Thomson whose poem, *The Seasons*, was to meet with acclaim and who later introduced him to Shenstone. It was to be an association upon which the poet was to set great store and after Thomson's early death he wrote, under the patronage of Sir William Lyttelton, his *Verses Written Towards the Close of the Year*, in memory of him.

It was not long after the Lyttelton visit that Shenstone was to be introduced to another new friend, Henrietta Knight, the black haired beauty and estranged wife of Robert Knight of Barrels in Ullenhall. Henrietta, or Lady Luxborough as she was later to become, was a friend of Somervile of nearby Edstone Hall and of the Reverend Jago of Beaudesert in Henley-in-Arden. She also knew Jackie Reynolds, soon to become Somervile's chaplain and as these gentlemen were also friends of Shenstone, their meeting would seem to have been more or less inevitable.

Shenstone first mentions a visit to Barrels in 1740 in a letter to Reynolds in which he comments upon losing his way as he returned home; but we know from a letter written by Mrs Knight in 1739 to the poet's friend, Jago, that by then Shenstone was already sending her his verses and that he had already visited her. In it she thanks the former for introducing her to the poet and expresses her pleasure in his poetry. "I must... entreat you" she writes, "to make known to your friend, the sincerity of my heart in the approbation it gives to his works."[3] Shenstone's friendship with Lady Luxborough was to blossom in a remarkable way. Their friendship was to become one of the most important of his life and is chronicled in their letters. But for the present he was to be content, with the rest of his circle and without too much commitment, to enjoy the hospitality of her welcoming home.

Although Shenstone had moved into The Leasowes in 1736, he did not obtain full control of his own farm until his tenant, John Shenstone died in 1745. Until then life at his farm was to be punctuated by long periods away from home: in Worcester, London, Cheltenham and of course, Mickleton. And by now, with Oxford a pleasant memory and his friends scattered: Whistler back at Whitchurch in Oxfordshire; Jago at Harbury in Warwickshire and Graves soon to be at Tissington in Derbyshire; he was beginning to understand the drawbacks as well as the advantages of country life to which he returned, not always enthusiastically, from his visits away.

Already it was clear that the sending and receiving of letters was to be a lifeline and an art form upon which Shenstone was to expend considerable time and energy. One in which he set out to amuse his correspondents and to make his letters as "Fantastical" and as personal as possible in the hope that his friends would reciprocate. This they did, but not always as promptly as he would have liked. "I did indeed give you up for lost" he grumbles on one occasion to Graves – and a little later to Jago: "I have been extremely mortified in my correspondence of late" and proceeds to name both Graves and Whistler as partners in error.

Shenstone would look for letters as a miser prospects for gold. He was on friendly terms with "old Emmie", the Halesowen post mistress and, in an age when postal services were both suspect and rudimentary, would, "... pay her irregularly and in the lump" to bring packets to his door. The alacrity with which he could, when he wished, respond to letters, epitomised his eagerness to keep in touch. "It is not above two hours since I received your obliging letter and I am already set down to answer it"[4] he writes, which must have been a little discouraging to those other members of the coterie who were not gentlemen of leisure and busy making their way in a career!

Shenstone's letters of this period demonstrate many of the skills that he later became so adept at implementing. The humour, with which he describes setting out for London with a brand new pair of elegant pistols: "You will probably see your old friend on horse back, armed at all points, and as a very knight to all appearance as anybody".[5] The skilled aphorism as he gives his unlikely definition of a hypocrite:

I think the hypocrite is a half Good character. A man ...who...is...to be commended for talking better than he acts, as he is to be blamed for acting worse than he talks.[6]

A comment which although not possible, sounds as if plucked from Lewis Carroll's *Alice in Wonderland*. And always there is the supreme regard in which he holds his friends: his friendship for Graves, which is "inviolable" and for Jago which "no time shall extenuate".

Already the letters begin to form a diary of events and provide a glimpse into the workings of his mind during these years when, as a young man in his twenties, Shenstone spent much time away from home and was at his most active. It was a period when he was to pen many of his songs and ballads and, more importantly, his masterpiece of memory and execution, *The Schoolmistress*. The stories of this and his several visits from home at this time are to be told in the following chapters.

Chapter 6

MAN ABOUT TOWN

During the early seventeen forties when Shenstone was settling down at The Leasowes, his aspirations were high and he lived enthusiastically as a poet and young gentleman. He continued his visits to Mickleton and we come across him in Worcester, in London where every young aspirant making his way was to be seen, and in Cheltenham Spa. The impression is of a young man at work and enjoying himself at play although the first hint of melancholy with its resultant apathy when he was "habitually dispirited" had already manifested itself.

In the summer of 1740, Shenstone visited Worcester and attended "a very full" concert which is likely to have been part of the Three Choirs Festival programme. The trip was important to him, for most of his aristocratic friends and a number of his acquaintances would also have been there and he would have felt that he was keeping his finger upon the social pulse. It was not long before he "observed" a friend of Somervile's talking to Sir George Lyttelton and moments later was himself discussing poetry with the latter and especially the merits of the hunting and shooting squire's *The Chase*. That the occasion was primarily social there can be little doubt, and one feels that it was almost with regret that the audience settled down to listen to the music as "the fiddles squeaked, the harpsichord jingled" and silence was imposed...

Shenstone was fond of Worcester and briefly during the winter of 1740, toyed with the idea of wintering there as preferable to the isolation of dark months in the country. The idea came to nothing and instead of a "little cathedral town" he was to visit the great metropolis of London where he remained for four happy months. On this occasion he stayed at the home of Mr Wintle, a London perfumer who augmented his income, as did many tradesmen of the time, by taking in a few, recommended paying guests. His house, which adjoined the King's Arms by Temple Bar in Fleet Street, was centrally placed and Shenstone, who liked the man, was to remain a loyal customer for many years. Later, in 1749, he was to recall this visit and recommend the perfumer to his great friend, Lady Luxborough, "as a very obliging man" and one with whom he has "dealt with... for lavender water, wash balls and havannah" ever since. It was not to be long before her Ladyship, also, was to patronise Mr Wintle. "...his havannah and lavender water are, I know, extremely in vogue", she was to respond before ordering from him the distinctive Eau de Mille Fleurs which she used throughout the rest of her life.

There is an interesting sequel to this. For over two hundred and fifty years later, in 1988, it would seem that a number of staff who then still lived and worked on the Barrels Estate were convinced that Lady Luxborough's presence still lingered.

According to the author Colin Hey, one of the resident grooms who lived in a flat built over the original stable block, was frequently conscious of "a strong fragrance of perfume" as she went about her work. She and other employees, including the gardener, would also often experience "a freezing sensation" and the feeling as they carried out their tasks, that they were not alone. Villagers from Ullenhall corroborated these stories with evidence of their own for the existence of a benign, scented, ghostly presence and, whether their stories were true or not, none of the people questioned was aware of Lady Luxborough's passion for Mr Wintle's perfume.

Shenstone was to stay with the perfumer for the full term of his London visit and his letters of the period are filled with news of where he has been and what he has seen. For much of the time during these early days he is full of joie-de-vivre, enjoying: "a sunshiny day (and) a tavern supper after a play well acted". On occasion the reality is disappointing and of a production of *The Merry Wives of Windsor* he finds it: "impossible to express how much everything fell below my ideas"; and even worse the entertainment, "falsely so called" which followed, was of three hours length. In total, he would have endured five hours of boredom which must have been excruciating!

But in spite of himself he enjoys Colley Cibber in *Fondlewife*; in fact is "highly pleased with him" although he admits to feeling a hypocrite for deriving amusement from such an "ostentation of ...follies". And he tells of a gentleman who, on another occasion, sat next to him at a production of *Comus* and admitted to not understanding a word; who frequented the theatre only "to see and be seen" and was, suggests Shenstone, probably representative of "a great number of (playgoers) if they would but own it".

He writes of the commonality: of the chair, the Hackney coachman and the black-shoe-boys who "cry up the genius of Shakespeare" and who all are "amateur poets and judges of literature". His letters paint pictures on a large canvas and the writing and receiving of them was as important to Shenstone on holiday in London as it was to him back home at The Leasowes. To this end he charges Jago "to set aside the sum of eighteen pence... for letters which you will receive whilst I am in London"[1]; a tidy sum which provides a clue to the trouble he took with his correspondence. For if the cost of postage is to be born by the addressee there is every incentive to make the content worthy of the expenditure.

It was also during this time in London that Shenstone became involved in the "riddle controversy", a phrase coined by Graves and a game which the former played with enjoyment. Fans of Jane Austin and especially of her novel, *Emma*, will know that during the eighteenth century, riddle writing had become a craze. That Harriet's struggle to decode a conundrum presented to her by the ubiquitous Mr Elton, "Can it be... a trident? or a mermaid? or a shark?" is representative of similar amusements pursued in the wider world: and who can tell but that the riddle was the precursor of our modern crossword?

So it was that many tried their hand at riddle writing: that from the late seventeen thirties onwards, a plethora of doggerel verses, posing the question "What am I?"; swamped the market and a number of them, of which the following is an example, were published in the *Gentleman's Magazine*:

I'm all kinds of vice both of age and youth
And of all sorts of virtue the seat;
Wherever I'm present ev'n error is truth –
When absent ev'n truth is a cheat.

and tantalisingly the last verse ends:

But still I my old habitation retain
Ev'n after I'm turned out of doors,
And whilst he is seeking to fetch me again,
Madam, say what I am and I'm yours.[2]

Riddle writing and solving for many was fun, but a number held contrary views. Consequently in October 1740 there appeared in that edition of the magazine a little poem which wittily derides the craze and holds it responsible for a lowering of standards. It was signed S.S.:

Tis thus with him who fond of rhime
In wit's low species piddles;
And tunes his thoughts and wastes his time
In explicating riddles.

Go learn of Pope; then judge aright
Which way to fame's the surer;
To put the truth in fairest light
Or render it obscurer.

It was a stance with which both Shenstone and his friends agreed; the former believing with passion that "obscurity was the reverse of good writing" and together they entered the fray, intent upon proving their point and demolishing the opposition. It is now and for the first time that we see the poet in his role as editor – one that in later years he was to fulfil with considerable success. "I like everything in Mr Somervile's (poem) but the running of the last line" he writes authoritatively and later: "Should be glad to have a line or two of yours (Jago's) that one may make a bold attack"[3] and such like. One begins to see, too, the way in which the friends worked together, seeking and offering advice. "I have a line or two which... I would send to you for your advice" writes Shenstone "but can't readily find them". How human: and when he continues: "I look on it as *fun* without the least emotion" he speaks for all.

At the same time Shenstone was also engaged in a much more serious affair. This was his long poem in heroic couplets, *The Judgement of Hercules*, which was to be priced at one shilling and published by Robert Dodsley in the spring of 1741. The work, with an incorporated extract from the poem "… which we believe will show the author has been no less happy in the execution of his design than in the choice of patron" (Sir George Lyttelton), was advertised in the April edition of *Gentleman's Magazine* and Shenstone awaited anxiously upon its reception.

The Judgement of Hercules is little read today and one can understand why. Firstly, it is a very long poem and secondly, its sentiments are not those with which the modern reader is in tune. But it does show Shenstone's concern with the opposing values of a carefree or indolent country life and those of the city where success is a goal to be achieved by hard work. Is the young man in his poem to retire "to cool grots and tumbling rills", to a life of ease? Or is he to opt for the "generous toils" of town which alone will lead him "through the gates of fame"? The choices presented in *Hercules* are those which concerned Shenstone personally at this time. Having recently inherited the family home he was in the process of concluding that country pleasures at The Leasowes outweighed all else: unlike the character in his poem, whose solution is to choose to work hard in the city. To quote a cliché, it was a case of doing one thing and saying another.

In its day the poem was well received; and especially pleasing to Shenstone was a complimentary letter from his old tutor, Dr John Radcliff, now Master of Pembroke College. Its accompanying admonishment that the poet's conduct should "with equal propriety and elegance", illustrate the (poem's) moral was not so welcome for, in Shenstone's case, it was one thing to write about the virtue of toil and quite another to practise it. There was a further pleasant surprise and it occurred one morning when the poet was "loitering" at George's Coffee House, an emporium which prided itself upon being "the acknowledged region of gallantry, wit and criticism". It was here that members paid their one shilling fee which entitled them to read: "all pamphlets under a three shilling dimension", including gossip columns with headlines that rivalled our own popular press today. "ARE THOSE THINGS SO?"; and "WHAT THEN?" were typical of the way these stories were presented and for Shenstone, who was always on the lookout for things unusual or fantastic, would have had a special relish.

Also to be perused were pamphlets of a more literary bent: recently published poems, sermons and essays which could be presented upon request… And this was what happened when two well-dressed gentlemen entered and asked to see, *The Judgement of Hercules*. Not recognising the author, and one can imagine how the latter would have felt, the two quickly read the poem and as quickly delivered their verdict. "The work (was) fine – very fine", a recommendation which was music indeed – except that the gentlemen continued their conversation by determining the work to have been written by Pope!

Even so, flushed with modest success, Shenstone's hopes were buoyed and his spirits raised. It would soon be time to return home – to a life away from the bustle of town and a future that he could face with a smile.

Chapter 7

THE SCHOOLMISTRESS

Back at home, it was not long before Shenstone began to miss the lively company of town. Instead he was obliged to accommodate his neighbour, W.W., who came to visit in an old coat and a dirty shirt without a stock. Who made the point that he was a practical man and in no need of his host's poetry by the dextrous twiddling of a pair of scissors on his begrimed thumbs.

But as always it was in the sending and receiving of letters that Shenstone transcended such limitations. He writes to congratulate Graves upon his ordination at Oxford and professes him "very capable of shining in a dark coat", the uniform of his new profession which can so easily engender dislike. He enquires after the sale of his Collection of poetry and as if accidentally, points the truism that, "fact… is the comfortable resource of dull people". There was much time to be filled and he read Richardson's *Pamela*, pronouncing it "too prolix" in a comment with which many would agree and amused himself by designing cuts for an edited version of the novel.

All this is recounted with good-natured humour, but at other times the landscape changed and Shenstone, instead, was to find himself "utterly dejected". It was a mental state accompanied by a feeling of extreme inertia or as he writes to Jago, "a disregard for present things". He diagnoses the problem with an accuracy that is meticulous and in a way that vividly presents his feelings. During these periods his, "rakishness… is checked by want of spirits". His "solidity… is softened by vanity (and his) esteem of learning… broken in upon by laziness, imagination and want of money"[1]. At these times he finds it easier to daydream than to translate his imaginings into reality. Today, so much more is known about depressive states of mind and the accompanying inability to make decisions or take action that the illness engenders. We are inclined to be sympathetic. But in Shenstone's day his bouts of depression and his "laziness", no doubt triggered by feelings of isolation and insecurity, were not understood and even his friends despaired of provoking him into action.

Fortunately these periods of dejection did not last and it was not long before the pendulum of his mood was to swing and his spirits rose as he contemplated another trip to town. Enthusiastically he paints a picture of a party of four: himself, Whistler, Jago and Mr Outing, Lady Luxborough's secretary, all "jogging to the big city". He anticipates the fun they will have: Jago's laughter, "as candid and singular as his friendship", as together they all enjoy a trip to the theatre. For as young men they are "of the proper age for pleasure", and yet, sounding a gloomier note, do not have "above four or five whimsical years left". An extraordinary comment for a young man of twenty-six to make, and one which underpins Shenstone's dispiriting view of the transitory nature of life.

That the visit, on this occasion, did not materialise is arguably a good thing. The idea of London cheered him and enabled him to concentrate, instead, upon his poetry and especially *The Schoolmistress*. For this is a poem extolled by Dr Johnson as "the most pleasing of… works" and one which down the years has given pleasure to poetry lovers of all ages. *The Schoolmistress* is a journey back in time to the poet's years at his dame school under the stern guidance of Sarah Lloyd and is full of treats. In it we are introduced to the dame, herself, "a matron old" whose cap "is whiter than the driven snow" and who disciplines her young charges by means of her cane – her "tway birchen sprays". The children view her cane with awe; imagine it as being "shaped into rods", and tingle with apprehension as they look at it. After its use, Shenstone describes the victim's response to a sweetmeat, proffered to take his mind off his troubles. A child who not unexpectedly:

Scorns her offered love and shuns to be caressed.[2]

But in her own way, the old schoolmistress is both kindly and wise: and Shenstone's is an affectionate portrait. She allows: "One ancient hen begirt with her chickens" into the classroom to be fed; and she is skilful enough to accommodate herself to the needs of each child. Her task is:

To thwart the proud and the submiss to raise – [3]

For who knows, but that under her tutelage there might be with the right inducement:

A little bench of heedless bishops here
And there a chancellor in embryo… . [4]

There are many happy images which have much less to do with discipline. We glimpse playtime as the older children gambol on "a patch of green" outside her cottage; a joy denied to the littlest ones who are kept inside by means of an "imposing bar" across the open door. We are introduced to the old dame's herb garden from where so many homely remedies are grown and are seduced by the children and their world as we enter the classroom.

This is a jewel of a poem upon which Shenstone lavished much of his time during the winter months of 1741. A briefer version had appeared in his 1737 Collection as mentioned earlier, but now he set about expanding upon his original idea by adding another sixteen verses. The work evolved in a series of stages. Originally it had been intended as a burlesque; that is, a simple or "low" subject made humorous by means of inflated or grandiloquent language – in this instance – in the manner of Spencer.

However, between the original 1737 version and 1741, Shenstone's attitude had changed. Originally Spencer had been for "trifling and laughing"; but now this approach was to be no longer possible. After many re-readings, his admiration for the Elizabethan poet had grown and he was to find himself, instead, "really in love with him". To Graves, he explains how he feels:

> *The true burlesque of Spencer...seems to consist in a simple representation of ...*
> *things... one laughs to see and observe rather than in any monstrous contrast*
> *betwixt thought and words.* [5]

So it was that the poem became less of a burlesque with its accompanying "monstrous contrast" between subject matter and language, and more an affectionate portrait penned with nostalgia. It was a change of direction that was to have repercussions. For it meant that verse nine in the original version, one of the stanzas which most obviously reflects "monstrous contrast", would now have to go. In it Shenstone describes the unselfconscious way in which the children run outside to relieve themselves:

> *Then squatten down with hand beneath each knee*
> *He seeken out not secret rock or wall,*
> *But cack in open street – no shame doth them appeal –* [6]

The lines are but one example among many which met with the same fate; for these changes brought more and Shenstone, anxious that his affection for such a "low" subject should not be misunderstood, now felt obliged to add his ludicrous index which would supply those very elements of burlesque which he had just taken out. He explains to Graves his rationale. "I have added a ludicrous index, purely to show (fools) that I am in jest". He continues; "You cannot conceive how large the number is of those that mistake burlesque for the very foolishness it expresses"[7]. One cannot but agree. An example from the ludicrous index relating to stanza sixteen shows how it works. It is the verse in which the poet introduces us to the old dame who is sitting in her chair in front of her class.

> *In elbow chair, like that of Scottish stem...*
> *The matron sate; ...* [8]

In the ludicrous index this becomes: "a view of this rural potentate as seated in her chair of state, conferring honours, distributing bounties and dispensing proclamations..."[9] and so on.

Not only did Shenstone spend this winter in creating and refining extra stanzas for his poem, but also he designed a front cover for its appearance in pamphlet form. Embowered in trees, he drew the cottage where the old schoolmistress lived and where she held her class. In front of it was the "patch of green" where the children played in their break time. Just in sight is the spire of the village church and in the distance beyond the Clent Hills, the setting sun sparks its cartwheel rays across the panorama of the landscape. Shenstone spent much time perfecting his picture which was to be a prototype for the engraving to be executed by James Mynde, an artist of some note, especially for his engraving of birds. He wanted it as a fitting vehicle to help promote the publicity of his poem and at one time came near to persuading himself that the two were of equal merit. Unfortunately, upon Dodsley's publication of *The Schoolmistress* in the spring of 1742, such hopes were to be dashed. For the illustration was greeted, not with approbation but with amusement, and described by D'Israeli in the second volume of his *Curiosities of Literature* as little short of a disaster when he likened the effect of the setting sun to that of "a falling monster". So it was that Shenstone, after his initial approval of Mynde's design, came to believe that the engraver had let him down. Nevertheless it has to be said that a reproduction of the engraving which appears in Dodsley's first edition of *The Works* published in 1764, bears little resemblance to what one has been led to expect – but rather – is a delight.

It was in the spring of 1742 that Shenstone again visited London. His trip was one which enabled him to see James Mynde concerning the engraving of his illustration for *The Schoolmistress* and he chose to remain in town for the publication of his poem in May. On this occasion he was to desert Mr Wintle, his perfumer, for Ernest Shuckborough, a London bookseller in Fleet Street, and a man with whom his friend, Whistler, frequently stayed: and as usual his letters to friends are filled with news and gossip. He has spent a whole evening gossiping at a coffee-house. He has been to see *All's Well That Ends Well* and describes Colly Cibber's son as Paroles, a part for which he dons:

> *A rusty black coat, black stock, a black wig with a Ramillie, a pair of*
> *Black gloves and a face – which causes five minutes of laughter.*[10]

He has spent time with Mr Outing who, in London, presents a different face. Who in the company of a Mr Dean, "… had laid his hand upon his sword six times and threatened a dozen men (with) death, one of which was Broughton, the prize fighter"[11]. Not very sensibly, one is inclined to think! And later, on another occasion, he was just about "to kick a fellow downstairs" when fortunately, he was talked out of it by a friend.

To take his mind off things and especially the publication of his *Schoolmistress* Shenstone has bought himself a magnificent belt which "captivates the eye of all beholders" and to further describe it he quotes some lines from a burlesque opera, *The Dragon of Wantley:*

> *No girdle nor belt, e'er excell'd it;*
> *It frightens the men in a minute:*
> *No maiden yet ever beheld it,*
> *But wished herself tied to me in it.*[12]

We come across him walking in the park with his companions, or strolling in the Mall sometimes as late as ten in the evening. It was on one of these occasions that he passes the Duke who stares at him "enormously". Was it, one wonders, anything to do with that resplendent belt? On another, "a tasteless fellow" spoils his walk when Shenstone suffers the indignity in conversation of being contradicted in "things I have studied and am certain of".

It was while still in town that the poet was to hear of the death of his old friend William Somervile. As a teenager Shenstone had been impressed by the older poet's expensive lifestyle; for he had never allowed a lack of money to prevent him from doing and having what he wanted. It was a situation with which Shenstone drew parallels, perceiving his own financial problems as similar to those which had faced the Edstone squire. "My old friend Somervile is dead", he writes to Jago of the man who had been "forced to drink himself into pain of the body in order to get rid of the pain of the mind"[13]. In an original and humorously anglicised version of a Latin phrase, he refers to the older poet's management, or rather mismanagement, of his finances. "I loved him for nothing so much as his flocci-nauci-nihili-pilification of money". It was a phrase later to become popular with writers from many different parts of the country, including Sir Walter Scott and William Hazlett who, in his role as critic, was years later to deride a book he was reviewing as "a work which, in Shenstone's words, the flocci-nauci-nihili-pilification… known to every competent judge is placarded into eminence".[14]

There is little doubt that Shenstone enjoyed his visit to London at this time, but there were anxieties; there were frustrations. His concern for the imminent publication of his *Schoolmistress* was constant. The poem was to be advertised in both the *London Magazine* and the *Gentleman's Magazine* of May 1742, but just prior to the deadline he was still anxiously awaiting advice from Graves which he hopes "will free me from much perplexity". And this in spite of the fact that at the same time he doubts whether "I can defer my schemes so as to make your criticisms of service". Then there was his status as a man of letters which he felt on occasion to be compromised. It distresses him when he is contradicted by the less educated which makes him, instead, keep his own council and "give up my *knowledge* to *pretence* or vent it with diffidence to fools". So his London visit progressed.

It was a time when, on a good day, his eye-catching belt matched his temper and he was ebullient. But there were other occasions, too, when already he felt that life was passing him by. His mood seesawed and yet, whatever he might feel, summer signalled; it was time to pack up and return home.

And what of the *Schoolmistress*? Even after the 1742 version of his poem was published, Shenstone was not satisfied. After a further reading of Spencer and several years later, in 1745, he was still working on it and having written "full as much more" sent the manuscript to Graves for comment. The response is of interest. For Graves, always tactful, felt the additional verses to be repetitive – pointed out that the work was already complete and could not be bettered. But Shenstone was undeterred and his reply is quintessential of the charm which many found endearing:

I thank you for your perusal (but) you will pardon my silly
Prejudices if I choose to read and show most of my new stanzas.[15]

Who was right? Graves was an astute critic and there is some weight in what he says. But there is no denying that the *Schoolmistress* in its present form with the additional verses is a joy. One must make one's own choice.

It was in January 1748 that this extended version of the poem was first published by Dodsley in the first volume of his popular series of anthologies, *Poems by Several Hands*. The story of this is told fully later; so it suffices here to mention briefly that Shenstone, who would have liked more time to "spruce her up a little", was far from pleased: that he offered to supply an "improved" version to Dodsley when a second edition of the volume was pending and would seem to have been incapable of leaving the poem alone. Even as late as 1750, he was still hopeful of, "furnishing a more complete edition yet…".

It is a human story – of delight and frustration. A story which irritates and yet one with which the reader can empathise. And there can be very few whose delight in literature does not enable them to enjoy this remarkable and poignant poem.

Chapter 8

MARY ARNOLD
AND MARY CUTLER

Summer called, but for a further few weeks Shenstone lingered in town. He was impressed by a parody that Graves had sent him and "had a violent inclination to print it …price 4.p". Adopting an editorial role he urgently requested "whether I print or no?"

The weeks slid by and he busied himself with editorial tasks that prefigured the important role he was later to perform for Dodsley; but finally he could put off returning home no longer. It was a return soon to be brightened by the arrival of an invitation to Mickleton where the "irregularity of the housekeeping" was much to his taste and the company of appreciative friends lifted his spirits. Mickleton, where there was no arbitrary summoning of the gong; where at meal times his conversation scintillated and his wit was given a free rein.

But all this, too, was to come to an end and back at The Leasowes he soon became unhappy in his "wintery, unvisited state". It was at these times that the burden upon his friends was considerable. For his dependence upon letters was such that he would take umbrage when they did not arrive as frequently as he would like. When he feels that "Whistler has not for caring to write", or he begins to fear that a delayed letter from Graves is because he has taken offence. Sadly he admits at these times he "must rely for happiness on the hopes of a never-ceasing correspondence" and he is not above the occasional reprimand: "I did indeed give you up for lost".

However, all this was surface froth and the foundation of his friendships remained steady. The friends continued to exchange poems and offer criticism. "I have" he writes to Graves, "your poem in front of me…and many observations to make". These were to include both the title and the preface which "is on no count to be admitted". The letters run on and are scattered through with thought-provoking and quotable comments. "Flattery among foes is…absolutely desirable…but among friends its consequences are of too dangerous a nature".[1]

The tone of the letters is conversational. "Have you read? …Have you tried? …What think you?" All recur frequently and are the exchanges of intimates. Shenstone gossips of local news: "Mr Lyttelton has built a kind of alcove in his park", he writes of his Hagley neighbour; and he has a nose for any entertaining story such as the one about an alehouse he visited in Wales with no glass in the windows. How, when questioned about the cold, the couple admit that they would like glass because it is "so very genteel"; a circumstance which as the poet relates, "struck me a good deal that they should discover the genteelness of glazing and never think of its expediency".[2]

In the early summer of 1743 Shenstone entertained a number of guests. Graves came in June, a visit which because of its success, plunged the poet into gloom when it ended. But not for long; for soon it was Jago's turn and together the two visited Dudley Castle which "has great romantic beauty" and where Shenstone felt the urge to quote from Shakespeare's *Henry V*. The days slipped away and soon, too soon, it was time for Jago also to return home, leaving behind his friend to mull things over on his own.

On his own, and in spite of the kind solicitations of his friends, it was around this time that Shenstone seems to have become quite seriously ill. His illness was the culmination of many less serious bouts of ill health which seem to have occurred from his early twenties onwards; "nervous fevers" which although possibly emotional in origin, nevertheless manifested debilitating physical symptoms.

> *When I was a school boy, I never knew there was any such thing as perspiration, and now, half my time is taken up in considering the immediate connextion betwixt that and health.*[3]

There is also the hereditary problem. For both Shenstone's parents had died when comparatively young: his mother aged thirty-nine and his father at thirty-eight. His brother Joseph, died when only twenty-nine and inherited weaknesses may also have played a part in some of the symptoms of illness that the poet experienced throughout his life. In fact it is likely that both emotional trauma and heredity contributed to the catalogue of ailments from which, during the early summer of 1743, the poet was seldom free.

He had problems in sleeping. "I can scarce get a wink of disordered sleep for a whole night together". It was a state of affairs which he made frantic efforts to remedy. He would ride every day until exhausted, but to no avail; for when on the verge of sleep, he would find himself, like a puppet on a string, "jerked" wide awake to endure the misery of another sleepless night. Not surprisingly it was a time when he felt "old" and had energy only for "lolling on the bank in the very heat of the sun". He suffered also with vertigo and dizzy spells, conditions that were to plague him intermittently throughout his life and render him incapable of concentrating. He experienced severe night sweats and digestive disorders: an unrelenting colic and wind accompanied by "a pale flux".

It was now that Shenstone came to appreciate the role played by his housekeeper, Mary Arnold, for this redoubtable woman was as caring and as loving as a mother. She sat with him for long spells during the night when he was feverish and could not sleep. She prepared him special, tasty and easily digested dishes to tempt his appetite. To keep up his spirits she regaled him with stories and during the evening was constantly on hand to move and adjust his candle. It is not surprising that the poet came to "prefer her to all her station!"

It is clear that Mary Arnold adored her master, and from references that Shenstone makes to her in the *Letters* it is possible to build an affectionate portrait of this loyal and uncomplicated country woman. We glimpse her in the farmyard, tending her beloved chickens or rushing excitedly and breathless indoors to report the joyful news of a clutch of newly hatched chicks. Her hens are "Poor pretty creturs" and she delights to bring one in her arms that "has gotten a speck of black upon her tail" or single out another favourite, "a great black and white hen" as an admirable mother. Mary Arnold's concern was with young chicks and egg laying hens. In birds for the table she took no interest and her response to any suggestion of slaughtering was as uncompromising as it was forthright. None of her birds was suitable, "ne'er a one".

On the other hand, a present from Lady Luxborough of eggs for hatching was a different matter. For "under the protection and auspices of the fortunate Mrs Arnold", they would be quickly placed under a suitable hen. And when, years later, another present of a couple of very fine geese arrived: Don Pedro,

> *"who has all the stateliness of a swan; and Donna Elvira his faithful consort (who) has filled my vallies with complaint for the long summer days".*[4]

It was from Mrs Arnold that Shenstone was to seek a solution. She offered two and one may take one's pick. Either the goose was expostulating about the loss of some young, ...or lamenting her removal from plenty and splendour (at Barrels) to poverty and obscurity (at The Leasowes). Fortunately it was not to be long before the bird, for whatever reason, settled down in her new environment, "she now seems content with both", and peace was restored.

Although built on mutual esteem, Shenstone's relationship with his housekeeper was not without problems. We read of his discomfiture when she persisted in visiting neighbours in her smock, a state of undress which he considered to be unseemly. He remonstrated to little effect, however, for Mary Arnold could be deaf when she chose and was prepared to go to war to protect her little freedoms. At one such time, Shenstone recounts her involvement in a verbal "battle" which lasted for over two hours! It took place inside the stairwell of The Leasowes with Mrs Arnold stationed, as befitted the victor, at the top of the stairs and her combatant, a female neighbour who had transgressed, cornered in the hall. Shenstone who is amused, describes the incident in military terms. "The fire lasted the whole space, without intermission; at the close of which the enemy was routed, and Mrs Arnold kept the field".[5]

All of Shenstone's friends who met Mrs Arnold liked her and admired the loyalty with which she served her master. To Whistler she was an "example of the simple force of moral beauty" and by providing for her care in his will, Shenstone was to demonstrate his appreciation of her in a tangible way.

Mrs Arnold was a country woman with a rich store of folklore. The poet tells of her repository of "charms" and "incantations" and there is little doubt that in modern terms she was also an excellent psychologist with an instinctive knowledge of sickroom management. On the numerous occasions when Shenstone took to his bed, not only would she keep up his spirits with tall stories and warm drinks, but encourage him on the earliest count to leave the sickroom and occupy his mind with something new: a visit to see the "pretty creatures in the barn" when one of the cows had newly calved, served her purpose well.

Sometime before his death, the poet was to write an appreciative inscription to her in Latin which she most certainly would not have understood! It was never published and was to surface decades later in the February edition of the *Gentleman's Magazine* in 1797. It was submitted by a resident of Halesowen as "a literary curiosity", copied from a small notebook, an original manuscript which he claimed to have in his possession:

"Hunc juxta locum	*"Near this place*
mortales fui exuvias	*Mary Arnold peacefully laid down her mortal coil*
LXX annorum invida	*finally torn from her*
tandem dilaceratas	*through the envy of seventy years;*
placide depofuit	*Mary Arnold*
M.A.	*a friendly slave*
Amicum mancipium domino	*which is just what a master wants."*
Frugi quod fit fatis"	

This interesting find poses problems. Why should the poet have provided for his housekeeper in his will if she had died before him? All the evidence points to the fact that she outlived her master, so perhaps this is a joke? Or refers, not to her death, but to her retirement? It is a puzzle. One thing it does, however, is to point the affection that Shenstone felt for his old retainer whom he had come to regard almost as "family".

Indeed, it is now worth looking a little more closely at the role of the "upper" servants in Shenstone's life. There were two women in the poet's household who would have fitted into this category: Mary Arnold and his maid, Mary Cutler. There was also the "trusty" Tom who was responsible for so much of the work carried out in The Leasowes park but who does not feature in this chapter. Both the women were devoted to him and both, because Shenstone frequently could not afford their wages, worked for very little money. In fact, when times were hard, and for Shenstone they frequently were, he would borrow money from the latter and at the time of his death was in her debt to the staggering amount of £500. So these women were not servants in the accepted sense but rather employees and there may well have been a romantic involvement with one of them. But which one? And where is the evidence?

In his novel, *Columella*, Graves models his plot upon Shenstone and The Leasowes' household. The hero, Columella, falls in love with his maid and makes the interesting confession that:

> *A man is never completely ruined till he has married his maid; yet... his ruin is nearly complete when he so far indulges the ignoble flame, as to take any freedoms with a servant.*[6]

Now when it is understood that the material in all his novels is meticulously replicated from life, and that Graves makes little attempt to disguise his sources, this is of interest. It becomes more so when it is placed beside an extract from one of Shenstone's letters written to his friend in 1745:

> *It is long since I have considered myself as undone. The world will perhaps*
> *Not consider me in that light entirely, till I have married my maid!*[7]

And when this is followed by a further letter detailing, "My amour as far as I indulge it, gives me some pleasure, and no pain in the world"[8], the picture becomes still clearer. So it is possible that Shenstone did become romantically involved with one of his servants.

It is unlikely to have been Mary Arnold for she was not only considerably older than the poet, but possessed little formal education. It is more likely to have been Mary Cutler or "Molly" as the poet affectionately called her. For we know that Miss Cutler was literate and highly regarded by Shenstone and his friends. In 1758 Dodsley was to send her, together with the poet and Mr Hylton, a signed copy of *Cleone*. He also gave her Christmas presents as in 1757, "to my good friend Mrs Mary a small canister of tea". On another occasion, in lieu of wages, Shenstone was to give her an illustrated manuscript copy of his Elegies and after his death she was to become the proud custodian of his library – although how this came about is a mystery. It is a mystery, too, how after Shenstone's death the two women came to live at Ivey Farm, one of the poet's numerous little properties: but that is a story to be told later when the poet's will is discussed.

It was at Ivey Farm, in 1768 that Catherine Hutton, the daughter of William Hutton, Birmingham's first historian was entertained. She was staying with a Mrs Fieldhouse, "A woman of excellent understanding, great reading and poetical taste": who had been a neighbour and a friend of the poet and who, with her twelve-year-old guest, was invited there to tea. It is from the child, Catherine, that we get what is possibly the only existing description of Mary Cutler. In her Journal, she writes that Miss Cutler:

> *Was about forty-five or forty-eight years of age; tall and thin, her face hard favoured,*
> *but not disagreeable, her manner grave, almost to melancholy.*[9]

She describes the room where they drank tea "which served for kitchen parlour and hall". It was a room with "a brick floor and one casement window" with furniture that was "neat and good". She continues:

> *A door on the left hand opened into a smaller room; and here was Shenstone's picture,*
> *in oil, as large as life, and in a handsome frame:*

Inscribed on the back were the words:

> *This portrait belongs to Mary Cutler, given her by her master William Shenstone*
> *Jan 1st 1754, in acknowledgement of her native genius, her magnanimity, her*
> *tenderness and fidelity.*[10]

Does this provide another clue to the nature of their relationship? Arguably it does, for it is not the kind of present that the poet would have given to an illiterate peasant woman. And surely, knowing that he was a man who would have chosen the words of the dedication with care, the choice of "tenderness" (a wifely tenderness?) amidst the role call of her other attributes, must be of some significance.

The little room where this portrait hung was also the "library"; for here "in excellent condition", Shenstone's books adorned the walls. It is of interest that Catherine believed Mary Cutler to have "idolised the memory of her master" and in an indirect allusion to the poet's housekeeper, Mary Arnold, mentions the former to have had either a servant or a sister living with her.

The episode is of interest because of the light it sheds upon how Miss Cutler was regarded within the wider community. That she was on visiting terms with the respectable and middle-class Mrs Fieldhouse, says much for the regard in which she must have been held.

That Mary Cutler was an educated woman and one with whom the poet would have had a degree of rapport, there can be little doubt. She was also a woman of means – not what one would expect of a servant. It has already been mentioned that Shenstone, on occasion, would borrow money from her and that when he died he owed her a considerable sum. In spite of this, Miss Cutler still had money to leave to members of her extensive family. In her own will she left her sister, Hannah Moore, the interest on a hundred pounds "of good and lawful money of Great Britain;" and to her niece, Elizabeth Derby, the interest on sixty. To this must be added the ten guineas left to Matthew Chandler "for the trouble I have given and services he has offered me" and a guinea to her godson, Richard Chandler, "to purchase him a good Bible". It would seem that she was a woman of sincerely held views and forthright opinions: someone who would have made a man a good wife!

There was a time, early in 1749, when Mary Cutler decided to leave Shenstone's employ. Was this because of money she was owed? Or because her hopes of marriage had been dashed? We do not know but it is probable that her decision would have had something to do with a personal grievance; and the timescale, a mere two years after Shenstone has hinted at an involvement, would fit well with the second option. We know that she changed her mind and appears to have been influenced by the poet's promise of an improvement in her status. He agreed to increase her salary from five to ten pounds a year and to offer her a post as housekeeper. Shenstone never married. Marriage would have impinged upon his relationship with Lady Luxborough, a friendship to be discussed later; and if he had married Cutler, it would have interfered with his social aspirations. The poet was not Richard Graves and his Molly was not the delectable Lucy.

Both Shenstone's employees, Mary Cutler and Mary Arnold, lived with him to the unexpected end of his life. In this respect he was fortunate for each would have been able to cater for his differing needs: and they must, for the most part, have been content, or they would not have remained. In the summer of 1743 when Shenstone was ill, both women had a role to fulfil; and it was Mary Arnold, as different from Miss Cutler as it is possible to imagine, who cosseted the poet back to health - a chastened man who now determined upon a trip to Cheltenham Spa, to drink the waters and consolidate his recovery.

Chapter 9

CHELTENHAM AND
THE PASTORAL BALLAD
– A CHAPTER ENDS: 1743-1745

By the seventeen forties, Cheltenham was becoming increasingly fashionable. Its popularity had been aided by the publication, in 1740, of Dr Short's *History of Mineral Waters* in which he maintained that Cheltenham waters were the most efficacious in the country. It was a claim which advanced the town's expansion and encouraged the publication of guide books trumpeting the waters as "a most commodious purge for those who do not bear strong cathartics" - an affirmation which would have appealed to Shenstone, whose search for the right purge to overcome his digestive problems was constant.

At the time of the poet's visit, Cheltenham's graceful Well Walk was newly planted with elms and limes; and when frequenting the Pump Rooms he would have passed the newly built Grove House where much of the Spa's entertainment took place. Unfortunately much of this would have involved dancing and card-playing – both leisure activities which Shenstone disliked. But he would have enjoyed the concerts promoted on a regular basis and, above all, conversation with "superior" people of whom there were a number that summer in 1743. Records show that his fellow guests included members of the aristocracy: the Duke and Duchess of Argyle, the Earl of Chesterfield and Sir Francis Dashwood among others.

Shenstone would also have been able to see a number of plays; for although, as yet, there was no resident theatre company in Cheltenham, The Warwick Company of Comedians was in town with a repertoire that included: Beaumont and Fletcher, Shakespeare and Dryden whose plays, before the construction of a permanent theatre in the town, were performed in converted malt houses or the back rooms of inns. So there was much to look forward to, and in spite of his recent illness, the poet set out for the Spa in high spirits. "I am in as good spirits this instant as ever I was..." he writes in one of those mercurial changes of temper which characterise his behaviour at the time.

But in spite of an auspicious beginning, his journey to Cheltenham turned out to be both fatiguing and expensive; a situation which he brought upon himself. For on the way he was tempted to call in at Mickleton to view the improvements introduced by Morgan Graves in his park. In his enthusiasm he stayed too long, refused an invitation to stay the night and set off again without a hope of reaching his destination in daylight. In the dark he lost his way, was fortunately rescued by "a waggoner's servant" who led him to "the worst Inn…I ever lay at", and arrived after a sleepless night, exhausted and a day late, in Cheltenham to begin the restorative of a holiday, which, by then, he needed more than ever.

Shenstone's stay at the Spa lasted two months and it was during this period that he fell considerably in love with a Miss "C". Unfortunately few letters survive from this time – possibly because his attention was otherwise engaged. There is a bravura little piece to Graves upon arrival; "My pen has run on a whole page at random" and then – silence. This is a pity because it means that one is dependent for information about the girl upon what the poet has to say when he returned home, by which time the affair has already taken on the glamour of the unobtainable. "I did not think it possible I could have been so much engaged by love as I have been of late – poor Miss "C" -!"[1] Why *poor* one wonders? And, as always, when Shenstone's heart is involved there is an ambivalence. On the one hand his emotions are engaged but on the other he is anxious to play down the episode before he is seen to appear too committed. "I know not what you have heard of my amour" he writes to Graves, and pointing to the roles played by gossip and exaggeration, "probably more than I can thoroughly confirm:" and then, as if to put an end to speculation: "marriage was not once the subject of our conversation".

While to his friends Shenstone was alternately rhapsodic or dismissive of the affair, in a letter to the girl, herself, he maintains a facetious front – his defence against hurt. "Perhaps you may remember to have seen an odd sort of fellow"… Or later:

You are a very wicked lady, you defrauded me of the crosslet you promised me, putting me off with a single bead; but it was yours, and that's enough".[2]

The truth is that Shenstone was both attracted to and at the same time afraid of the commitment of marriage. That in all his affairs of the heart, it was fear that ultimately won: an emotion which obliged him to concoct fragile excuses such as his own lack of money or the girl's imaginary reluctance which encouraged him to retreat when the situation was beginning to look hopeful. So it is not unexpected that young Miss "C" at Cheltenham was destined to go the same way as all the others, except for one important difference, the *Pastoral Ballad*.

Graves tells us that Shenstone first conceived a poem along these lines when he fell a little in love with Mary Graves in those early days at Mickleton. It was never completed and the germ of the idea remained with him until at Cheltenham he became captivated with Miss "C" or Miss Carter as she probably was; an experience which seems to have acted as a catalyst. For no sooner home, and upon a flood tide of creativity the poem was drafted; although with the poet's obsession for "improvement" it did not arrive at the form in which it now appears in the *Works* until a number of years later.

This lovely poem is divided into four parts: *Absence, Hope, Anxiety* and *Disappointment* which together span the spectrum of emotions that he has so recently experienced. He has parted from a love with whom he "has prized every hour that went by"; but is buoyed by the hope that she will one day join him at The Leasowes where:

My banks are burnished with bees
Whose murmurs invite one to sleep;
My grottos are shaded with trees
And my hills are white over with sheep.

The lines are well known and justly so, as is a later quatrain from the same section:

I have found out a gift for my fair;
I have found where the wood pigeons breed;
But let me that plunder forbear,
She will say 'twas a barbarous deed;

For here is shown a remarkable concern for bird life at a time when such sentiments were rare. However, a poignant triplet from the poem's final section, *Disappointment*, is often overlooked:

Perhaps it was plain to foresee
That a nymph so complete would be sought
By a swain more engaging than me.[3]

It is a passage which iterates Shenstone's underlying insecurity in his dealings with women; and in lines that are tender, wistful and sonorous, he leaves one with the feeling that an unhappy outcome is inevitable – almost wished for.

In this ballad Shenstone uses a conventional literary form, the pastoral, as a vehicle for the outpouring of genuine emotion. For while his swains and nymphs may appear as divorced from the realities of life as their filigree counterparts upon the mantelshelf, his understanding of country life is born of a personal experience which enables him to write with a conviction not found in some other works belonging to this category. And this, in spite of the line taken by Dr Johnson who argues that the "intelligent reader" who understands the reality of life in the country, "sickens at the mention of the crook, the pipe (and) the sheep...". *The Pastoral Ballad* is one of the poet's most delightful and readable poems; and without the elusive Miss "C" it is likely would never have been written. Who was she? Was she the daughter of a Mrs Carter who Shenstone also met at Cheltenham? A lady in whose gift was the prize of a clergyman's hat for the best preacher of the season? It seems likely; and if not provable at least one thing is clear. Whoever she was we owe her a debt for the part that she, no doubt unwittingly, played in the execution of a work that deserves to be enjoyed as much today as when it was first penned.

As the memories of Cheltenham began to fade, Shenstone's letters tell something of how his life at this time proceeded. He was not only working on his elegies, songs and ballads, but was becoming increasingly interested in the improvement of his estate. He has improvised "a serpentine river" out of a little stream and is in the process of "raising a greenhouse" from the remains of one that his friend, Lord Dudley, has pulled down. He recounts a charming story concerning his friend's father whose decision to mix business with pleasure must have caused amusement. For in the middle of a wedding reception, when the Grange, the Dudley's family home, was filled with "feasting and high Jollity", this old gentleman suddenly remembered a quantity of timber that had caught his eye and the possibility that it might prove suitable for conversion into "gunsticks". He did not waste time; but thereupon sent out for samples and had them delivered, not to his door, but inside his house where his guests were obliged to pick their way over and around them, that oblivious to their discomfiture he might finally come to his decision.

But in spite of this humorous little tale, there is no disguising the fact that Shenstone was melancholy. That his house "does not receive a sufficient number of polite friends and is not fit to receive 'em (even) were they so disposed"[4]. That he is lonely and "now and then impelled by the Social passion to sit half an hour in my kitchen"[5]. Is this, one wonders, how any possible romance with Mary Cutler might have started?

It is also a time when Shenstone has "little health and frequent mortification:" and is, "sensible of the daily progress I make towards insignificance". Even so, on occasion his acerbic wit can still resurface. He has been reading the fifth in the series of Edward Young's *Night Thoughts* and does not think that the contents measure up to the standard of his earlier work. Indeed, he considers it "wind in great measure" and recommends treatment: "rhubarb in powder, with a little nutmeg grated in it as I do".

So the months passed until, after the usual procrastination and in the throes of a severe cold, he was to set out again, in May of the following year, for London. On the way up he visited Lady Fane's Grotto at Basildon which, at the incredible cost of five thousand pounds, in the region of over half a million pounds in today's money, had been entirely decorated with sea shells. By contrast, Shenstone's own estimate of a mere three hundred pounds as sufficient to implement his own plans at The Leasowes was extremely modest and placed the former's achievement high up upon the Richter scale of extravagance.

Upon arrival in London, Shenstone took lodgings with a goldsmith who like the perfumer, Mr Wintle, had premises conveniently situated between the two coffee-houses, George's and Nando's, where he felt most at home. It is from the latter that his letters paint a lurid picture of how life in the capital has deteriorated over the last couple of years. He tells of pickpockets who now openly carry "bludgeons" to knock their victims down; and he points out that both Fleet Street and the Strand are no longer safe to walk down alone. In the theatre hinterland of Covent Garden things are even worse. Here, as people pour out of the theatres they are attacked by gangs who are armed with knives: a circumstance which was to make the poet hesitant about frequenting play-houses which he had previously so much enjoyed.

It was disappointing; and the fact that he had no companion with him led to feelings of isolation such as he experienced at home. But he cheered himself up by recounting gossip gleaned from coffee-houses. There is the story of Sir Thomas Knight who was to find himself knighted against his will, and who before being allowed to leave St James' Palace, was subject to a demand of one hundred pounds for the privilege! who was to leave in a violent rage and whose comments upon departure: "G-d Jack, what dost think? – I am knighted – the devil of a knight, e'faith", provide their own humorous commentary.

Dependent for companionship and gossip upon fellow frequenters of the coffee-house, Shenstone, for a while, made the best of things. He writes of debate in the House: "My Lord Carteret said yesterday…"; of theatre news and a translation of Voltaire's *Mahomet* at Drury Lane of which he has "no great opinion". He has heard that Pope is upon his deathbed; but the news is at third hand and one feels that Shenstone is at the periphery of affairs and with "but slender inducement to stay". So he lingered on in London for a further month, grappling with a melancholy to which, upon his eventual return home, he was to give full rein.

Then he pours out his frustration to his friends. His poor health; his lack of recognition; and a supposedly lost happiness which he dates, in a glorious phrase, from the time when he "first deviated from the turnpike road of life". In a final excess of misery, he recognises that to whatever heights others may aspire, he "must aim at nothing higher than a well concealed ignorance". So he does what so many of us do when we feel depressed; he exaggerates and his very exaggeration seems to have a cathartic quality. For fortunately it was not to be long before his mood was to swing; and his long-suffering friends who had recently appeared as "lost" were back in favour. Soon he was looking forward to the Spring visits of Graves and Whistler who now, as each stepped over the threshold of The Leasowes, would afford him "a climax of happiness". Now he could talk of "jaunts", of "public places to visit… to peep at and renew my idea of the world's vanity".[6]

With his emotional and physical health restored, the following summer of 1745 passed agreeably. After visits from friends, he was again to spend time at Broom with his cousins, the Dolman children who had recently lost their father and for whom, in consequence, he felt a special concern. Together they visited Lichfield and attended a service at the cathedral where they were, "confined and crammed… and served God after the manner of Popes and Cardinals!" They also took a trip to Worcester whose cathedral, by contrast, does not get a mention and they visited the Fletchers of Aston in Birmingham where the family lived. The three Fletcher sisters, and especially Winnie, were great friends of Shenstone as was their brother who asked to borrow the poet's set of pistols, for there was talk of him volunteering to fight against the Young Pretender. It was a request with which Shenstone was delighted to comply for he had both a fear and dislike of Roman Catholicism which we, today, might find hard to understand. He believed, as did many of his contemporaries, that the rebels would be defeated in "less than a fortnight" and like many mild mannered men, admired the dash cut by the soldiers of the Legionnaires' Horse when he saw them march through Birmingham, "with vast spirits and alacrity".

Winnie Fletcher, especially, was good for Shenstone for she boosted his confidence with her admiration of him as a man of letters and taste:

I think it would be inconsistent with gratitude as well as good manners, not to return thanks for the pleasures your writings have given me.[7]

So she replied to one of his many letters. And he would respond in kind by thanking her for her "elegant letter"; or upbraiding her for escaping him at Birmingham by concealing the time of her visit. It was a light-hearted, pleasurable friendship which was beneficial to both and did not have the complications of a love affair.

But to return to the Dolmans and their home at Broom. The visit there in the summer of 1745 was a happy one. Maria Dolman who, for her age, had achieved "great things" was a favourite of Shenstone's and her brother, Thomas, an agreeable companion. Then they presented a united family front which later was to be destroyed: first by Maria's tragic death, and second by Thomas who was to embark upon lengthy litigation in an attempt to increase his share of the Penn estate. It was to cause Shenstone much distress but that belongs to the future. At this time there was no such cloud upon the horizon and the poet was free to enjoy the company of his young cousins during a pleasurable holiday which was to mark the end of what might loosely be termed a chapter in his life. For from this time onwards, it was to be his blossoming friendship with Lady Luxborough and his increasing involvement with plans for his garden that were to occupy so much more of his time.

Chapter 10

THE LUXBOROUGH LETTERS

Background

Shenstone first met Lady Luxborough in 1739. He was twenty-five, a talented but insecure young man and she at thirty-nine, a raven haired beauty of considerable intellect and charm. By this time Henrietta Knight, as she then was, was already well established at her home, Barrels Hall, in the village of Ullenhall near Henley-in-Arden and numbered among her intimates the poet, Somervile, of Edstone Hall and Shenstone's close friend, Richard Jago. It was through the latter that the poet had first met Somervile, and it is likely that Jago facilitated his introduction to Mrs Knight. Welcomed into the Warwickshire circle of this remarkable woman, there is no doubt that life for Shenstone took on a gloss that it would not otherwise have had: that their friendship which burgeoned into increasing intimacy, was to bring solace and enormous satisfaction to them both.

One thing is clear; the woman who became Shenstone's friend bore little resemblance to her earlier self, for she had matured and blossomed since the separation from her husband, Robert Knight, three years earlier. Then there had been rumours of a romantic interlude with John Dalton, who later was to court acclaim with his adaptation of Milton's *Comus*. At the time he had been employed as tutor to Lady Hertford's son, Lord Beauchamp, and an intercepted letter had brought disgrace upon Mrs Knight and fired her husband's fury. Henrietta had always denied authorship and maintained it to be the copy of a translation she had made and intended to burn; but of course the explanation raised further questions.

What is certain is that the husband was a womaniser who did not follow the dictates that he set out for his wife; that the last thing he appeared to want was a well-read and intelligent wife, and that he seized upon this opportunity to rid himself of her as expeditiously as he could. In vain might she beg his "pardon on my Knees". In vain might she, "swear the passion was platonick and is no more". A legal separation was initiated and Henrietta banished to a country estate which, by London standards of the time, was conveniently in the middle of nowhere. Now her home was to be Barrels Hall, "a damp ditch" of a house in need of considerable repair; for the roof leaked, doors hung drunkenly on their hinges and a number of windows were missing. Out of her five hundred pounds a year allowance Mrs Knight was responsible for turning all this around; and by the time Shenstone came on the scene, Barrels Hall was an elegant and tasteful home. It speaks much for her pluck and ingenuity.

Under the terms of the settlement Henrietta did not fare well in other ways either. She was not allowed access to her two children, a son and a daughter; she was not allowed to visit Percy Lodge, the home of the Duchess of Somerset where she had first met John Dalton; and she was forbidden to set foot in London, her husband's stamping ground. It was a state of affairs which demonstrated more clearly than any novel, the considerable power of the eighteenth century husband even if, like Mrs Knight, you happened to be half-sister of Henry St John, Viscount Bolingbroke, a man with power and influence.

Although separated, the Knights remained legally married. In 1745 Robert Knight was created Baron Luxborough, an honour which, whether he liked it or not, had implications for his estranged wife. Mrs Henrietta Knight metamorphosed into Lady Luxborough and in so doing became a great social asset at the dinner tables of her friends. Shenstone was not immune to such an attraction and was to write to his friend, Jago, of the thrill of pleasure when he first saw her coronet emblazoned coach at his door! "A coach with a coronet is a pretty kind of phenomenon at my door; few things prettier..."[1]

In middle age Shenstone was to recall the early days of his friendship with Henrietta Knight as she then was. He writes of a balmy summer's evening in 1739, when he first shared with Somervile a bench under the canopy of Barrel's famous "double oak". By then he had already created a favourable impression for Mrs Knight "enjoyed" the wit and sparkle of his conversation. They surely must have discussed poetry and it was not long before he was sending her his own verses which throughout their friendship were to provide her with such "agreeable entertainment". This was in the early seventeen forties and from then on life at The Leasowes and Barrels, increasingly was punctuated by keen anticipation of visits and letters which were as important to the friends as the telephone is to us today. For letters were like gifts to be savoured. They were read and re-read and treasured, not only for their contents but aesthetic qualities such as the texture of paper, or the colour of sealing wax. As Shenstone puts it:

> *I know the want of gilt paper is of little moment to persons who, like your Ladyship, can make their letters shine by dint of genius...; but 'tis otherwise with me. I love to have my scrip of paper well ornamented without, in fear it shou'd have no merit within. I love to have the impression of a seal well taken off; and I am not entirely satisfied unless the sealing wax itself be of a lovely orange-scarlet.*[2]

All this goes some way towards explaining Shenstone's concerns. Sometimes he would include in his letters a minute but superb pencil sketch of a garden "skreen" or folly, or a design for a seal. Henrietta, too, would send letters that are a joy to behold. Often she would illustrate them by hand with expertly coloured and crafted flowers or eighteenth century society figures; on at least one occasion, even a woodcut. But whatever the trappings, it was with the contents of their correspondence that both, and especially Shenstone, took such care. Years earlier he had set out his stall. His aim, he told a friend, was to make his letters as "odd and fantastical" as possible. Later, in his *Pensées*, he was to expand upon this and comment that a good letter "perhaps should not rise higher than the style of a good conversation". So there we have it. His aim was to converse on paper, an aspiration triumphantly realised but sometimes only after numerous attempts at recasting. For this was a man who would delay a letter if "I had not expressed myself in it to my mind": and it explains why when one reads the letters today with their, "What think you?" and, "I have a mind to…" and their stream of chit-chat and gossip, one gets the impression of a telephone conversation with Shenstone on the other end of the line!

Shenstone took such care with his letters to Henrietta because he so looked forward to her replies. He was mindful of their merit and when she died, he carefully bound the collected manuscripts and commented upon the front that they were "Written with abundant ease, politeness and vivacity; in which she was scarce equalled by any woman of her time".[3]

The admiration was mutual. During her lifetime, Lady Luxborough was to write of Shenstone's letters that they:

> *Give innocent pleasure to yourself and instruction as well as pleasure to others… Your pen, your taste…give such an example, as it were wished, might be more generally followed… .*[4]

It was an opinion shared by Robert Dodsley who in his preface to the *Collected Letters* writes: "…they cannot fail… to afford an agreeable entertainment to such as can relish an animated display of a fine imagination"[5]: and he quotes Shenstone, himself, who believed that "any pretensions to style or sentiment" was to be found "principally in my letters…". It is a view with which Marjorie Williams, editor of the *Collected Letters,* agrees. For her he is "the prince of letter writers", a compliment that would have given Shenstone much satisfaction. But it is to Dodsley that we owe a great debt for it is he who also published the Letters of Lady Luxborough, so enabling us the better to understand how life was once lived in a corner of Warwickshire and its environs by a coterie of well informed and well-read gentle folk.

* * * *

Shenstone's letters to Henrietta exude a peculiar charm. A delight that is to be found in their apparent spontaneity as he tailors his craft to accommodate her. It is because Lady Luxborough has difficulty with Latin that he offers her instead and without the aid of his beloved Virgil, the trivia of provincial gossip which is more to her taste. To please her he adopts an approach which enables him "to jumble some very different spots of news together in the manner of a Gazette".[6] He writes of a "very formidable" locust with wings like a dragonfly that has landed in Birmingham. He discusses the relative merit of quill pens, a subject in which they both have a vested interest and one which becomes a peg upon which he is able to hang the bravura of his wit. Lady Luxborough uses crow quills, so the crow can "never be esteemed inauspicious" because it enables him to read of her "health and welfare": unlike the turkey, a bird "remarkable for empty noise and ostentation" whose quills are therefore "singularly proper for your military men!"

Because he knew where her interests lay, Shenstone writes to her Ladyship of his neighbours, the Lyttelton's, and their "gothic" castle; a truly monumental folly that they are in the process of building. He sends her his friend Whistler's poem, *The Shuttlecock*, and begs leave when the young man is next staying at The Leasowes, to "introduce him to Barrels…", and soon the latter, too, is welcomed into that exclusive little club which we, today, know as the Warwickshire Coterie. He writes to her of his friend Dick Graves and Lucy, "a farmer's daughter", who after their child is born, is sent to a London finishing school to learn how to become a "suitable" clergyman's wife. And here her Ladyship detects an inconsistency. For as Graves "may be supposed to despise the opinion of the world" and "since he marries so much beneath himself and what the world would recommend", why then obtain for her an education to, "please that world which he seems to despise?"

There is a logic here of which Shenstone would have been uncomfortably aware as he penned his response. Indeed, he must have felt like a tightrope walker without a safety net. On the one hand he would not have wished to offend a woman of judgement and a lady of quality. On the other, he could not compromise his loyalty to Graves. For in spite of his foibles, Shenstone was deeply loyal and, as he once said to Dodsley, could never be "half a friend". How he dealt with the situation is masterly. He writes:

> *Your Ladyship's sentiment is very ingenious; but we will suppose he prefers his Lucy to the good opinion of the wise world, yet he doesn't so entirely despise that opinion as not to wish to compromise matters…*[7]

This is what the poet is doing here. He compromises by steering a middle course. He credits the acuteness of Lady Luxborough's perception and at the same time offers an acceptable explanation for the action taken by Richard Graves. It is a formula for peace – and it worked. It saved his conscience and opened the way for Graves, Lucy and Lady Luxborough to become the best of friends.

In spite of rare problems like this, Shenstone's aim is to entertain and this he does in a number of ways. One of these is by means of flattery. "I have had such frequent reason to be convinced of your Ladyship's great penetration". Or when she playfully upbraids him for being dilatory: "I cannot but observe that your menaces afford me greater pleasure than I could receive from any courtier's promises…".[8]

A variation upon the theme was to flatter by seeming to belittle oneself. It was a game extensively played in the eighteenth century – and one which Shenstone embraced with a will. It explains how he is able to conclude a letter by describing its contents as "a rhapsody which – not unlike a beggar's garment, consists of mere rags and trumpery ill-tacked together".[9] How it is that his verses become "mere trifles" and one of his greatest poems, *Verses Written Towards The Close of the Year 1748,* "a little autumn song I…scribbled yesterday". Lady Luxborough played by the same rules. Shenstone is to "pardon this stupid letter...which...in its lowly way is very sincere". Her letters are "not much worth reading" and she is "ashamed of my slovenly garden". Henrietta also flatters. She contrasts Shenstone's letters with her own. "...Sir...you (who) love good writing, good impressions to seals, and all other proper decoration of a letter..."[10] must be ashamed, she argues, to receive "such a scrawl" as she is about to send.

Today, all this seems strange; but in eighteenth century England it was an accepted mode of address, understood as the "game" that it was. Today the rules have changed. We are encouraged to "project" ourselves and consequently in the Luxborough correspondence see the cringing humility of a Uriah Heep where none exists. This is a pity.

The letters show Shenstone to be a master of style for he picks his words with care. During a poor summer, and they seem to have been as frequent then as they are now, the weather is a mere "coquette"; and when there is rain, "the weeds begin to rebel". Then there are the coal carriers who are "transported into angels of light" when they bring good news about the state of local roads. He describes one of his frequent bouts of depression and uses his condition as an excuse for being less amusing than he would have liked. "It is out of my power" he writes, "to send an amusing letter"; and he explains why. "There is not a single cloud or dimness in the sky, but has its exact image or counterpart in my imagination".[11] Few would disagree that as an apt description of melancholia this is incomparable: a comparison which he deftly concludes by pointing out that although the weather may affect his "vivacity", it cannot dispel his "sincerity". He is still, "her Ladyship's most obliged and obedient servant".

* * * *

Apart from their wit and their language; Henrietta, for example, coined the word "frummery" to describe the world of the social climber, the letters are interesting primary source material. Their pages have much to tell us about the life of the eighteenth century country clergyman: of the relationship between master, mistress and servant as well as, among other things, those curious "crazes" which swept the country from time to time as they do today. One can be prepared for a number of surprises.

By Shenstone's day, the social standing of the clergy had vastly improved. Gone was the illiterate peasant priest of earlier times, and in his place, as well as the younger sons of the gentry, could be found the aspiring, university educated young man from a middle-class background. Later, a close friend of the poet's was to be the Reverend Pixal, son of a prosperous Birmingham upholsterer. Many, like Parson Thomas Hall, Shenstone's old school friend, perpetual curate at Henley and from 1741 vicar of Beaudesert, people the pages of the letters, and one comes across him playing bowls by moonlight with the Reverend Holyoake, or riding over eight hundred miles in a single fortnight: to Bath, to Rugby and to London in "view of a good living": Indeed this "little round, fat, oily man" seems to have been a favourite with them both; even though he did once walk off with Shenstone's greatcoat by mistake, leaving the latter "almost starved to death" before he could get it back.

The saga of Parson Hall's preferment is one which illustrates Shenstone's concern about the poor stipends of "journeymen" clergy. He was unhappy that poorly paid clergy were obliged to acquire if they could, a number of livings; and felt that better pay would make this unnecessary, releasing more posts for other applicants. However, Parson Hall had set his sights upon the additional living of Harborough, at that time in the gift of Sir Edward Boughton. It was one that the poet, understandably, held to be "By no means...worth Mr Hall's acceptance" but no matter, and upon hearing that his application had been successful, the latter set off in high spirits to be inducted by the Bishop of Lichfield and Coventry.

It was not to be. He arrived to be told that his Lordship was dead - that he had died at five o'clock on the morning of that very day! Neither Shenstone nor Lady Luxborough mention the unfortunate bishop; but both are vociferous in their concern for the "trouble and expense" to which the unlucky parson has been put; and to the fact that the whole sorry business of obtaining preferment – there had been thirteen other applicants for the post – will now have to be gone through again. Bureaucracy triumphed then, as it does now. So for the time being Parson Hall remained at Henley and Beaudesert and continued to augment his stipend with fees from the occasional sermon given at Warwick Assizes. A transcript of one of these was circulated among the friends and drew from Shenstone the oblique comment that "he applies scripture phrases very spiritually". A remark worthy of many present-day politicians!

Hall's duties seem to have been less then onerous. He spent much time being wined and dined both at Barrels and The Leasowes and on one occasion at the latter, Shenstone was to accuse himself of rudeness towards the young man because he had not properly introduced him to other guests. But he did not like it when another parson, the Reverend Perry, suggested that he appeared to be "sneering"; and to her Ladyship writes that the latter must have been "nettled...at what I said about his preaching for Mr Hall at Henley...". It is all greatly inconsequential; but it shows that the pettiness and jealousies of human nature do not change. Hall was popular and proffered his views on subjects as disparate as stucco wallpaper and garden obelisks; and he was missed at The Leasowes when, because of family problems he failed to visit as frequently as formerly:

> *Why won't Mr Hall take an afternoon's ride to see me now and then?*
> *Were it not good-natured? And then, were it not in character?*[12]

Often the parson would visit Shenstone with Lady Luxborough and, on occasion, be offered a bed for the night. Upon the death of his brother he was invited to spend a week at The Leasowes and when, after a number of years, he eventually did obtain the living at Harborough, Shenstone's "intimate acquaintance and school fellow" had less time for socialising and was much missed in consequence.

Other clergymen who figure in the pages include: the Reverend Holyoake, rector of Oldberrow, Parson Allen of Spernal, and the already mentioned Reverend John Perry. Holyoake was a loyal friend of her Ladyship's and it was from him that Shenstone was to hear the sad news of her illness and death in 1756. Allen and Perry are frequently included in the guest lists of the early 1750's – indeed Perry,

> *"who had dined on a paltry dinner the day before, was told that if he came the following day he wou'd partake of a better".* [13]

An invitation which he accepted with alacrity. Allen, on the other hand, who thought himself as something of a scholar was, on occasion, a trial to Shenstone. *Mr Perk's Dedication to Lady Luxborough corrected by Parson Allen*, tells its own story and the latter's objection to the line of a motto, submitted by Shenstone brought a response which prickles with irritation:

> *... if Mr Allen will not allow of that alteration (tho' 'tis often done) why then you are to desire him to think of some* other *expression of the* same thing". [14]

In other words, get on with it!

Finally, there is the case of "poor" Mr Belchior, a rather unpleasant clergyman who got into debt and who wrote to Lady Luxborough asking for help. He had been unable to obtain preferment, she writes to Shenstone, "at last getting a trifling one to live upon". Subsequently he had been harshly treated by his creditors and it is suggested that Shenstone bring influence to bear upon his friend, Lord Dudley of the Grange at Lapal, in the hope that the latter might "be able to give him a chaplainship". Hopeful that Lord Dudley would not "refuse any request that your Ladyship is pleased to make", Shenstone responded immediately. His letter, with a servant and coachman, was dispatched with instructions to wait for a reply which was duly forthcoming. But it did not please Belchior who let it be known that he thought, "Lord Dudley's lawyer a little too scrupulous in his objections..." and insisted that, "there are many precedents for gentleman in orders receiving the favours he asks". The friends were surprised. Help had been proffered and deemed insufficient – by a man who was not in the strongest of bargaining positions: whose health had deteriorated (by now he was tormented with ague) and in hiding from his creditors! One can but imagine the problems for his young wife and their two children. At last even the kind-hearted Lady Luxborough ran out of patience. Belchior becomes "our troublesome little parson" and all concerned were heartily relieved when, complete with his baggage of debt, he "has set sail for America", never to return. It is a story which illustrates the problems which could beset the "journeyman" parson, however likeable or unlikeable, he might be. One which throws light upon the willingness of the friends to be of help, for they took their social responsibilities seriously and nowhere is this more apparent than in the way they cared for their servants.

* * * *

The Letters provide insight into the workings of three households: The Leasowes, Barrels and also Lord Dudley's Grange: and one gets the impression, that contrary to expectations, the master or mistress with a hierarchy of servants formed a "family" in which there was much laughter and all manner of communication which frequently crossed the class divide. A state of affairs which took place against the backdrop of an age which, by modern standards, was peculiarly class ridden, a time in which one might have expected much less mutual concern, less loyalty than there was. Lord Dudley and Shenstone both remained unmarried and Lady Luxborough was without her husband. It is arguable that the servants, therefore, were looked upon to provide a stability that would otherwise have been lacking.

Whatever the reason, stability there undoubtedly was and it seems to have been provided by a combination of respect and familiarity which prevailed in all three households. One reads of friendly rivalry. Of Lord Dudley providing tuition on the French horn for one of his household and of Shenstone taking up the challenge by providing a similar facility for one of his musical tenants. One reads of laughter, joke telling and merriment and although there was a less appealing side; both Shenstone and Lady Luxborough, on occasion, were unable to pay their servants' wages, it is clear that, on balance, life in these three households was beneficial to all.

Shenstone's housekeeper, Mary Arnold, and his maid, Mary Cutler already have a chapter to themselves, but there was also Hannah, his scullery maid. It was Hannah's valentine that caused amusement and no doubt teasing at The Leasowes. She was understandably secretive about it, but the poet "with difficulty" managed to obtain a peep before it was snatched away! And he was amused enough to write of the incident. He also pens a request to her Ladyship on behalf of Hannah's sister who was trying to find work.

> *(He) would take it as a great favour if you wou'd please to make tryal of my servant's sister. She has a good sense, good temper and a good person and it is of my opinion that she would please...*[15]

It was a plea with which her Ladyship was more than ready to comply although, as things turned out, work in the cold dairy at Barrels was soon to become a stumbling block. For it was not long before the girl became ill, "seized with pains in all her limbs...which grew worse and are more fixed in one arm now".[16] A doctor was called who diagnosed "severe rheumatism" and Lady Luxborough decided that it would be "imprudent" to keep "one so tender" in a job that required her to spend so much time out in the cold. So she was returned to The Leasowes in her Ladyship's own post chaise; and who was sitting beside her but Hannah, sent for to look after her on her way home.

It was a caring gesture and one which illustrates how well the servants were treated in both households. Servants, it has to be said, who repaid this concern with loyalty, and versatility and who were extremely hard working. Shenstone's Tom Jackson is a case in point, for he was employed in so many different ways. It was Jackson who was responsible for much of the landscaping carried out in The Leasowes park. Under the poet's supervision, it was he who constructed Shenstone's root houses and who built the much admired turf seats. And his skills were also, on occasion, employed by her Ladyship at Barrels.

Then there was Tom's role as messenger. He was frequently required to play postman and would often wait while letters were in the process of composition, for a reply to bring home. Lady Luxborough's Joe fulfilled the same role and one gets a snapshot impression of Shenstone, who acutely disliked being hurried, as he struggled to shape a final paragraph to his satisfaction against the backdrop of a ticking clock. "I trespass upon Joe's patience", or "Joe tells me he is in haste", writes the poet as he reaches the close with a mixture of frustration and relief. There was also Tom the agent who, having both "punctuality and management", would be sent to Woolcott upon Tenant's business", or to Harborough to negotiate the letting of a farm. We find it is Tom who "cannot be spared" when Joseph Shenstone became ill and needed his assistance in moving from room to room. But his loyalty was rewarded. When Tom himself became ill, it was Shenstone who supervised the taking of his pills and discouraged him from working out of doors in case he got chilled.

It was an intimacy mirrored at both Barrels and at Lord Dudley's Grange. Mrs Lane, Lady Luxborough's housekeeper, was especially popular. Shenstone writes of her "admirable taste" and was anxious to show her Ladyship's gardener, the Scottish Mr Hume, personally around his walks in the hope that a good report from him would encourage a visit from her. "I hope that your Ladyship will…give her leave to come over", he writes and the impression is that he valued Mrs Lane as a friend.

If Shenstone were fond of Mrs Lane from Barrels, at the Grange it was Sally Rock who caught the eye. Mrs Rock was Lord Dudley's housekeeper and her combination of efficiency and personal attraction was sufficient to entrap John Scott Hylton who would have liked to become romantically involved. There was also the complication of Miss Lea, Lord Dudley's sister. Shenstone gleefully writes of the prevailing emotional merry-go-round, for the latter:

> has a regard for Mr Hylton; Mr Hylton, on the other hand is enamoured of Sally Rock (a servant) and how fortune is to manage the catastrophe of this tragi-comedy, is past my comprehension to determine.[17]

Soon there is mention of an alternative match for Miss Lea, a Buckinghamshire gentleman who is considerably older than she, but who offers "a landau and four (and) unlimited indulgence". It is the stuff that Jane Austen's novels are made of; but unlike an Austen heroine, Miss Lea did not marry Mr Hylton which was where her fancy lay.

Other servants at the Grange are also mentioned in a way which paints that household as convivial. "The Grange Ministry (to wit Baker, Mrs Rock and Coley) are, I hear in high spirits…" imparts Shenstone in a way that manages subtly to hint at class distinction while at the same time demonstrating an interest in "below stairs" frivolities.

For the lives of master and servants were part of an intricate pattern which dictated both how much communication was acceptable and the manner in which it was expressed. In the eighteenth century, each needed the other and perhaps, after all, it is not so unexpected that bonding occurred as it did.

* * * *

The Luxborough Correspondence is full of plans for proposed visits and when either set out they would take a number of servants with them. They would also take friends; Parson Hall often accompanied her Ladyship and Shenstone would take his niece Maria, or any one of the coterie who might be staying with him at the time. So it was that the poet has, "agreeable hopes…of waiting upon your Ladyship at The Leasowes" and is busily occupied in preparing his garden so as "to render my environs less unworthy of your notice": and inside the farmhouse the allocation of sleeping accommodation is of interest because beds are at a premium:

> *There will be a bed for your ladyship, another for Mr Hall, a third for Mrs Ann and one and a half for your servants of the other sex.*[18]

Clearly, beds provided for the "lower" servants would have to be shared.

If entertaining was enjoyed, then so was being entertained. Shenstone eagerly anticipated his visits to Barrels and her Ladyship looked forward to his arrival with an eagerness that matched his own. A crie-de-coeur from her pen at a time of acute disappointment when one of these was delayed: "Whether you are well or ill, alive or dead… remember that you have a sincere friend… impatient for the pleasure of your company"[19], is one that typifies the feelings of both. Each liked the other to visit at a time when their garden was at its summer best, and to encourage her guest Lady Luxborough pens an entrancing portrait of a summer's evening at Barrels where she sits beneath a canopy of oak, "looking at the neighbouring hills, hearing my mowers whet their scythes (and) seeing the troop horses"[20], to which she has given a temporary home, "scamper about my avenue".

Gardening was a pastime that gave much pleasure to them both. Their heads were full of plans for the design of new walks, for opening vistas, creating waterscapes and all manner of what was new. Like Shenstone, her Ladyship was actively involved in directing operations. Over a period she has "stood from eleven to five each day in the lower part of my walk…displanting and opening views"[21]. She seeks Shenstone's advice and sometimes his responses are baffling. In what way can her "hermitage become part of her shrubbery?" And the poet is resolved that only "upon the spot" will he be able to clarify the situation.

Much ink was expended upon discussion of memorial urns. Her Ladyship was to raise one to her departed friend the poet, Somervile, and was anxious that the inscription should express admiration and friendship but nothing more. She has had sufficient of scandal. Its siting, in the fork of the famous Barrel's double oak, was a happy choice for in summer it is "beautifully shaded by its canopy…". Following her example Shenstone was to raise an urn in Virgil's Grove to the bard, James Thomson. Almost big enough for the "bacco stopper of an inhabitant of brobdignag", it was to have "a charming effect", but when sited looked rather small and the poet is obliged to anticipate the spring when:

> *The area will appear so much contracted when the trees that encircle it are thickened with leaves that it will not seem deficient in size… .*[22]

The friends bring or send each other gifts. Her Ladyship gives Shenstone a greyhound; his favourite, Lucy, who appears with him in the Alcock portrait, and guinea fowl eggs. He offers her books. They ask favours: he for a "receipt" for the making of sealing wax and she for advice over the design of the Somervile urn.

Entertaining was expensive but both lived extravagantly on their limited incomes; she on her five hundred and he on his three hundred pounds a year. They discuss "economy" even if they do not practise it. "I am frightened at the expense of common decencies" Shenstone protests and warming to his theme:

> *I never walk beneath my roof, but one room cries out, "Pray why I am not papered?…", another… "Why am I not stuccoed?" a third, "Why have not I a chimney-piece?"*[23]

He tells of his problems with tenants who on occasion would take advantage of his kindness. Of one man who owes him two years' rent and who, after an afternoon spent haggling, agrees to pay off six months of his arrears only to recant "because he was unwilling to break his promise"! Shenstone draws a parallel between his situation and "a butter dish with a spout at both ends" - or later, with "the sluice of a pond which lets out twice as much as comes in". These are images with which her Ladyship can all too readily relate and she suggests that perhaps because she is unable to cultivate "a proper veneration for sixpence", she is better acquainted with the theory of economy than its practice.

* * * *

It was from Shenstone that Henrietta learned of that extraordinary example of frivolity, the Pantin, a craze briefly popular among London's society ladies. Mr Pantin turns out to have been a life-sized cardboard figure like a puppet: "a sort of Scaramouch made with card which ladies bring into company and the playhouse".[24] His purpose was to make "their compliments for them" and it would seem that as the craze grew, ladies overnight were to turn themselves into puppeteers and develop skills that they did not know they possessed; much to their own and others' amusement.

It was not long before Lady Luxborough acquired one of these toys. It was a present from one of her nieces and reckoned "to make as genteel a curtsy as any Pantin in Europe!"

The Leasowes; birthplace of William Shenstone by W.J. Child.

The Leasowes by William Shenstone.

1

Malvern House, Solihull, where Shenstone went to school.

Shenstone's dame school.

Broom church and bell.

William Shenstone as a young man.   *William Somervile.*

Harborough Hall, the home of the Penn family.

The haunted churchyard at Harbury.

Mickleton Manor today: a rear view.

Entrance to Mickleton Manor.

St Lawrence's Church, Mickleton.

Memorial urn to Utrecia Smith in St Lawrence Church, Mickleton.

The first Lord Lyttelton.

Hagley Hall.

Shenstone's illustration of his dame school for The Schoolmistress.

Richard Graves.

Thomas Arne's setting for The Pastoral Ballad.

Sadly, she had little occasion to employ him and frequently mentions him as the only "company" she has. How different was Barrels from London - for there the craze spread even to the men! Indeed it was said, so Shenstone tells his friend, that Lord Melbourne appeared one day with his Pantin at a cabinet meeting!

Not to be outdone, Henrietta responds with gossip of her own: "ladies of fashion…who crow like cocks" to attract the attention of any gentleman who catches their eye: and she tells of how he reciprocates by "braying like an ass" as a means of signalling his acceptance. That such things happened is undoubtedly true. Shenstone's informant was Richard Graves, who on a visit to the capital had seen Monsieur Pantin in action. Lady Luxborough obtained her story from a close family friend, Patty Meredith, who wrote home from her holiday lodgings in London of the numerous "cocks" and "asses" who were to be seen exhibiting themselves about Vauxhall in the early evening. Such antics may seem incomprehensible to us; but there is no denying that eighteenth century stupidities like these are colourful enough to make us view our own eccentricities – like the wearing of outrageous hats at race meetings or face painting at football matches – as rather tame.

We are treated to numerous "snapshots" of the time. Of their mutual friends, the Merediths, who like the characters in *Mansfield Park* are keen amateur actors. Shenstone is entranced with Patty Meredith's portrayal of Ophelia; and when one summer they stage an excellent production of *Tartuffe,* he writes that there is even talk of taking their version of the play to London! He tells of the practice of guests arriving in time for breakfast, a custom which would horrify many today: and it is clear that the host would frequently write to thank his guest for visiting and to enquire after the journey home. "I cannot content myself… till I have the addition of satisfaction of hearing that you got safe home",[25] pens the poet after an especially rewarding time with her Ladyship at The Leasowes.

Other trends of the period included those of busto making and decorating with papier-mâché. Shenstone tells of an impromptu visit on his way home to the Baskervilles in Birmingham where he had hoped "to beg a draught of Perry". There he had found both husband and wife seated in their front parlour with a busto maker hard at work who, for the price of two guineas, could produce likenesses that were "well managed in point of hair (and) draperies". It was a time when everyone who could afford it was having a busto made and the poet who never liked to be left out of things, was in two minds whether to follow suit. "I should make the frightfullest of bustos" he writes, "or I do not know but I should employ him". In the end he did; and the result, far from flattering, appears as a frontispiece to the *Collected Works*. Strangely, the letters make no mention of the incident although they recount in some detail the history of the Alcock painting which is discussed in a later chapter. They also make little mention of Shenstone's friendship with Baskerville – but the two men, nonetheless, had much in common. The poet for his dislike of bigotry and the printer for his horror of superstition. Ironically, Shenstone's funeral was to be conducted by the Reverend Pynson Wilmot of whom the poet intensely disapproved. The printer, on the other hand, chose to be buried on the site of an old mill in his garden in "unconsecrated" ground away:

From the idle fears of Superstition
And the wicked arts of Priesthood.[26]

But to return to the subject of eighteenth century novelties. Also fashionable was papier-mâché now so popular that it was used to adorn the interiors of houses belonging to the rich, replacing the "lead carving" that earlier had been cut out by ladies with sharp scissors and fixed into rosettes upon the walls and ceilings of their homes. Now it was papier-mâché that Lady Luxborough required and it was to Shenstone that she turned for advice. The poet advises where she can obtain the material: "from Mr Bromwich at the Golden Lion upon Ludgate Hill". He explains that for her drawing room ceiling she will require "an ornament for the middle and four spandrells for the corners". And so that she can see the effect, he takes down his own "pineapple" centre piece and sends it to her, complete with "corner ornaments".

As well as recounting such frivolities the letters also provided a platform for serious discussion. New novels were eagerly digested and commented upon. Henry Fielding's *Tom Jones* is much admired and his Squire Weston "a natural picture of thousands of his Majesty's rural subjects". But of Samuel Richardson's *Clarissa,* the critic in Shenstone is harsher. In a delicious phrase he points out that although the author "is a man of genius and nice observation", the novel is too verbose and consequently spun out into "an extravagant prolixity"! There are some who might agree.

Shenstone ponders the nature of evil. "...Evils there are in the world which affect individuals and also Society but which are, no doubt connected with the good of the whole".[27] Or he muses upon the recurring admixture of pleasure and pain which, like stinging nettles and dock leaves, are experienced frequently together. For her Ladyship, these are the "chequered scenes of life" of which she has had much experience: but for the poet, who also has had his share of disappointment, it is become the expectation that every pleasure will have "a pain to balance it". So it was that the two friends discussed their views and exchanged philosophies and were able to support one another in times of distress.

* * * *

In December, 1751, Shenstone suffered a dreadful blow when his beloved brother, Joseph, died. For months he was incapable of articulating his feelings, or of putting pen to paper, so it was only after an interval that Lady Luxborough was finally informed of what had happened. Only then, and after briefly explaining the reason for his silence, is Shenstone able to lay bare a heart which "is well-nigh broke". He explains how, since his brother's death, "every object round" reminds him of the pleasures they shared and engenders feelings that he is "unable to support". How his recurring "nervous fever" has returned, a condition emotional in origin and for which he is now "taking medicines...to cure anxiety of mind".

Her Ladyship received this most genuine and pathetic of letters while she was visiting Bath. Arthritic and weary, she had been persuaded of the efficacy of such a visit and her condition greatly improved; but whether due to taking the waters or the fact that for several months she was away from the damp which so adversely affected her at Barrels – who can tell? She, too, was grieving; for her half-brother, Lord Bolingbroke, had also recently died. But unlike Shenstone who is neither, "in a condition to receive relief…or even pretend to give it", Lady Luxborough manages somewhat better and her response is both apt and genuine. "Your grief for your brother I feel in its full force, and am persuaded you feel the like to mine".[28] And she even sends her servant, Joe, with a "packet" of toys: buttons or buckles or something of the kind, to cheer him. Roused from his despondency, Shenstone's acknowledgement is one of carefully crafted good manners. "Your Ladyship honours me with your friendship, revives me by your letters, and amuses me by a succession of elegant presents".[29] But there is a correctness here, a politeness, as it were, through gritted teeth; and her Ladyship has to try again.

She invites Shenstone to join her at Bath and paints a most delightful picture of the activities there. She writes of how he would enjoy himself. Of the friendly booksellers he might visit and especially Mr Leake of number five, The Walks. For here, not only could he while away a morning in polite conversation, but meet literary giants like Samuel Richardson whose *Clarissa* was the talk of London, and who happened to be this gentleman's brother-in-law. Here the novelist Richardson was a familiar figure in his plum coloured waistcoat, with his "kindly, flabby face" and his yellow wig. She writes of the plays Shenstone could see: the "Othellos, Falstaffs, Richard the Thirds and Harlequins who entertain one daily for half the price of your Garricks, Barrys and Rich's!"[30] And of Beau Nash, "our law-giver", whose white hat, "commands more respect and non-resistance than the crowns of kings". Her admiration for him is considerable and she describes how successful he has been in his aim "to promote…good manners, to suppress scandal and late hours".

It was to no avail. Shenstone, emotionally drained, was unable to comply even if he wished – which he did not. But as always, he tempers his refusal with possibility. "Nothing could attract me thither so powerfully as the satisfaction…in conversing with you". But then again: "Before I must think of this expedition I have…business to pass thro' which is a task as necessary as it will be painful".[31]

Even so, as the days passed his emotional health, little by little, began to improve and there came a time when he at last began to think of papering his living rooms; to this end was contemplating, "patterning paper" as we today bring home pattern books. At this time, a matter of weeks after his bereavement, he had even indulged his passion for antiquities by buying "An old Romish Missal on vellum", yet this was carried out guiltily as if he were in some way "defrauding sorrow of its lawful claim".

Bereavement was not the only grief that the friends shared, for they both had other family problems, too. Shenstone writes of "young Dolman", his nephew, who has instigated legal proceedings against him in an attempt to obtain a larger share of the family property. Dolman was Shenstone's only remaining relative on his mother's side, and as a child and adolescent had spent happy hours in the poet's company. He would also have been next in line to inherit Harborough Hall, the property to which, for some reason, he now decided to lay claim. "Were I to relate but half of my story, I am sure you are too much my friend not to sympathise in my distress"[32] confides the poet of "this little fellow (who) may have malignity enough to cut my throat!". The affair, first mooted in the early seventeen fifties, was to drag on for over a decade although when Shenstone was seriously ill in the winter of seventeen fifty seven and not expected to survive, Dolman briefly halted proceedings until the spring of the following year when the poet recovered. Undoubtedly all this caused Shenstone distress and ironically was resolved in his favour only just before he died.

It was a scenario with which Lady Luxborough could empathise. For now having restored her home, she has reason to believe that both her husband and her son-in-law have designs upon Barrels. To Shenstone she confides her concerns and the fact that she dare not meet with them unless in the presence of a solicitor. So, uncannily, it would seem that their circumstances, those "chequered scenes of life" continue to mirror each other and that the friends were each to need the other's support, not less but more as the years passed.

By the middle of the seventeen fifties, and in spite of the continuing vivacity of her letters, it is clear that her Ladyship's health was deteriorating. The friends were now unable to visit and the letters became less frequent. Soon the correspondence was to stop altogether and so was pointed the way for the inevitable end. But before this happened, one feels obliged to consider more closely the nature of their extraordinary friendship and anything which passes between them that sheds light upon their relationship. Immediately an interesting little poem, Shenstone's *Song XI*[33], written and despatched to her Ladyship in seventeen forty four springs to mind, for its contents is especially revealing. In it Shenstone uses the refrain which takes the form of a repeated first line, "Perhaps it is not love", to argue that it is possible to appreciate the "beauties" of a "polished" mind without falling in love. Quite so. But what, he poses, if these qualities are combined with "a form that is fair?" The answer is found in a change to the last verse where, "Perhaps it is not...", gives way to "It is... it is...".

One cannot achieve greater clarity than this. Either Shenstone fancied himself genuinely "in love" or he flirted with the idea and it is more likely to have been the latter. Undoubtedly he was very fond of her Ladyship as she was of him. He also found her attractive; but more importantly, because she was legally still married she posed no threat and he was free to indulge his fancy. Shenstone was also grateful to Lady Luxborough for the roles she had played – both in bringing his poem, *Rural Elegance* to the attention of the Duchess of Somerset, and in the publicity by means of her acquaintance that she was able to bring to The Leasowes.

And as for the lady herself? Her "esteem and friendship" for the poet were "unlimited". She especially enjoyed receiving letters from him that were written in instalments over several days. For such a letter:

makes a little journal [and] is the more agreeable because it imitates conversation.
and makes one fancy one's self upon the place, and in the company described.[34]

Although there is no evidence that there was romantic involvement on her side, it is clear that each appreciated the other and that their relationship was a close one. She wanted no scandal and he wanted no commitment. It was a situation that suited them both.

Her Ladyship died at the end of March, 1756, and Shenstone was to hear the sad news from the pen of the Reverend Holyoake who, with his wife, and having proved the most loyal of friends, was with her at the end. Due to failing health she had "not attended church nor the sacrament very lately" but the night before she died her chaplain had read her the Recommendatory Prayer which he hoped had offered comfort. Shenstone, not unexpectedly, "on the loss of so intimate a friend…(was) anxious to become acquainted with every little known circumstance that attended"[35] her death and it comforted him to know that the Holyoakes had been present when they were most needed. His grief was tempered by the knowledge that "her mortification" would have increased with every year that passed and his reaction, after the initial shock, was a desire to perpetuate her memory. As has been seen, it was to this end that he carefully collected up her letters which sparkle with a love of life and demonstrate a not inconsiderable intellect untarnished by pedantry. For she had been a most valued critic of his poetry, and that she well understood what the poet was successfully attempting in his garden is clear from a verse that she penned at The Leasowes in 1749:

> *'Tis Nature here makes pleasing scenes arise,*
> *And wisely gives them Shenstone to revise;*
> *To veil each flaw, to brighten every grace;*
> *Yet still to let them wear their parent's face.*[36]

Most importantly, it was predominantly because of Lady Luxborough's encouragement and interest that Shenstone's imagination came to be fired by a vision of Arcadia; a fantasy to be realised by means of poetry and emblem within the parameters of the landscape surrounding his farm. It was to be a remarkable achievement which is considered in the next chapter.

Chapter 11

A GARDEN OF POETRY
AND EMBLEM

"I have seen nothing in all England to be compared with it"
John Wesley

It is not possible to be precise about how and when Shenstone's vision of Arcadia and the development of his garden into a country idyll first began; for such ideas germinate slowly and the arbitrary use of dates, like fences round a field, is unhelpful. Life, unlike land, does not fit so easily into compartments. But in Part Three of his autobiographical poem, *The Progress of Taste*, Shenstone does give us some clues, for in it he tells of his love affair with "Fancy". He writes of how she would lead him in those early days at The Leasowes "o'er hill and mead", show him their beauties and then "prescribe improvements of her own". In an age when every educated man would have been familiar with classical literature, he explains how she would encourage him "to raise a dome to Venus there" or elsewhere to place "Minerva's sacred seat" or an altar to Apollo and so on. How she fired his imagination so that he:

> *… dreamed he saw the Fawns*
> *And Nymphs distinctly skim the lawns,*
> *Now traced amid the trees, and then*
> *Lost in the encircling shades again,[1]*

He tells of what happens when we follow such "bright visions". For only then can we begin to understand how such a "fairy landscape" charms to become, if anything, more "real" than the one that it replaces. This was the key to full enjoyment of Shenstone's garden: the imagination, a faculty to be motivated in a number of ways including the poetry of his inscriptions. For the poet did not, at the click of a switch, stop writing poetry in order to turn his attention to his garden as has been suggested. Instead, his interest in gardening, which he had enjoyed since the early Mickleton days, and his interest in poetry were, during the seventeen forties, to develop in tandem as Shenstone the poet and Shenstone the gardener, each pursued his complementary craft. For complementary the two undoubtedly were and without an appreciation of this, an understanding of The Leasowes is incomplete.

It was in 1743 that Shenstone first writes of his plans to Jago. "I am taking part of my farm upon my hands to see if I can succeed as a farmer",[2] and half jokingly, "but I am afraid I am under the sentence, 'whosoever he taketh in hand it shall not prosper'". He need not have worried; for at a time in the eighteenth century when interest in garden design had never been keener Shenstone was to create at The Leasowes his ferme ornée, one of the most sought after, influential and eagerly visited parks in Britain. It was unique – and garden design was never to be the same again.

Shenstone created his Leasowes at a time when formal gardens like Hampton Court and Versailles were distinctly out of favour. In England, at least, they were perceived as too artificial, too "studied" in their execution. No longer were gardens to resemble parade grounds with their plants and trees, like soldiers, marching in straight lines or wheeling in geometric patterns. Instead the new English School prompted a more natural style of landscaping, its precepts to utilise the natural contours of the land and to work with materials like wood, rock or stone indigenous to the area.

These were ideas with which Shenstone felt most comfortable and he used them as a springboard for his own innovations. At The Leasowes, they led him to eschew anything that smacked of artifice, so straight paths were replaced by ones which meandered along the slopes of his groves and hills: and judicious planting meant that new vistas were continually opened up while at the same time an impression was created that the new trees or plants and shrubs had always been there. Alcoves were placed where they might best draw attention to, or enliven the view. "I have an alcove, six elegies, a seat, two epitaphs…three ballads, four songs and a serpentine river to show you when you come"[3] he writes to Jago in 1746 in words which demonstrate the division of his labours at that time; for by then his tenant, John Shenstone had died and the poet had a free hand to do as he pleased. It was the implementation of these new concepts that he later described in his great poem, *Rural Elegance:*

> *Nature exalt the mound where art shall build;*
> *Art shape the gay alcove, while nature paints the field.*[4]

But this was not all, for ultimately, Shenstone was to combine elements of the Roman garden with the "new" ideas of the English Landscape School, a concept that Philip Southcote, a friend of Morgan Graves, had first put into practice at Woburn Farm. It was Southcote who first encircled a large area of his land with an ornamental belt; a device that he diversified with grottos, waterscapes and woods and which successfully "married" a working farm with its environs. The Leasowes, also was a working farm and it was along these same lines that Shenstone was to proceed: "I am employed in extending my path so that it will now in a short time lead around my whole farm",[5] he writes to Graves in 1748; and any subsequent similarity between the two estates, serves only to show that the poet knew and was able to capitalise upon a good idea when he came across it.

In fact, Shenstone's ungravelled paths were simply constructed and in wet weather they became extremely muddy; a special hazard for ladies, which was one of the reasons why he hated the rain and why, when the sun shone, his spirits lifted. An extended letter to Lady Luxborough written during the summer of 1750 charts the progress of his feelings. He had been looking forward to his visitors arriving but:

> *'Tis now Friday morning, seven o'clock; the sky dark and lowring, and the ground wet; so I suppose, no Lady Duchess, Lady Die, Lady Caroline, or Lord Fielding; no colonels, admirals or fine ladies today...*[6]

His disappointment is acute and drips from his pen. But then, as happens today, the weather changed and at a stroke his depression turns into jubilation. For by one o'clock in the afternoon...

> *A sudden change! The day has cleared up and here arrives in the first place Lord Fielding and Miss Lyttelton on horse back, in the last place Monsieur le Colonel and Lady Die in a chair...*[6]

He notes with evident satisfaction that his walks "proved dry enough" and they all seemed to enjoy themselves. Even so, it is difficult to imagine ladies in their long dresses and tightly laced stays, undertaking any walking at all – except under the most benign of weather conditions.

Shenstone was a practical gardener but his interest in gardening is also expressed in his prose works. In his *Unconnected Thoughts on Gardening* he discusses garden design and the similar aim of both landscape gardener and landscape painter. "Landscape" he says "should contain variety enough to form a picture upon canvas". And he stresses the importance of water which should "ever appear as an irregular lake or winding stream in an infinite pattern of form and shape".[7] It was an imperative which enabled him to make use of the Leasowes' abundance of meandering streams, irregular waterscapes and imaginative cascades. A decade on, the poet was to write to Graves of a new cascade which "is a very great thing for the size of it", and was to prove a most popular draw for his visitors. The "Mr Bisley or Dingley (who) came hither with his wife and a large party to see my new cascade by moonlight..."[8] was only one of many newcomers attracted to The Leasowes on account of it.

In Shenstone's day, a walk around his garden was infinitely rewarding. Its meandering paths took the guest through grove and meadow, past thicket and woodland into "secret" green places. They invited him beside cascading streams whose banks were "enamelled" with wild flowers. Or, where, along winding ways his ruinated priory, a folly partially hidden by firs could be seen; and again, later "down a green slope and thro' tall oaks".

On occasion, and by means of a strategically placed seat, Shenstone would direct his visitor's eye beyond the confines of his immediate garden to the outline of the Clent Hills: or on a good day to Welsh mountains silhouetted some thirty miles distant. For The Leasowes was like a precious gemstone which is rendered even more beautiful by the design of its setting and one of Shenstone's innovations was to exploit the beauties of the countryside on his doorstep to the advantage of his farm.

Shenstone's success at The Leasowes was due to a variety of skills. Not least of these was his imaginative vision – the poet who enabled the gardener to see and execute things differently. When necessary, he could be quick to make use of the ideas of others; but always he gave them a dimension of his own and nowhere is this more apparent than in Virgil's Grove.

* * * *

Named after the Latin poet he so admired, Virgil's Grove was one of Shenstone's favourite walks. It was here on warm summer evenings and under a full moon that he would sometimes entertain. Then he would hang tin lamps from the trees to reflect the moonlight as it played upon his sparkling stream and cascades: and he hired local musicians to entertain his guests as they picnicked in the grove. Here they could sip the healthful waters of his chalybeate spring or puzzle over his inscribed obelisk at the walk's entrance. Also sited here was the urn that Shenstone had raised to the memory of "that right friendly bard" the poet, James Thomson.

Virgil's Grove was one of the earliest walks at The Leasowes to be completed and Shenstone's letters, full of plans for its improvement, also provide a diary of their implementation. "I have made a great improvement in Virgil's Grove since you were here and have finished paths from it to the house",[9] he writes to Jago in 1747. And later, to Lady Luxborough: "I have made two little islands in the stream that runs through Virgil's Grove"; and he records with satisfaction that they make it appear, "considerably larger". When entering the Grove, visitors could have been forgiven for imagining that they were in "fairyland", an idea perpetuated by its winding and wooded ways; its streams and sparkling cataracts.

Shenstone makes use of this analogy in one of the most delicious of his inscriptions, *In Cool Grot.* For this is a poem about fairies and was to be found on a tablet placed at the base of a root house in the Grove. To Lady Luxborough Shenstone explains his technique for the preparation of such poems in this way:

> *My method is a very cheap one. I paste some writing paper on a strip of deal and so print with a pen. This serves in Root-Houses and under cover.*[10]

The story of how *In Cool Grot* came to be written is a delightful one. It was fashioned one morning over an extended breakfast, in what turned out to be a successful attempt to put a stop to persistent pilfering of wild flowers planted along the banks of the stream there. The lines, as the poet explains to Jago:

> *Are… for the admonition of my good friends the vulgar of whom I have multitudes every Sunday evening and who very fortunately believe in fairies and are no judges of poetry.*[11]

That the verses achieved their objective cannot be in doubt, for the pilfering, much to Shenstone's relief, stopped as suddenly as it had begun. They demonstrate, too, how well the poet understood the minds of simple people, for the psychology of the poem is admirable. First, in a setting redolent of Puck and Titania and all the host of Shakespeare's fairies, a fairy-world is engaged:

> *Here in cool grot and mossy cell*
> *We rural fays and fairies dwell...*

Second, having feasted the imagination, there is the exhortation:

> *...Tread with awe these favour'd bowers,*
> *Nor wound the shrubs, nor bruise the flowers;*

Finally, should even this fail, comes the warning of the last couplet:

> *But harm betide the wayward swain*
> *Who dares our hallow'd haunts profane.*[12]

Many will argue that the verses of *In Cool Grot* are both evocative and delightful; but still one is left wondering how it was that so many of Shenstone's "the vulgar" were able to read!

However, literate or not, these were the people who visited The Leasowes and, especially, Virgil's Grove on Sunday evenings. One of many such occasions is described to Jago:

> *It is now Sunday evening and I have been exhibiting myself in my walks to no less*
> *than a hundred and fifty people, and that with no less state and vanity than a Turk*
> *in his Seraglio.*[13]

In fact Shenstone enjoyed their visits. He revelled in his reputation for being a local "character", as dressed in a favourite red waistcoat and wearing his own hair drawn back in a ribbon he mingled with the crowd and stopped to speak with locals who were personally known to him. The poet took his responsibilities as a local landowner seriously and was frequently instrumental in aiding those who were out of work or in need of money as the following extract from one of his letters to a Mr Milward of Harborne shows."The Bearer, M Rice has a number of children, and one whom I recommend to Lord Foley's Hospital": and he admits himself ready, "at all times...to acknowledge my share of the obligation".[14]

Meanwhile among rich and poor, the fame of Virgil's Grove continued to spread: and during the summer of 1748 Shenstone was further encouraged in the implementation of his improvements there. He received a visit from the fashionable

Thomas Smith of Derby whose well known speciality was the engraving of scenes chosen from a selection of the great country estates. These had included Byron's Newstead Park and much nearer to home, Lord Lyttelton's Hagley Hall.

Shenstone was excited about the visit, for he appreciated the benefits that such publicity might bring. And when upon entering Virgil's Grove, Smith's admiration gave rise to action and he, there and then, sketched a draft view for an engraving to be included in a forthcoming collection of his "smaller scenes", one can easily imagine the pride and satisfaction that the poet must have felt. It is hardly surprising that the visit was an unmitigated success: that Shenstone believed Smith to have behaved with "a complaisance that made us wish to serve him". As the artist was leaving, he presented the poet with his sketches of "five charming ruins". It was a shrewd gesture, for the latter responded by buying, for the price of half a guinea, a considerable sum in those days, a set of the artist's "grander scenes". So was the encounter completed to the satisfaction of both men for each believed himself to have benefited from the exchange.

The occasion must rank as one of the highlights in Shenstone's gardening career and for weeks to come his letters are full of the visit. Like this one to Jago:

> *Mr Smith...takes other little views...of particular beauties which will form a drawing book... would you not be surprised to see a draught of my Virgil's Grove inserted among the latter?*[15]

To Lady Luxborough Smith becomes:

> *... the designer of the prints of Hagley Park...(who)...called here last week...he took a draught of Virgil's Grove here (which) he purposes to insert in a similar collection; a kind of drawing book...*[16]

And he concludes with a wry honesty that, "He must needs imagine me to be a person of greater influence than I really am".[17]

But no matter, for the Grove continued to impress all who visited, and from contemporary records, it is clear that it was especially striking. Robert Dodsley, Shenstone's publisher and friend, was to believe it the most perfect spot of all in the poet's "arcadian farm". In his *Description of The Leasowes* he paints the picture of a small but deep valley overshadowed by "lofty trees rising out of the bottom of the dingle". He writes of "a copious stream" and the "mossy banks enamelled with primroses and...wild wood flowers" through which it flows. From a vantage point at the top of a steep bank overlooking the valley, he proffers a bird's eye view of the various cascades which enliven its meandering way; and of Shenstone's "dripping fountain", a spectacular effect created by the tributary of a small rill which trickled down, "a niche of rock work through liverwort and aquatick weeds" into its parent stream.

Most spectacular of all, was Shenstone's great cascade. It was "seen...through a kind of vista or glade, falling down a precipice overarched with trees". In fact, Dodsley is here describing a waterfall which cleverly had been engineered to appear more striking than it actually was, both by means of strategic planting, and by the opening of sluice gates higher up in the valley as visitors approached. As if this mattered – for it was the successful effect that counted.

Over the years, it was to the perfection of his entire garden that Shenstone was ultimately to aspire. But as always, there was a special place in his heart for the "pleasing melancholy" of his Virgil's Grove which, with its winding waters and "fairy" dells, was to bring him and countless others the most absolute of satisfaction.

* * * *

Shenstone's garden was personal to him, and in many ways presented a collection of moods and memories. In the first place it was a typically English garden and the poet was proud of its patriotic flavour. Of the fact that its design was modelled along English lines: using English plants, rock and wood. The Leasowes was a working farm and its hills were grazed by English sheep. In his Eighteenth Elegy, Shenstone extols their wool, "the rich growth of British hills" and contrasts it advantageously with "the extraneous twine" of their French counterparts.

Shenstone peopled his garden with statues and furnished it with seats and other artefacts such as his "Gothick" screen, his memorial urns and the obelisk and chalybeate spring in Virgil's Grove. So were his visitors encouraged to contemplate a beautiful view or with melancholy remember a departed friend. With "calm delight", they were exhorted by the lines of a poem on the back of his "Gothick" seat to "seek no more – the rest is vain".

Two of the statues deserve a mention. Shenstone's Venus de Medici, "who has a more bashful attitude than any other", and who in keeping with her mood was "hidden away" at the entrance to his shrubbery which surrounded the farmhouse. The inscription, denoting, a young woman to whom, "every bosom warms" had caused him problems and was only satisfactorily completed with the aid of Graves. The poem was fixed to a large basin of goldfish beside her and referred to the "sweet concealment of her charms" which would allow, "fancy (to) point the rest". In fact Shenstone's concern here was with the spiritual dimensions of physical beauty, but one might be forgiven for thinking otherwise; that he was suggesting a partially clad young woman to be more seductive than a naked one. In 1761 the poem was published in the January edition of the *London Magazine* when Shenstone was annoyed to discover that his punctuation had been altered. He had not contributed the poem himself and spent considerable time and energy in trying to find out who among his friends had – but to no avail.

Another delightful statue was the Piping Faunus, a present from his publisher, Robert Dodsley. Shenstone had it placed "in a natural bower" where its charms could be seen from the house, and where, on a tablet, placed beneath the merry woodland creature, Shenstone's inscription showed his appreciation of his friend's dual role both as publisher and poet.

Come then, my friend, thy silvan taste display,
Come hear thy Faunus tune his rustic lay;
Ah, rather come, and in these dells disown
The care of other strains and tune thine own.[18]

The Leasowes' garden was a tranquil place of "peaceful shade" and "pleasing melancholy", alternating with a more robust delight to be found along the perimeter of its meadows and pastures. From seat and grotto, and some of the former were spectacular like the one "enclosed with handsome pales" to the memory of Lord Lyttelton, Shenstone's inscriptions sang of the various delights to be found there: of the kingfisher's "sapphire plumage" and, in the stream, "the trout bedropt with crimson stains"; of rills and "leafy bowers" along which the traveller would do well to turn away from the ugliness of ambition and the money-grubbing toil of the city. Or he might pause in reflection before any one of the poet's memorial urns: to the poet Somervile or, most beautiful of all, one that was "richly gilt" and placed at the end of Lover's Walk in memory of Shenstone's niece, Maria Dolman, who died at twenty-one from smallpox. Then there was the urn raised in memory of the poet's brother, Joseph, and inscribed with a quotation from Virgil's Eclogue V which in translation read:

When fate snatch'd thee away
Pales no longer swell'd the teeming grain,
Nor Phoebus fed his ascent on the plain.

Or the one in Virgil's Grove to James Thomson, "that right friendly bard", which was in memory of what might have been rather than what was. For the two men had met at most a trio of times and the latter's early death, from a chill caught riding home one night in wet clothes, had deprived Shenstone of a future rather than a present friend.

The two men had first met in the summer of 1746 when they were introduced by Sir William Lyttelton. The three enjoyed a pleasant walk around The Leasowes' garden and Thomson's fulsome compliments, soon to be expressed in sexual imagery, had at first greatly pleased Shenstone. "You have nothing to do", Thomson addressed the poet from the bench upon which they were seated, "but to dress nature – you only have to caress her; kiss her...and then descend into the valley".[19] Soon the metaphor was extended to include the "two boobies of Clent", and then Lyttelton espied a "nipple", to which was added "the fringe of Upmore Wood" and so on. Finally came Thomson's "naughty" allusion to the gushing stream at Shenstone's door! How much the latter contributed to all this is unclear; but undoubtedly he presented here a different face from the one he showed his close friend, Lady Luxborough; and the fact that he recorded the episode in a private memorandum, indicates that he viewed the occasion with some unease. Even so, Shenstone was pleased to obtain an invitation to Thomson's Richmond home: and to direct his departing visitors along a route beside the pool, which framed his farm to advantage.

After this, and although the two men enjoyed a number of mutual acquaintances, they did not meet again until the following year; and twelve months after that, Thomson was dead. But his death did provide the catalyst for one of Shenstone's greatest poems. Dedicated to Sir William Lyttelton, *Verses Written Towards the Close of the Year 1748...*[20] discusses the raising of a votive urn against a backdrop of the seasons. Spring will return each year, "To call forth flowers around", but there can be no recompense for the death of a friend, "this loss to Damon's bower". Later, Shenstone came to view this poem with distaste. He felt it to be insincere and not a little contrived as, it is arguable, was the raising of the Thomson urn, signalling that he knew the man better than in fact he did.

But none of this detracts from the urn as a signal to memory and an object of beauty and to the fact that at The Leasowes the wide deployment of these artefacts invited the visitor to become more personally involved in the poet's life than might otherwise have been expected. Today the raising of an urn is foreign to our thinking but in the middle of the eighteenth century such a practice among the wealthy was commonplace and much thought was given to the design, placing, inscription and size. An example of how pleasing a well proportioned and suitably sited memorial urn could be, is to be found in the one raised to Maria Dolman of which there is a picture in this book.

Shenstone is much concerned with the correct siting of artefacts within his garden. In his *Unconnected Thoughts on Gardening* his ultimate concern is for the character of the land; only then may "a suitable appendage" to enhance the beauty of the scene be considered. Suitability is paramount and he gives as an example a lover's walk with its assignation seat; with "proper mottoes", "garlands", and "urns to faithful lovers". He writes of the important association between the placing of a seat and the scene to be viewed so as to stimulate the imagination by any proper means. An excellent example of this must surely have been the poet's octagonal seat, which was placed on the summit of "a circular green hill" from where a view of the Wrekin could be seen as a series of scenes framed and divided into eight "compartments" by a similar number of fir trees. At the centre of this seat was:

> an *elevated table which serves as a pedestal for a large goblet...with one handle on which is the inscription "to all our friends round the Wrekin".*[21]

In his *Letters* Shenstone criticises Sanderson Miller's estate at Radway. For there he could find no "suitable appendages" to commemorate the Battle of Edge Hill: "not one Motto, urn or Obelisk that might impress..."; and this, in spite of the fact that the park overlooked the land where the historic event took place. The poet found Radway distastefully impersonal: unlike The Leasowes where the visitor was directed around his garden in the most intimate of ways: where his thoughts, his mood; his eye and ear; were all subject to Shenstone's "presence" – exhorting, directing and encouraging. Most of all he disliked Miller's tower, an example of all that he felt a folly should not be. But we have yet to discuss the folly; the grandest of all the poet's "suitable appendages"; grand enough to deserve a section to itself.

* * * *

The eighteenth century was the age of the folly, the extravagant fake in the form of a castle, temple or suchlike that was rising up in the gardens of the rich. The folly was built to be striking and the more authentic its appearance, the greater would be its capacity for attracting admirers. Its concept was one of nostalgia – the child of a love affair with the past. In the form of a ruined castle or temple, it was an instrument for the contemplation of glorious, or if one preferred, amazing feats of architectural dexterity and extravagance. The folly had enormous curiosity value and sited where it would not dominate the scene, was intended to provide an eye-catching focus. Unfortunately, not all of these curiosities were to fulfil such requirements and in one of his letters to Lady Luxborough Shenstone describes such a one, Sanderson Miller's "Gothick" tower at Radway.

The poet had visited Radway when he was staying with his friend, Richard Jago in the winter of 1749. At the time, he was unhappy that Miller had earlier visited his neighbours at Hagley Hall without bothering to include a visit to The Leasowes in his itinerary, so his view which he subsequently modified, was disgruntled. Even so, a number of points that he makes are valid. First he complains about the height of the tower which, "is so excessive that I could not endure to look out of the windows". He grumbles about its turret which in reality is "some Poor body's chimney" and the tower, itself, the "top of which is detestable". He complains that the folly, "attracts the eye too strongly and takes from the variety of which his Scene was capable".[22] When Shenstone came to build his own follies, he was to take care that he did not perpetuate the same mistakes.

In his *Unconnected Thoughts on Gardening*, the poet writes about "Ruinated structures (which) derive their power of pleasing from the irregularity" of their shape. In love with the concept of the folly, he believed it to be one of the most important ways of creating atmosphere and introducing variety into his garden. If one discounts his summer house which came in for criticism and which he subsequently demolished, Shenstone, throughout his gardening career was to build three follies: his hermitage, his "gothick" alcove and his ruinated priory.

Shenstone's hermitage, later to metamorphose into the Temple of Pan, was constructed in the early seventeen forties before his tenant, John Shenstone had died. It consisted of "a small building of stone" and was approached by means of a "straight walk through his (upper) wood". Above its entrance, and in an attempt to provide a limited degree of religious "authenticity", the poet first placed "a rough hewn wooden cross", but as his vision of Arcadia ripened so, too, was the concept of this folly to change; his hermitage becoming a pagan temple, and the Christian God making way for the classical deity of Pan.

Later, in 1749, Shenstone constructed a second folly; his "Gothick" alcove, "a very handsome building" with a floor "paved carpet fashion with black and white pebbles". He describes its situation.

The ground about it is turfed but wants Rain; a new path is made to it, I think,
much for the better; by the side of...(it) is a little rock with a tree that I think is
picturesque...[23]

To the rear wall of this building Shenstone placed his inscription, *O You That Bathe in*
Courtly Blysse[24] a poem which makes a distinction between those who "Toyle in
fortune's giddy sphere" and those who are content, like the poet and his friends, with
simple, rural pleasures. A familiar theme and one to which he frequently returns in the
elegies, it is summed up here in the final couplet:

For faults there beene in busye life
From whyche these peaceful glens are free.

The story of its "posting" and reception is recounted to Lady Luxborough. He "had just
fixed up the lines...when who should arrive but Mr Lyttelton, Mr Pitt and Mr Miller".
The verses were duly admired by his visitors but with the exception of a couplet that
now makes up the last two lines of the second stanza:

Nor yet deryde the beechen bowle
In whyche he quaffs the lympid springs.

It was Lyttelton who first questioned their suitability; a response with which Lady
Luxborough agreed, maintaining them to be "Vastly pretty (but) in some other place".
Possibly she felt "gothick" and "pastoral" to be an unlikely mix. In any case, the
honesty of Shenstone's response was typical of the man. It would appear that he had
suspected all along the "offending" lines to be "flimsy" but had hoped that their
"Autient guise" would disguise the fact! How valid this criticism was is difficult to tell;
for today the poem is greatly changed and neither is it "posted" inside a "gothick"
alcove. But it is of interest that Shenstone finally kept the queried lines, even though he
moved them from the final stanza into the second verse.

This was completed only after much thought, for wedded, as were his
contemporaries, to the didactic concept of art, he took his inscription writing seriously.
He saw the function of these poems as both to instruct the mind and to stir the emotions
and he had a clear view of what was acceptable and what was not. "I do not like your
bee motto", he was later to write to his friend, Thomas Percy. "As being neither moral
nor affecting; which when mottos are not, they had certainly better be quite omitted".[25]
From the evidence, it would seem that he contemplated his verses written as
inscriptions, with the same care as that given to the elegies, odes and ballads.

As well as his "Gothick" building, Shenstone was later, in 1752, to build the most
spectacular of the three follies, his ruinated priory. This was fitted with windows from
the nearby ruins of Hales Abbey to make it look more "authentic" but, behind its
"Gothick" façade it was also to double as "A tenants' house that pays me tolerable

poundage". In fact the tenants, who were an old man and his wife, paid rental for the privilege of living there of four pounds a year; not an inconsiderable sum. From Shenstone's friend, the actor/manager, Thomas Hull, who visited The Leasowes in 1759, we learn how successful a "ruin" the "priory" was. "It appears a ruin of a chapel built some hundred years ago", he writes, "whereas it has not been built two years".

Upon Shenstone's death, his one-time great friend, John Scott Hylton, compiled an inventory of contents which demonstrates even more clearly, how "real" a chapel the single downstairs room would have seemed. In his *Letters* Shenstone was to mention the numerous "Gothick" shields that he had placed around the cornice but there was much more. To these were added a "Gothick" stone chimney piece, above which hung a "Brass relivo" (Basso relievo) of the crucifixion fashioned in alabaster. Over the stained glass window was a carved figure of Christ, crowned with thorns, and to balance this, over the door, the carving of a martyred bishop. Added to this was a painted wooden triptych, the middle panel depicting the Adoration of the Magi and the two outer ones a different saint on each. To complete the picture, there were two "Gothick" and four cane chairs to encourage visitors to sit down awhile and contemplate.

Shenstone was justly proud of his ruinated priory and of the added interest that it introduced to his park. It was eye-catching, and unlike Sanderson Miller's tower at Radway, it did not dominate. The siting of the poet's priory was superb. It could be seen nestling in between, and partly concealed by trees which made it appear more impressive than it was. Or alternatively it could be viewed in the distance, "at the bottom of a green slope" and spied "through a narrow opening" which provided an alternative picture of enchantment. Shenstone's priory was to cost him comparatively little and its success was due, not to money, but his own powers of imaginative invention.

His neighbours, the Lytteltons at Hagley, on the other hand, were wealthy landowners who could afford to pay for the design and construction of follies on their land. There in 1748, and under the auspices of Sanderson Miller, a most magnificent folly in the form of a "Gothick" castle was under construction. Shenstone charted its progress. "Mr Lyttelton has near finished one side of his castle" he writes to Lady Luxborough. "It consists of one entire tow'r and three stumps of towers with a ruinated wall betwixt them"[26]: and although he approves of the siting of the building which gives it "a charming effect", he is critical of the proportions of the chief tower which is "too low" and of the design which has neither "art" nor "variety". To prove his point, he adds a small pencil sketch for full measure. Whether or not his opinion was coloured by the behaviour of Sanderson Miller, seen by Shenstone as dilatory in not finding time to pay The Leasowes a visit, it is impossible to tell. But others, like Bishop Pococke, find "the ruins (to) have a beautiful effect". And, in any case, it was not long before the poet changed his mind, deciding that a glimpse of the Hagley folly from his own park would be no bad thing. "Hagley Park is considerably improved since you were here", he writes to Jago: "…they have built a castle by way of a ruin on the highest part of it which is just seen from my wood". He continues that "…by the removal of a tree or two…I believe it may be rendered a considerable sight here".[27] So was Hagley's castle put to good use as a spectacle for Shenstone's own visitors.

The following year, another of Lyttelton's follies at Hagley, costing two hundred pounds and in the form of a stone dome balanced upon Ionic pillars, called forth a different response. This was to come in the form of a "gothick seat, on the bank above my Hermitage". For the modest sum of "fifteen shillings and six pence three farthings", it was to be a sight at which, "all the Pitts' and Millers' castles in the world shall bow their heads abashed". Dodsley describes it as a "Lofty gothick seat" and it undoubtedly commanded a magnificent view of a lake in the valley; of the Clent Hills and of Halesowen: even of Lord Dudley's house, the Grange, and of the Lyttelton woods! Such was the result of friendly rivalry between neighbours; of a two hundred pound rotund and a vastly scaled down alternative, as delightful as it was imaginative.

Shenstone's explanation to Lady Luxborough of how his plans for his park first came into being shows how far he had travelled;

> *At first I meant them (paths etc) as melancholy amusements for a person whose circumstances required a solitary life. They were so; but I ever found the solitude too deep to be agreeable. Of late, encouraged by your Ladyship and others, I began to covet to have my place esteemed agreeable; in its way to have it frequented... to enjoy even the gape and stare of the mob... but above all... to have it honoured with the company of your Ladyship's acquaintance.[28]*

This was how it all began; and as his vision of Arcadia grew, he sourced from a common reservoir of classical antiquity the Roman poets and deities appropriate to his need. He conceived the idea of posting his own inscriptions – of guiding his visitors by means of them around his garden in the most personal way. He used his verses to enhance their responses especially to the differing moods engendered by an ever changing panorama of scenes; whether the "pleasing melancholy" of Virgil's Grove or the "calm repose" of Priory Walk. He also used them to exhort and instruct all who came upon the merits of country life and the importance of using the imagination to interpret what was seen. On the back of a seat within earshot of the "harsh clamour of a cascade" was a Latin inscription from the *Aeneid*. They are lines which stress the imperative of "fancy" and an English translation reads:

> *Thro' various scenes we rove*
> *As fancy guides, from verdant grove to grove,*
> *Or stretched on flow'ry turf extended lie,*
> *Lull'd by the tinkling rills that murmur nigh.[29]*

These are lines which encapsulate Shenstone's own feelings of how his garden should be enjoyed. One in which poetry was to play an important role. For without its verses and its emblems The Leasowes garden is incomplete – the imagination remains unstimulated and the charm of a "fairy" landscape unappreciated. In response to a request from Graves, Shenstone's own view about his poetry is categorical. He would rather that the verse his friend is in the process of writing should contain a compliment without "so much emphasis upon any skill I have in gardening; but in some sort (be) divided betwixt that and poetry".[30]

Shenstone did not want his poetry to be forgotten. Indeed, without his poetic vision The Leasowes, conceived as a garden of emblem and poetry, could not have triumphed – would not have been a magnet for the multifarious visitors who were, at that time, to derive such pleasure from his unique experiment: one which was to include also The Leasowes' farmstead.

* * * *

It was not long before the trickle of visitors who came to view and stayed to admire Shenstone's Leasowes became a flood, and he felt it necessary to make improvements to his farmhouse for the reception of ladies and gentlemen of "quality" so dear to his heart.

At first these were little more than cosmetic. "Pray, how do you like the festoons dangling over the oval windows?" he writes to Jago in 1748. But it was not long before major structural changes for the provision of larger rooms was under way. By December, 1748, with the aid of a stonemason and a number of carpenters, Shenstone was busy converting his kitchen into a parlour, "a room measuring seventeen feet by twelve feet six inches", with a ceiling height of a fraction over ten feet. This he considered to be of "tolerable size" and the walls of plain stucco decorated with a "cornish" or cornice, were thought by his friends to be tasteful.

Today, Shenstone's "parlour" would be described as a dining kitchen; for at one end was a lead pipe, "with a basin for water over a slobb". No such word appears in Johnson's Dictionary, so one must suppose this to be a bastardised version of "slab" and the description here to be of a primitive sink. At the other end of the chamber a door led into a favourite front room from where, "visto fashion" could be seen a hint of the Clent Hills, a view enhanced by its reflection in a suitably placed pier glass opposite. To achieve continuity, this front room was also decorated with stucco wallpaper and, for added cosiness, a niche chimney piece from his former summerhouse was installed to make a focal point and enable him to arrange his books on either side. These together with a busto of Pope, were to provide the finishing touches to a room that could be enjoyed by the gentry who cared to visit as well as provide homely accommodation for himself.

Encouraged by what he had so far accomplished, it was not long before Shenstone devised other plans. By the following May he has had a second living room enlarged; this time to around nineteen feet by twelve, and as yet is undecided as to whether it will eventually become the library or the drawing room. He is at this time also implementing other improvements of a more "convenient kind of which my servants will more sensibly reap the benefit": an end to which he is employing: two carpenters, a painter, plumber and glazier. No wonder he feels the demands of his house to be: "a bottomless pit... or rather... a whirlpool which sucks in all my money".

But it was all with an aim in view and by 1750 he was able to receive his "superior" visitors in a manner which he felt befitted their station: a necessary improvement made clear to him upon returning home from a visit to Lady Luxborough in the summer of that year. For on this occasion he was delighted to find a roll call of local gentry and their friends who emerged from both rooms and on all sides to greet him; among their number being Miss Lyttelton, Lady Caroline Egerton, Admiral Smith and later – even Sir Thomas Lyttelton, himself!

The refurbishment of his house and embellishments to his park were ongoing. In the autumn of 1753 he is "making a little alteration in the room over my hall which is now my library"[31] and has a looking glass in his "little breakfast room" which is in the process of being turned into a dressing room. It is one of a number of permutations as apparently endless as the resultant pleasure he derives from them. Earlier, in 1748, Shenstone was to feel that he had brought "my place here to greater perfection than it has ever yet appeared in". Now, a couple of years later, his aspirations have grown to include his farmstead and upon returning home he would ask, as we today might enquire after telephone messages, whether anybody had called. To meet a pleasant stranger along his walks was a delight and to have his old friends introduce new ones into his house and park was a minor triumph.

Improvements to his farmhouse did much to raise his self esteem. Visitors upon arrival there were likely to have been entertained in the parlour with green tea before being escorted around the walks, often "en famille", by Shenstone and his upper servants. For although he had always, in theory, considered the house and its environs to be an integral whole:

> *In designing a house and garden it is happy when there is an opportunity of maintaining a Subordination of parts; the house... placed as to exhibit the whole design.*[32]

It was only now that his plans for his farmstead were complete that he was sufficiently confident to invite comparatively unknown but important guests inside. And indeed, as requests for his advice from the local gentry continued to grow, he was encouraged to reflect, as well, upon the inside of their houses as well as consider their parklands. When in 1754, Lord and Lady Plymouth thanked him for his, "emphatically and ingenuously given" advice; to relocate their lake, have it "thrown into a broad serpentine river, the fens drained; and the grounds sloped down to it"[33], he was also encouraged to view the interior of their home, Hewell Grange, with a critical eye. Fortunately, the management of his Lordship's rooms was not found wanting. They were all to receive his "thorough approbation", otherwise one can but imagine what might have ensued.

It was not new to believe that great houses and their parks should complement each other. What was new was the way in which this could be achieved – for fashions change. In Shenstone's farmstead, views of his garden were reflected in mirrors which also augmented light from the windows. The use of uncluttered, stuccoed or stone coloured wallpaper helped to create a "natural" effect which married well with the apparent spontaneity of his garden. He had contrived a partnership which like all successful marriages brought advantages to both; a single entity of farmstead and land.

Chapter 12

SONGS, BALLADS AND ELEGIES

Shenstone and Lady Luxborough shared many interests and these included, not only their houses and their gardens, but a love of poetry, literature and ideas. Shenstone's own poetry which has attracted an undeservedly poor response over the years, and his stimulating prose works, *Men and Manners*, which have been ignored, are each now to have a chapter to themselves.

As early as 1739, Shenstone had begun to send verses to his friend, Mrs Henrietta Knight as she then was, and her appreciative response is clear from a letter that she pens to Jago at that time.

> *It will be impossible for me to return Mr Shenstone sufficient thanks for the honour he does me – and for the agreeable entertainment his verses afford me.[1]*

It was a pattern that was to continue for well over a decade as the poet supplied her as he did all his friends, with a constant supply of his work for her appraisal.

At around the same time he was also to send one of his songs, *"When Bright Ophelia Treads the Green",[2]* to Richard Jago with a hint that the chief musician of Birmingham (possibly Barnabus Gunn)[3] was to be asked to set the words to music. As with so many of Shenstone's plans nothing came of it, but a glance at one of its verses will quickly convince of its suitability, for the poem is brief, rhythmic and evocative:

> *"When bright Ophelia treads the green*
> *In all the pride of dress and mien;*
> *Averse to freedom, mirth and play,*
> *The lofty rival of the day;*
> *Methinks to my enchanted eye,*
> *The lilies droop, the roses die..."*

The song was first published in the *Works* in 1764. By then the name of the girl has been changed from Ophelia to Roxana but a few alterations to the text do not change the theme of the poem which tells how love with its "wild delusive flame" can change our perceptions.

That Shenstone thought of a number of his Songs in musical terms is evident and he had strong views concerning how this should be achieved.

*"... in musical composition, sound ought as much to answer sense as one language
does another... such and such thoughts ought to bring into our heads such and such
sounds and vice versa..."[4]*

So ideally, the words are enhanced by the music in a "marriage" which is of benefit to
both as for example, in Purcell's vocal music, but not apparently in Handel's *Messiah*.
For although the poet held this to be "the best composer's best composition", he was not
so happy with the word setting. Indeed he:

*Could observe some parts in it wherein Handel's judgement failed him: where
The music was not equal, or was even opposite to what the words required.[5]*

Who would dare voice such an opinion today!

Another of Shenstone's Odes, "To be performed by Dr Brettle and a chorus of
Halesowen Citizens, the instrumental part a viol d'amour", demonstrates how he wished
to achieve this. The poem is presented in dramatic terms; with a variety of characters
and even stage directions. There is a chorus, a solo by the "Doctor" and a duet
accompanied by "soft" and later, "war-like music".

The setting is the rehearsal of the local choir. Encouraged one Christmas to enjoy
themselves, the citizens are quick to "stir the tipple" and as a result soon find it
impossible to focus upon their singing. One by one they slip away from the rehearsal
and it is not long before the Maestro, Dr Brettle, after pleading with them to stay, is left
conducting to an empty room.

*Hear but this strain – 'twas made by Handel
A weight of skill and judgement deep!
Zoonters, thet're gone-Sal, bring a candle –
No here is one, and he's asleep!"[6]*

It is a lightweight piece of froth, but it is fun.

Over the years, a number of musicians were to set Shenstone's verses to music.
These were to include Samuel Howard, the composer, organist and choir master who set
Florello and Daphne to a tune that merrily trips away. Later still Charles Dibdin, best
known today for his sea song, *Tom Bowling* which is played every year at the last night
of the Promenade Concerts, also set *The Western Sky is Purpled O'er*. This was to
become popular with the Victorians who would frequently include it in their soirées.
Most important of all was to be Thomas Arne's setting of *The Pastoral Ballad* which
appeared in the first volume of Dodsley's Miscellany in 1752.

Some of the poems that Shenstone sends to Mrs Knight are written especially for
her; as when she is, "Queen of May" and:

The parsons round her praises sung!
The steeples with her praises rung – [7]

There are his lines *Upon a Visit to a Lady of Quality* whose company will "charm the dull eyed spleen away" and from whose "social hearth" he is too soon to return home: a poem graciously accepted as "extremely pretty and very poetical".

Shenstone's *Pastoral Ballad* is discussed elsewhere but in 1748 he sends Lady Luxborough his *Jemmy Dawson,* "a most woeful ballad founded on a paragraph in the newspaper" and written to supply words for a melancholy tune popular at the time. The poem's concern is with the execution of Captain James Dawson, allegedly a traitor, who was hanged on Kennington Common that same year. The final stanza evokes a mixture of sadness and relief. Sadness for the death of a young man and relief that justice has been carried out. And such was the febrile climate of the day, that Shenstone begs her to show the ballad to no-one lest the zealous might "elicit treason from this humble song".

At the same time he sends her *The Dying Kid* in which his Disney-like description of the little billygoat and the cartoon quality of his antics:

… with what delight he stood
To trace his features in the flood:
Then skipped aloof with quaint amaze
And then drew near again to gaze:[8]

only serve to makes the poem's theme, that the young animal is destined for slaughter before he becomes destructive and "the vines his wounds deplore", all the more poignant. Shenstone wrote the verses "one afternoon, thro' a propensity to write something on whatever delighted me." And he admits that he hardly knows "whether 'tis pretty or ugly". In fact it is both: a pretty description of a delightful creature before its ugly death.

Many of the poems contain wistful descriptions of the uncertainty of love: "Love is an April's doubtful day". Or the misery of an unrequited love that cannot be forgotten:

And the more I, with study, my fancy refined,
The deeper impression she made on my mind.[9]

A favourite from this group of poems must be *Slender's Ghost*. In her nineteen thirty five biography of the poet, Dr Marjorie Williams is so delighted with the work that she quotes it in full and writes of "a charm which lingers and defies criticism". It is a comment true of many of the songs. Shenstone was a passionate admirer of Shakespeare and it is no accident that the comic character of Slender should have enabled him to create a poem which delights with its imagery and rhythm, its repetitious reminder that:

> *'Tis Slender's voice 'tis Slender's way*
> *Expresses all you have to say.*[10]

Also occupying his mind were the elegies, poems to which he attached considerable importance. Most of these were composed in the seventeen forties when six of them form part of a list of his accomplishments at the time. By 1748, the number has grown to "a pretty large collection of elegies on almost every melancholy subject that I could recollect"[11] and it is clear that Shenstone has been devoting at least as much time to crafting his poetry as he has been expending upon his garden.

At this time he was toying with their publication, but upon the advice of friends was relieved to drop the idea in favour of "something else... of more general acceptation" which is how he attempts to rationalise his position to Lady Luxborough. For from now on, and until the end of his life, publication of a Collection of his poetry, like a mirage in the desert, was to prove both desirable and at the same time unattainable: desirable because part of him longed for recognition and unobtainable because fear of adverse criticism was to make him dilatory. Indeed, so great was Shenstone's ability to procrastinate that his friend, Jago's witty pastiche on the Hamlet soliloquy springs to mind:

> *To print, or not to print – that is the question.*
> *Whether 'tis better in a trunk to bury*
> *The quirks and crotchets of outrageous Fancy,*
> *Or send a well-wrote copy to the press,*
> *And by disclosing, end them.*[12]

Instead, he was content to circulate his poems in manuscript among his friends before transcribing the "corrected" ones into his green and later his red writing book ready to send to Lady Luxborough. Transcription was laborious and time consuming for, as he writes later:

> *My Pegasus is one of those dull horses which will not bare to be*
> *Hurry'd. Allow him but his time and he may jog on safely; but urge*
> *him to move faster, and he is sure to break one's neck.*[13]

In the meantime he was keen to obtain critical comment from friends and his request to Graves in the summer of 1748, "I want to correct my elegies by your assistance", is representative of many made at around that time. By the autumn of the same year work was progressing and he has, "wrote out my levities and... Sonnets with many ornamentations of the pencil". For Shenstone was a fine draughtsman and much of his work in manuscript was accompanied by illustrations designed to delight the eye in the same way that the poems were to delight the ear. The way ahead was clear and: "the next thing... will be to transcribe my elegies"; he is even confident enough to protest that, "I am vain enough to imagine that the little merit I have, deserves somewhat more regard than I have met with from the world".[14]

By November, the "Green Book" was nearly filled and the poet felt sufficiently encouraged to write to Lady Luxborough of "some very solemn elegies which I shall shortly put into your hands". Unfortunately the "shortly" turned out to be premature, for he was to have trouble with the writing of the preface and finally forced to admit that part or even, on a bad day, the whole of it might have to be omitted! In the meantime, Lady Luxborough waited. "I am impatient for the Green Book", she reminds him and a week later, "the Green Book will add greatly to my pleasure". Shenstone continued working and remained silent, but one can have little doubt that he was already regretting the ill-considered "shortly" of his earlier letter.

On 12 December, 1748, Lady Luxborough begins a letter with an image of Shenstone at work; no doubt in an attempt to encourage him:

> *Methinks I see you by your chimney piece, your pen in your hand and the*
> *Red or Green Book before you, just going to express with poetical elegance*
> *Some refined or sublime thought...*[15]

The poet could prevaricate no longer and was finally persuaded to part with the precious manuscript; but he has to be confident that his friend "will not expose them" and points out that "the outside of the Book seems to promise more perfection than will be found within".[16] He begs her, "to make some kind of mark on such as you should least dislike", for over the years he had come to know the quality of her Ladyship's mind and admire her perception - a view that is supported by the reading of her letters in which she demonstrates an astuteness uncluttered with the paraphernalia of intellectual word-play.

So it is not surprising that Shenstone was anxious for her approval which, if a little muted, was duly forthcoming. "I am persuaded they (the poems) will please better judges as they do me", and she singles out Elegy VII which, in the published *Works* becomes Elegy XIV, for special comment as its theme is patriotic and one with which she can empathise:

> *While others lost to friendship, lost to love,*
> *Waste their best minutes on a foreign strand,*
> *Be mine, with British nymph or swain to rove,*
> *And count the genius of my native land.*[17]

But she does not like the contents of the Preface which is too long and likely to induce readers to "lay down the book before they got to what (it) is meant to introduce them to!"[18]

However, in spite of her Ladyship's protestations, Shenstone's *Preface* to the poems is of interest, for in it he discusses the aims of elegy which are twofold: to celebrate a good name in death, and to present a show case for the virtues of rural seclusion. He writes of elegiac style which "should imitate the voice and language of grief; (be) flowing as a mourner's veil": two glorious phrases which, after considerable re-casting of the remainder of the essay, were to remain. *Elegy XXVI* is one which must surely come nearest to fulfilling these requirements. Called *Jessie* and "Describing the sorrow of an ingenuous mind on the melancholy event of a licentious amour," it was much praised by John Ruskin who quotes verses from it which describe the young man's state of mind:

> *Amid the dreary gloom of night, I cry*
> *When will the morn's once pleasing scenes return?*
> *Yet what can morns returning ray supply,*
> *But foes that triumph, or but friends that mourn?*[19]

These he places alongside lines from Wordsworth's *Ellen* as: "two most exquisite instances from masters' hands".

Upon reading the poems, correspondences between Shenstone's verses and his ornamental farm spring to mind. There is the "pleasing melancholy" of Virgil's Grove, analogous to the sadness portrayed in *Verses Written Towards the Close of the Year 1748*. Another of the poems, *Rural Elegance,* is the celebration of a way of life which has parallels with his own at The Leasowes. For it is dedicated to a particular friend of Lady Luxborough, the Duchess of Somerset who, "cloyed with merited applause" has retired to rural seclusion upon her country estate at Percy Lodge. An elegy concerned with "the pleasures of solitude and rural amusement", it presents "the person of true taste as the only adequate spectator".

The history of *Rural Elegance* is a chequered one. In March 1751, Shenstone sent copies to several friends for critical comment, but by February 1753 can no longer remember where they are. "I would be glad to correct that Ode to the Duchess" he writes to Jago early in the year, "when once I can find in whose hands it is deposited". By June the Ode is recovered and "after an unavoidable delay and some difficulty", together with some lines to her Grace, is included in a packet to Lady Luxborough with the insistence that the work is presented to the Duchess properly; "I mean with all that respect and deference... for her exalted character". Her Ladyship's response was encouraging. She writes that she has "read the Ode and thinks it can receive no amendment": that she "will not fail to send your packet to the Duchess...and obey all your commands".[20] All of which would have gladdened Shenstone's heart.

At this time it was to be gladdened further. For his morale received a further boost in the form of an invitation to Hagley Hall where he was to have the honour of reading "at table" three of his greatest poems: *A Pastoral Ode, Rural Elegance* and *Verses written Towards the Close of the Year 1748*. The reading of verses at table, like the listening to music on the harpsichord was common practice in the houses of the gentry at this time; and in Shenstone's case, one can but imagine what impetus the setting of the crystal glass and polished silver might give. In August, 1753, Shenstone gleefully writes of the reception his performance met. A stanza from *A Pastoral Ode* in which Dean Lyttelton is celebrated as "Philo", "made Lord Temple laugh abundantly" and the other verses, too, "were all more extolled than they had any pretence to deserve".

For the poet it was a proud moment in an age when patronage of the rich still played an important role in the literary life of the nation. In modern terms, what happened at Hagley on that day was a great publicity exercise, and the importance of the role played by word of mouth could not be overestimated. It was all most gratifying, but then – as so frequently happened, the period of elation was to be followed by three months of anxiety. As Shenstone writes with a grim wit: "Pleasure and pain continue to interfere! And I could be well enough content if they would come separate".[21] On this occasion, the poet's "pain" was to be due to the months that elapsed without any word from the Duchess of Somerset, a lady upon whose illustrious name he had set such store. As the weeks passed, his anxiety grew – a situation made all the more acute because he dared not enquire into the reason for the delay.

It was not until November that her Grace's response finally came and much to Shenstone's relief, revealed the long silence. Her letter was dated 20 November 1753 and its contents made clear her delight in his "two excellent poems". The second was "an additional fragment" of an earlier poem to which he gave no name. She explains that his packet had not arrived until the previous Saturday and is concerned lest Shenstone should think her "the most ungrateful and tasteless of all mortals" for not replying earlier. This was a great relief. The Duchess's silence was due to the fact that his packet had not been received; it was not because she disliked his work. But her Grace had a request to make. It was that her name be erased from the Ode, together with that of her home, Percy Lodge: and this so that "the world in general" will not be tempted to "draw mortifying comparisons" between the poem's ideal and the reality which is far less inspirational. Both, she suggests, be supplanted by asterisks, a convention frequently adopted. The Duchess also wrote to Lady Luxborough and although the contents of her letter remains unknown, the resultant action does not. For her Ladyship is ashamed of herself and writes to the poet to explain the cause of the delay. "I did not meet with anybody I could trust with it that was going towards her Grace's habitation, and the little book was too big and heavy for a frank".[22]

Shenstone was vastly relieved that the whole business was cleared up. The Duchess had signalled her approval and the best intentions of his friend were not in doubt. But the illustrious name of the former, which would have presented his poem with a gloss and aided its popularity, was not, after all, to appear and that was a disappointment – one with which however, in the circumstances, he would come to terms...

Today Shenstone's elegies are no longer read for they are longer than much of his other work and the Cynthia's, Delia's and Philomels who people their pages appear to the modern reader artificial characters from a culture of which they know little. Even so, a number of the poems are rewarding. Elegy XI, for example, that tells of the fleeting hours of youth:

Ah me, my Friend! It will not will not last,
This fairy scene, that cheats our youthful eyes;
The charm disolves; th'aerial music's past;
The banquet ceases, and the vision flies.[23]

And how sad it is; not so much that youth passes – but that the poet believes our youthful aspirations to be in some way thwarted by the world's false promises. There is also Elegy VIII, in which Shenstone points the mistake of listening to the over partial judgement of one's friends:

Not the poor veteran, that permits his foe
To guide his doubtful step, has more to fear.[24]

But always it is to the shorter songs and odes that one returns. For it is these that have a musicality and a lightness of touch that is frequently entrancing. His advice to a young girl whose manner of speaking is artificial in *Ode to a Young Lady*:

Survey my Fair! that lucid stream
Adown the smiling valley stray;
Would Art attempt or fancy dream,
To regulate its winding way?[25]

The pen portrait of himself as a school boy:

Who then more blessed than I,
When the glad schoolboy's task was done,
And forth with jocund spirit I run
To freedom and to joy?[26]

These examples, and there are many, serve to reinforce the truth which is that Shenstone down the years has received a bad press. His critics have remained blind to much that is good in his work and have honed in, for the most part, on the weaknesses. It was an imbalance of which, in his lifetime, the poet was only too well aware.

Chapter 13

THE PENSÉES

Shenstone's Pensées, or *Men and Manners*, as is their given title, reveal the man most clearly of all. For in them, penned throughout his life and given a free rein, are his thoughts upon people, politics and religion. Shenstone's comments spring from acute observation and from his own experiences as he journeys through life; and what he sees and says is as fresh and pertinent today as it was when first recorded. For although fashion may come and go and today we talk of "progress", the basic stuff of human nature is the same yesterday as it will be tomorrow.

In his Pensées, Shenstone pens the thoughts of a remarkable man in a way that is both palatable and readable. He lived at a time when class consciousness and religious bigotry were rife and his ability to cut through the pettiness of received opinion, shows him to have been both compassionate and wise. He writes of what was important and of apparently trivial matters too. He writes with humour and in a style commensurate with the greatest of the French exponents of the genre, a fact that has not escaped the notice of the late Havelock Ellis in a re-appraisal of Shenstone as a writer, written in the nineteen twenties.

The poet's pen ranges extensively and some of what he says relates to life at The Leasowes as do his lines concerning the importance of letters. "In an heavy oppressive atmosphere, when the spirits sink too low, the best cordial is to read over all the letters of one's friends".[1] In his own correspondence he writes of idleness, posing that: "There is something like enchantment in my present inactivity". It is an idea which in the Pensées becomes: "It should seem that indolence would incline a person to be honest; as it requires infinitely greater pains and contrivance to be a knave".[2] More pertinently, he writes of the responsibilities imposed upon those with intellectual talent and if there is irony here, for he did not always live up to his own strictures, one must remember that Shenstone is here promoting an ideal:

A man possessed of intellectual talents could be more blameable in confirming them to his own private life, than the mean spirited miser that did the same thing by his money.[3]

Much is sauced with wit: "A miser grows rich by seeming poor, an extravagant man grows poor by seeming rich".[4] Or it comes from a compassionate heart:

One should not destroy an insect, one should not quarrel with a dog, without a reason sufficient to vindicate one through all the courts of morality.[5]

83

Some of the comments are born of chagrin. Shenstone never managed to become proficient at card playing, no doubt because he was not interested enough to try very hard; and his lack of skill meant that he always lost, even when playing with children! So here he vents his spleen:

> *...cards...seem invented for the use of children; and among the toys peculiar to infancy, the bells, the whistle, the rattle and the hobby-horse, deserve their share of commendation.[6]*

If this were not sufficient, he continues that card games are favoured by those: "who come nearest to children in understanding; (who through) want of ideas grow enamoured of them as...suitable entertainment".

But in spite of this froth, much of what Shenstone writes is both thought-provoking and salutary: especially so are his concerns with religion and politics. About the established church of his day he has this to say: "Perhaps we should not pray to God 'to keep us steadfast in any faith'; but conditionally, that it be the right one".[7] It is, he believes, "peculiarly the Church that makes a jest of God Almighty", and he has nothing but scorn for "Christian" nations who attribute the success of their armies to "the peculiar favour of a just Providence". He muses upon the doctrine of Hell Fire and concludes: "If anyone's curse can affect damnation, it is not that of the pope, but that of the poor".[8]

These are the same progressive and moderate views that he maintains when he considers the problem of crime and the nature of punishment; the latter a sphere in which the Church wielded considerable influence. "It is difficult to be angry at beings we know incapable of acting otherwise than they do",[9] are words more likely to be those of a twentieth century Behaviourist than an eighteenth century gentleman of letters. Then there is: "vice is the proper object of compassion", or his views on celibacy among the peasant classes:

> *One scarce sees how it is possible for a country girl, or a country fellow to preserve their chastity. They have neither the – pleasure of books...nor the refined amusement of building, planting, drawing, or designing to divert their imagination (which is) continually...stimulate(d) by provocative allusions...[10]*

Words which tempt one to ponder how, if he were alive, he would react to a number of our television programmes today.

The political scene also comes under scrutiny. For the man who could write to Thomas Percy in 1763 that "I profess no party but moderation", is the same who repeats in his Pensées: "If a person ought heartily to stickle for any cause, it should be that of moderation. Moderation should be his party".[11] And he has contempt for governments that employ incompetents. "A government is inexcusable for employing foolish ministers; because they may examine a man's head, though they cannot his heart".[12] Who could disagree?

So a portrait of the man emerges. A compassionate man. A man of quirks and foibles who has; "often viewed my watch, standish, snuffbox, with…regard; allotting them a degree of friendship, which some men, do not deserve".[13] And the warning that follows is as uncompromising as it is inarguable: "There are a sort of people…with whom one could by no means share one's time".[14]

Shenstone is much concerned with writers and writing. There is: "a sort of masonry in poetry". Or, "Long sentences in a short composition are like large rooms in a little house".[15] He writes of the skills of an editor with poetic fervour as one: "who collects the merits of different writers and, forming all into a wreath bestows it on his author's tomb"[16]: and of the pitfalls confronting the biographer who should remember that: "a mere relation of matters of fact, is fit only for evidence in a court of justice".[17]

Sometimes the point is made by means of a story, as in the tale of a sixpence. For wealth and our perception of it is relative and the coin appreciated by a shoe-shine boy will be treated by contempt when offered to the butler of a nobleman. Shenstone writes about class; the way in which we see ourselves and expect to be addressed accordingly. In an essay, he considers the vice of envy and is persuaded to view it differently. Seen in a more positive light it arises from: "contemplation of the superior advantages of another" which in turn, can be translated into "emulation" and an encouragement to do better.

The Pensées are unique. They were not written for publication and although Shenstone on occasion was content to plunder them for material in his *Letters*, they give us a more accurate picture of the man behind the pen. They are written with wit, understanding and compassion and, as the late Havelock Ellis has pointed out, are well worth our study. In them, as one would expect, there is much about garden design; but as this is discussed elsewhere, it would be repetitious here. Instead, one's concern must be with Shenstone's humour that has the sparkle of champagne:

…it seems as much a piece of justice to commend a man for talking more honestly, than he acts, as it is to blame a man for acting more dishonestly than he talks.[18]

With perception as keen as a sharp blade: "Humility to genius is as an extinguisher to a candle"; and much drollery: "There is nothing more universally commended than a fine day; the reason is, that people can commend it without envy." So Shenstone speaks; and one can but marvel that his pen has so long remained silent when he has much to say that is relevant for today and all time.

Chapter 14

FRIENDS AND FAMILY: 1745 – 1755

The mid-forties saw Shenstone established both as a poet and a landscape gardener. The publication of the *Schoolmistress* in 1742 had raised his literary profile: and his garden was attracting many visitors and much favourable comment. It was during this period, too, that his friendship with Lady Luxborough was to bring him ample satisfaction and generate that unique correspondence already discussed.

In the summer of 1749, the poet was to make a new friend in the person of the Reverend John Pixell, a young clergyman from Birmingham. The grounds of The Leasowes were open to the public and Pixell, like so many, enjoyed walking there and was in the habit of introducing his friends to its beauties. Shenstone had first met him in Virgil's Grove and upon the latter's repeated visits the two had formed an empathy born of similar tastes and interests. For the clergyman not only played the harpsichord as did Shenstone, but also the violin which he would later perform outdoors on summer evenings for the entertainment of the poet's other guests. "A young…man of taste and ingenuity" was Shenstone's verdict upon his newfound comrade and it was not long before members of Pixell's Edgbaston music club were prevailed upon to exercise their skills on behalf of the Shenstone circle.

Another of the poet's local intimates was Lord Dudley of the Grange whose ancient house is now the home of the Halesowen Somers Sports and Social Club. Whose grounds, instead of today's tennis courts and football pitches, were once spiked with vicious man traps to deter poachers and trespassers by means of a posse of eagle-eyed gamekeepers. All of which seems out of character with the owner, who according to Shenstone at any rate, was an easy going man with few pretensions. Centuries earlier, Dudley's ancestors had been the power wielding Lords of Dudley Castle and it was from his illustrious friend, who was also a very distant relative, that Shenstone was able to beg franks for his letters. When Lord Dudley was in town, however, the supply dried up and the poet's friends were obliged to pay for the privilege of hearing from him: "Lord Dudley is gone and franks are no more" ruefully records Shenstone in 1747.

The franks were welcome, but the poet sought Dudley's company because he genuinely liked the man. And he seems to have been good for Shenstone in a number of ways. In the first place he had no literary pretensions and, surprisingly, this was a relief. Dudley "who often drinks your health" as Shenstone writes to Lady Luxborough, was a drinking companion and the two would frequently sit up together until the small hours. Their conversation would have been inconsequential, for the owner of the Grange was not educated in English literature or the classics. Shakespeare and Virgil would

Lady Luxborough.

Lady Luxborough's autograph.

The Old Chapel, Ullenhall.

The Luxborough coat of arms in Old Chapel, Ullenhall.

Illustrated letter from Lady Luxborough to William Shenstone.

if you please till Mr. Pixell arrives.

I beg my Thanks to Mrs. Weymondesold for her kind Remembrance of me: am a little fearfull her Visit will be too late in ye year; but 'tis in Mrs. Weymondesold's Power to make all seasons pleasing.

My Lord Dudley will be extreme glad to wait on Mr. Outing. But He must come hither first, & we will adjust ye Remainder.

I have taken ye Liberty to send this by my Servant Girl, who is desirous to see her Sister & Barrels; & really my Man is so much afistant in ye way of fitting up my Room (wch engages me) yt I could very ill Spare him.

I hope Mr. Price is recoverd, by ye mention you make of his going again to London. I did not merely ask, but wish to see him here. And now I must leave ye Ladyship for ye Company of my Carpenters; Yet am ever uniformly your Ladyships
most oblig'd   W Shenstone.

Page of a letter from William Shenstone to Lady Luxborough, 6 June 1752.

Virgil's Grove from an engraving, by Thomas Smith.

The Leasowes and Priory Seat, by D. Jenkins.

The Old Priory in 1761, by David Parkes.

A Gothic Alcove at the Leasowes, by David Parkes.

Gothic Seat in the High Wood, by
David Parkes.

The Temple of Pan, by David Parkes.

All friends round the Wrekin, by
David Parkes.

Memorial urn to Maria Dolman, by
David Parkes.

View of Leasowes, by David Parkes.

Memorial urn to William Somervile.

Memorial urn as reproduced in volume one of The Works.

Sanderson Miller's folly at Radway.

James Thomson, artist unknown.

The "Castle" at Hagley Hall.

have meant as much, or more precisely as little, to him as financial advice to a pauper. But instead of finding this irritating, Shenstone describes him, instead, as "a very honest, humane and hospitable neighbour". For he was pleasant and appreciative; posed no threat and was wholly untrammelled by care. Everything about him, including the overgrown yews in his park which obscured the view – was just as it should be: in sharp relief to Shenstone's situation at The Leasowes where he was constantly striving, very successfully, and not a little stressfully after perfection. With Lord Dudley, Shenstone was released from the straightjacket of care. With him life became less complicated and the friendship an antidote to melancholy.

Shenstone recounts some delightful tales of the man. There was the occasion in 1753 when he came to spend the night at The Leasowes. As the evening lengthened he decided against dressing for possible visitors and elected instead for an evening in his nightcap and slippers. One can guess the outcome. For no sooner had he changed than a knock at the door was to admit Lord Temple and Miss Banks both suitably attired for their evening visit! Another tale is more intimate and concerns a nocturnal accident. Shenstone describes with relish how:

> *My Lord Dudley has much irritated his great toe by hitting it against*
> *The bed's foot whilst he was strolling thro the dark in full quest of the*
> *Chamber-pot.[1]*

To the friendship of Pixell and Lord Dudley must be added another – that of John Scott Hylton who was to come to live at Lapal House in Halesowen. Shenstone was introduced to Hylton by Lord Dudley who had met him in London and who, together with his sister, Miss Lea, brought him to visit The Leasowes one fine summer afternoon in 1747. The poet immediately took to the man, finding him both "modest" and "ingenious": and it was not long before the acquaintance blossomed into friendship. By October of the following year Shenstone is writing to assure him of "your usual place in my affection and esteem".

Little is known of John Scott Hylton but he clearly came from a family of means. Later he was to refer to his unsuccessful lawsuit against "the faithless guardian of my younger days" which destroyed his fortune. This was to lead to the loss of a place at court which he had bought for the sum of a thousand pounds – in those days a very large sum. But no matter, for in Hylton Shenstone had found a friend with a similar interest in "toys": someone with whom he might indulge his passion as a collector and who, from his London base at the home of a Mr Evans in Brook Street, was happy to advise upon the "management" of his poet's snuffbox. The box was to be repaired; but whether in the cheapest way, "with a figured tortoiseshell on the top and a plain tortoiseshell on the bottom", was the subject of discussion.. In the end, neither of these options were to be taken up and it was decided to embark, instead, upon a new gold clasp and rim; work which Hylton was able to expedite because of his long-standing patronage of the jeweller concerned.

Hylton's letter informing Shenstone of the completed work: "your glass is done and I have got the gold clasp from the chaiser's", also contains some racy gossip. "I can furnish you with few particulars concerning Mrs W's amour" he writes and then fills in the details:

> *...her husband and other people had ocular demonstration of her guilt, by a servant boy's boring three holes in the wainscot, which afterwards cut into one...*[2]

By today's standards a sex scandal of tabloid proportions.

Sometimes Hylton's enthusiasm as a collector would run away with him and he would buy items for their curiosity value. This was to lead to a subsequent cooling in the relationship, a sad outcome to a friendship which, in the seventeen forties, still had many years to run.

Shenstone, for whom the role of collector was one which brought its own responsibilities, addresses himself to the problem of these "counterfeit" collectors in his essay *On Taste*. In it he describes "a kind of counter taste...which maintains a sort of rivalship with true": a comment, some might feel, with relevance for today. At any rate, he believes the trend to be both common place and of no value: one to which he gives the alternative name of "concetto".

But in the meantime the friendship flourished. "Mr Hylton has no...despicable share of Politeness, Genius and Literature" Shenstone writes to Lady Luxborough after a visit with his friend to Barrels; and when this carefree young man is dilatory in writing letters, he feels responsible:

> *If Mr Hylton have not acquitted himself of his letter to your Ladyship, pray notifye, that I will wrap a large Flea in a piece of white paper, and will cause the Post Boy to put it in his ear.*[3]

On such good terms were the two men in 1754, that Hylton stayed at The Leasowes for two months while work at nearby Lapal House where he had recently moved, was carried out. London had lost much of its magnetism and like Shenstone, he had come to prefer the peace of the countryside and despise those, "sordid wretches! – whose only God is Gold": who were perceived as devoted to "collecting a bag of shining cinders". A view that was all very well if like Hylton, one were still comparatively rich, even if not sufficiently so to maintain his place at court. Hylton's enthusiasm was boundless. He tried his hand at writing poetry and his letters show a vivacity, coupled with a genuine regard for Shenstone, which made their friendship while it lasted, of benefit to both.

During this period of the poet's life, Hylton, Lord Dudley and the Reverend Pixell contributed to what may be conveniently termed "the good times". But Shenstone's frequently articulated view that the emotions of pleasure and pain were in some way linked was to prove sadly accurate. Some time during the winter of 1749, the poet had paid an enjoyable visit to Jago at Harbury, but the following year, a February visit to Whistler was to prove disastrous. Since their undergraduate days the two had corresponded and their friendship had been cemented by summer holidays together: at Oxford, The Leasowes and Whitchurch, the Whistler family home. But on this occasion and upon returning from a week spent with the Whistler family, Shenstone was to voice his opinion that the friendship had dwindled – that it might even be at an end. Fortunately as events were to prove, this was not the case although it is clear that a serious disagreement had arisen.

Earlier letters from Whistler show how genuine his regard for Shenstone was. " 'Tis more than Garrick playing Richard to see you", he writes and upon the poet's gift of a watercolour; "The flowers were the finest I have seen…and superior to this…(as) they will not fade".[4] So as the friendship meant a great deal to both men, one wonders what went wrong? Was it Whistler's concern over his mother's illness that had made him ill at ease? or, for that matter, Shenstone's own worry about the health of his brother? Perhaps it was the venue, Whistler's "bandbox", the new and smaller establishment into which he had recently moved to be near his family. For here space was limited and the poet's faithful servant, Tom, had been obliged to stay at the local inn, which had proved unsatisfactory.

Then there was the perceived orderliness of the Whistler menage. Meals heralded by the summoning gong and punctuality, not a word included in Shenstone's vocabulary, maintained with vigour. All of which would have proved irksome, for the latter to whom even the fixing of a date was to be seen as an infringement of personal liberty, was incapable of living by the clock or, indeed, by the calendar. This reluctance to commit himself, already observed in his dealings with women, was but another aspect of his dislike of social obligation as was his "violent aversion to card playing", a pastime he found popular at the Whistlers. Indeed, he writes that "At Whitchurch I think they do nothing else". His unwillingness or apparent inability to master the rules of quadrille meant that he was to find himself relegated to playing "Pope Joan" with the children and even worse, of losing to them and having to keep paying out his stake!

The atmosphere was further soured by an unappreciated joke. Anthony Whistler might deride his own new property by calling it his "bandbox", but it was not acceptable for his guest to repeat the analogy; and Shenstone's continuance of the metaphor with an added alliterative dimension – that his host was now literally "a beau in a bandbox", met with a proportionally cool reception. All this conspired to spur the poet to leave as soon as he decently could…

"Too much trivial elegance, too much punctilio" is how Shenstone sums up this visit. But as the weeks passed and each came to attach less importance to misconceptions which arose from the trivialities of the dinner gong and the card table, the mending of the fracture in their relationship can be charted. For what begins in September 1751 as:

> *I have never received a single line from Mr Whistler, and I believe my journey to Whitchurch has given the final blow to our friendship:*[5]

has become by the following October: "Mr Whistler and I are now on good terms and two or three friendly letters have been exchanged between us".[6] One of these from the former shows him to have been a man incapable of bearing a grudge.

"I never did nor ever can mean ill or disrespect to dear Mr Shenstone, but shall ever be his most sincere friend and humble servant...".[7]

Words of conciliatory charm which played a large part in the healing process.

But more importantly than this, the Whitchurch visit is of special importance for the role that it played in Shenstone's creative life. For it was when homeward bound, and during a welcome respite at a roadside hostelry that he first conceived the lines of the most famous of all his poems: *Lines Written at an Inn at Henley*. In fact, the "Henley" of the title is misleading. Dodsley used it in his 1764 first edition of Shenstone's poems, but the venue is mistaken. The inn of the title could not have been at Henley-in-Arden for that would have been too near to Barrels, the home of Lady Luxborough, where the poet would have undoubtedly stayed had he been in the area. Neither could it have been an inn at Henley-on-Thames, for that would have been in the opposite direction to the route he would have followed to The Leasowes. Instead, it is more likely that the inn in question was the Sun Rising Inn at Edgehill, an ancient hostelry which obtained its name from the direction it faced on the brow of the hill which caught the early morning sun. It was an inn with a long history. An early reference to it appears on Ogilvy's Map of 1745 and by the time of Shenstone's visit it was already many years old and had earned its reputation as a coaching inn where passengers on their way from Kidderminster to London would spend a night en route. A private house now stands on the site.

Lines Written at an Inn is a poem that has graced many editions of Palgrave's *Golden Treasury* as well as numerous other anthologies over many years. It is a poem, according to James Bosworth, that was much loved by Dr Johnson and one which was recited by him with emotion when they were both staying at Henley-in-Arden's White Swan on their way up north to begin their Scottish Tour. Shenstone's poem is a tour-de-force. One in which its message of loss, like a mantra, is carried forward with increasing urgency in each of its five brief verses.

In it, the poet contrasts the freedom and friendliness of an English hostelry with the artificiality of the social round from which he has just fled. It is a point hammered by repetition, for every stanza ends with the word "inn"; and this is what drives the poem forward to the "pleasing melancholy" of its climax. It is with a "sigh", both of sadness and relief, that Shenstone realises he will find acceptance, if not among friends, then always in the company of mine host and his customers in the friendly atmosphere of an ale house.

Whoe'er has travell'd life's dull round.
Where 'er his stages may have been,
May sigh to think he still has found
The warmest welcome at an inn.[8]

Such was the outcome of the Whitchurch visit which has proved a bonus for countless poetry lovers. *Lines Written at an Inn* which is the last major work that he penned, has brought us, down the centuries, a minor masterpiece to savour. The poem is also of interest as a divide between his old life and the new – from his role of poet to that of editor. For although Shenstone was to continue to revise his poetry throughout his life, from now on, he was to write nothing of consequence. Instead his love of song and verse was to be maintained in his capacity, as editor, a function in which he was to excel.

And what of his continuing friendship with Whistler? By the spring of 1754 it was Shenstone's dearest wish that:

> *If Mr W. would give me a visit in the height of my season...I should look upon it as one of the most pleasing events that could happen to the remainder of my life;*[9]

How sad that such hopes were doomed to remain unfulfilled; that by June of that same year a letter from John Whistler should bring dreadful and unexpected news. Anthony Whistler, one of the poet's closest friends since those early Oxford days – was dead! He had caught cold, contracted a severe sore throat which worsened, developed into an "inward mortification", and died. Could this have been diphtheria? If it were it would make some sense of what to us, today, might otherwise seem inexplicable. It seems likely and even by eighteenth century standards when death, from the cradle onwards, was an ever present concern, this unexpected advice was to cause Shenstone much grief. For Whistler's loss was irreparable and overnight the poet's world darkened. To Graves he writes with moving eloquence of their common loss. "The triumvirate which was the greatest happiness and the greatest pride of my life is broken!"[10] And he opines that their recent and occasional "bickerments", were not of a sort "that touched the vitals of our friendship". He ends with an exhortation; that he and Graves should put shared memories of their friend to good use, "as the strong and everlasting cement" of their own friendship. It is a brave letter and one which demonstrates an inner strength not always apparent in the tenor of his daily life.

With this, one might confidently feel that the sad business was ended: but there was more to follow. Over a period of twenty-five years Shenstone had written frequent letters to Whistler and to his other close friends, Graves and Jago. The friends treasured these letters for the minor masterpieces that they were and, with an eye to posterity, kept them safe. But as the days after Anthony Whistler's death turned into weeks and then months, the poet, who had expected his correspondence as was the custom to be returned, became uneasy. By the end of July he is voicing these fears. "Pray what will become of our letters to Mr Whistler?" he asks Graves and continues, "methinks I could wish that they might not be destroyed". It is for their content as well as their literary merit that Shenstone prizes the correspondence. "It is from a few letters of my own...that I am able to recollect what I have been doing since I was born",[11] he writes in justification of his concern.

Sadly, Shenstone's worst fears were to be realised; for by October and much to his chagrin, came the first intimation that the letters, along with the rest of the "unimportant" papers, had been destroyed. His response is understandable for by now he had come to regard his letters as some of his "chefs d'oeuvres", and these particular ones as "records of a friendship that will always be dear". More importantly they are also, "the history of my mind for these twenty years past": and to Graves he admits that in order to have prevented their unnecessary destruction, he would have bought the letters back, even if it had meant giving, "more money than it is allowable for me to mention with decency!" But by then it was too late.

The death of Whistler, and the consigning of his letters to the flames were sad events during the middle years of Shenstone's life. Unfortunately they were only two in a further catalogue of catastrophes which were to undermine his health and darken his perception. But the love and esteem in which he was held by his friends and neighbours at this time was to provide the support which enabled him, though falteringly, to carry on.

The visit to Whitchurch took place in 1751 and Whistler's death in 1754; but the years between were also to bring sorrow including that of the death of Shenstone's beloved brother, Joseph. The closeness of the brothers was born out of shared tribulation – the death of their parents; and of similar tastes and leanings for they both enjoyed literature and music and shared a life of books, friends and song. Often it was Joseph, mentioned frequently by Lady Luxborough in her letters with affection, who, less frugal with his money, was the first to obtain a new book, pamphlet or sheet music that they would both play. He was a kindly, generous and literate man whose ill-health had prevented him from pursuing a strenuous legal career and one who provided Shenstone with companionship both perceptive and amiable.

Joseph had never been strong and first mention of a serious illness was made in June 1748. Few details can be gleaned except that he seems to have made a faltering recovery which unfortunately was not maintained. By 1751 his condition had deteriorated sufficiently to cause real concern. The letters are not always dated but in what is likely to have been the Spring of that year he developed "a very serious inflammation upon his lung". Medical advice was sought and Dr Hervey, a family friend and brother-in-law to Lord Dudley was to pronounce the illness "a true perineumony" or pneumonia as we would call the condition today.

The symptoms were severe and rapidly deteriorated; the patient suffering from "such inexpressible difficulty in respiration" that by late evening, Shenstone in consultation with Hervey, determined upon a second opinion. A servant was dispatched to Dr Wilks of Hagley, a man aptly described by another patient as "without dispute a good physician but no charity...". The choice proved to be unfortunate; for the doctor, who lived up to his reputation, chose to ignore the plea for help and in so doing, wasted valuable time. In desperation, Shenstone then turned to the aid of a mutual friend who personally turned out in the middle of the night and knocked at the gentleman's door.

Meanwhile, and in a state of near collapse, the poet could only watch and wait; listen with growing alarm to his brother's stentorian breathing until, with the coming of dawn, it was again clear that there was to be no response. There remained now only one hope in the person of Dr Wall of Worcester, Lady Luxborough's own physician and a most eminent doctor. As the clock ticked one can imagine the urgency of whispered debate before the decision to set out again for help was finally taken. And then a seeming miracle occurred. For at the very moment when the horse was again saddled in preparation, the patient's breathing became easier and his pain with each breath less acute. Unbelievably it dawned that the crisis was passed.

Shenstone writes of his brother's convalescence and the toll upon his own health. Joseph was soon to recover sufficiently to be carried "sedan chair" fashion around the grounds, but not surprisingly the poet was again subject to "the return of my nervous disorder" which always resurfaced when he was under stress: in this case the "sleepless nights (and) sudden alarms" and the burden of almost "constant solicitude" while his brother's life was under threat. Indeed, he was in such a debilitated state that extra support in the house was required. For now, with two invalids upon their hands his housekeeper, Mary Arnold, and his maid, Mary Cutler, were unable to carry out their other duties efficiently. Consequently, Shenstone was obliged to apply for help, "to a gentlewoman in my neighbourhood…a good motherly sort of woman", a second Mrs Arnold, in fact, to look after him.

The household struggled on, and Shenstone was even able to find time and strength to drink tea with a Captain West and his family in Virgil's Grove and entertain a party of well dressed men and women around his walks. But this was a false dawn. For in a few weeks Joseph's health again deteriorated and in November of that same year he died. A traumatised Shenstone was so grief-stricken that for several weeks he was unable to communicate his loss – even to his closest friends. And when he did feel the necessity of putting pen to paper the words that spill over are from his heart: "Alas dear Madam!" He writes to Lady Luxborough, "I have lost my only brother! A more sincere or truly affectionate one never bore the name".[12] And he explains how his grief affects his view of things.

> *I find all my views intercepted… Every Object round me every source of my former amusement, revives a train of ideas which I am not able to support.*[13]

Poor Shenstone! But he limped on, and by the end of the following January had come to realise that his dependence upon liquor to induce "stupification" was counterproductive . The first step towards rehabilitation taken, he was soon even beginning to think again about "patterns of paper for my drawing room" for, mercifully, such intense grief is not sustainable. His friends all rallied and none more so than Lady Luxborough whose own dearly loved brother, Bolingbroke, had recently died. "Your grief for your brother", she responds, "I feel in its full force and am persuaded you feel the like as to mine".[14] And in order to banish his melancholy, she encourages him to visit Bath where she is taking the waters for her arthritis and Beau Nash is king . It was of course in vain; for at such a time Shenstone was unable to rouse himself and the stress of meeting with a sea of new faces would have been too burdensome for him. He explains his position to Graves: "though my reason forewarned me of the event, I was not the more prepared for it"[15] and he still needs time to come to terms with his loss. Now that he has experienced *real* grief he refers to lines from his "idle" *Elegy upon Autumn* with new insight:

> All can I bear the motley cast
> You sickening leaves retain
> That speak at once of pleasure past
> And bode approaching pain.[16]

Autumn was a season that he always disliked for it signalled the departure of friends; heralded loneliness and the steeps of muddied walks. Now he has a "more important cause to hate and condemn it", one to which will be compounded, "the glare and gaiety of the spring" synonymous with regeneration, for all "but my poor brother".

Even so, by February he has roused himself sufficiently to invite Christopher Wren's young son from Wroxall to pay him a visit and also to take an interest in the future of young Hannah's sister,[17] who is to take up a post at Barrels. He has chosen new wallpaper and Tom is unable to be spared because he is "so much assistant in the way of fitting up my room". In his own way Shenstone was coping and he remained closely in touch with his young cousins at Broome where, it will be remembered, the two Shenstone brothers had gone to live after their parents had died. The daughter, Maria, was a particular favourite of the poet's. He believed her capable of "great things" and from her early teens she had impressed him with her manners, taste and discernment. Later, she was often included in parties at Barrels where she also won the approval of Lady Luxborough.

In 1749, Shenstone sent her for her eighteenth birthday the present of a "letter case" and her acknowledgement of it demonstrates how adroitly she can turn a pretty compliment. She writes of her "two obligations"; for the "neat and valuable" present and for "the honour of your letter". She comments upon the "two amusements" of reading and music which never fail to entertain and she tells of a new spinet that the family have recently acquired. The content of her letter is wide-ranging. She mentions the book of *Proverbs* of King Solomon and later, Vanburgh's stage comedy, *The Relapse*, in a way which shows how much she has in common with her better known and older cousin.

During this period in the late forties, there seems to have been a good deal of communication between The Leasowes, Barrels and Broome, and much time was taken up in both looking forward to and organising trips to these various establishments. Parties to Barrels would often include, not only Shenstone and his brother, but the Dolman children, Maria and Thomas, as well as any house guest and a number of "upper servants". Attending at Barrels would be Lady Luxborough herself, and possibly her housekeeper, Mrs Lowe, with her secretary and general factotum, Mr Outing, who the poet seems to have liked and encouraged as a friend. On occasion the vicar, the Reverend Holyoake, and his wife would also be invited.

Upon arrival and in the company of Hume, Lady Luxborough's Scottish gardener, the party would then, weather permitting, have been conducted around the grounds with special interest taken in the season's innovations. The rest is intelligent guesswork. They are likely to have been offered green tea in the drawing room and an elegant dinner is likely to have been lubricated not only with wine but Shenstone's smooth tongue as he contributed to a discussion of literature, music and poetry interspersed with London and local gossip to provide an added piquancy.

These were occasions heartily enjoyed at a time when no-one could have realised that Joseph's death, was soon to be followed by another. But it was so. For Maria Dolman, a healthy, happy young girl of twenty-one was to be struck down and die from smallpox which she contracted while on a trip to London in the spring of 1754. John Scott Hylton, who was also in the capital at the time was the first to alert Shenstone to her illness and Shenstone's response, "of dreadful anxiety concerning her" was such that he "shall dread to look into the letter that I expect by tomorrow's post". His fears were to prove justified. Hylton had promised to chart her progress and in a matter of days after the illness was diagnosed, the awful news arrived. "Poor Miss Dolman expired yesterday at three o'clock". He continues that two medical men, "Dr B – and Mr S – were called up to no purpose" and that Miss Millward, her young friend, became hysterical, which in the circumstances is not surprising.

By April of this same year, 1754, Shenstone writes to Graves "of the death of my best beloved and…most accomplished of relations". It was a tragic blow that could have been avoided for she had youth on her side; "risqued going to London for the sake of finding something new, was seized with the smallpox, and died in all her bloom".[18]

Again, Shenstone was desolate. Later, in memory of Maria he was to raise a most beautiful memorial urn and the task was to bring him some solace. But for the moment, life was black indeed. He had lost a brother, the dearest of one of his friends, and now his talented and dearly loved cousin. Two young men in their early thirties and a girl, little more than a child. Even by eighteenth century standards it was a heavy toll.

When Shenstone writes that "the regular succession of pain and pleasure becomes every day more clear to me" he is, without knowing it, penning a fitting epitaph for these middle years – the decade of 1745-1755. For during this time he achieved great things at The Leasowes which, with a gardener's eye and a poet's ear, he sums up in one of his greatest Odes, *Rural Elegance*. With consummate success he had set out:

To catch soft hints from Nature's tongue,
And bid Arcadia bloom around;[19]

It was a time of achievement – of enjoyment and sadness. A time when pain as well as pleasure was meted out in equal measure.

Chapter 15

"PEOPLE IN OUR PARISH"

Although reluctant to admit it, Shenstone was as much at home with his neighbours as he was with his more aristocratic friends. "I have neither a single neighbour that is fraught with politeness, literature or intelligence", he writes with typical exaggeration; but facts speak otherwise. Amos Green and James Woodhouse were two local young men of talent who the poet was pleased to help.

Amos Green was a native of Halesowen and employed as a painter by Matthew Boulton to illuminate gift boxes. It was through the latter that Shenstone came to know Green who was frequently invited to The Leasowes during the seventeen fifties: who found in the poet a friend who was "singularly agreeable" when in good spirits, but full of "faults and foibles" when he was not. Shenstone, who also painted, was struck by the young man's talent and when there was talk of Green setting up as a painter in Bath, supplied him with a letter of recommendation to Graves whom he felt might be in a position to help:

> ...the bearer of this letter has, by dint of mere ingenuity, risen to considerable eminence in fruit pieces...has been employed by Lord Lyttelton and is much admired in Oxford.[1]

It may sound a little thin, but a second reference carries more weight. "He is esteemed inferior to no-one in England for fruit". In fact Amos Green did not go to Bath but the considerable talent with which he painted arrangements of fruit, flowers and game, can be seen in his compositions at London's Royal Academy.

The second young man, James Woodhouse, brought himself to Shenstone's notice in 1759 by sending him an elegy.

> *Pardon O Shenstone! An intruding strain*
> *Nor blame the boldness of a village swain,*
> *Who feels ambition haunt the lowliest cell,*
> *And dares on thy distinguished name to dwell...[2]*

Woodhouse was twenty four years old at the time and plying his trade at Rowley as a shoemaker which is why he later became known as the "cobbler poet".

Shenstone's response was to invite the young man to The Leasowes where Woodhouse was shown his library and park – and grant him immediate access to both whenever he should so wish. It was a kindness which the young shoemaker never forgot and was to mention in 1764, in the Introduction to his first Collection of poems: *Poems on Sundry Occasions*. With Shenstone's help, Woodhouse was to persevere in his literary aspirations. His was to be an interesting and successful life and in spite of Dr Johnson's not unexpected: "He may make an excellent shoemaker, but can never make a good poet", was to live to see the doctor modify his judgement. How this came about is best left to Woodhouse, himself:

> *I was informed at the time that Dr Johnson's curiosity was excited by what was said of me in the literary world as a kind of wild beast from the country and (he) expressed a wish to Dr Murphy, who was an intimate friend to see me.³*

The meeting was a success, and when in 1765 the young man became land steward to Edward Montague, the husband of Elizabeth, a leading literary figure and close friend of Johnson, his career as a poet was further encouraged. For at the Montagues' he was to meet many important figures from the literary establishment, including James Dodsley, the brother of Robert, who was responsible for helping the young man establish a bookselling and stationery business in London's Grosvenor Square. By 1788, he had become an establishment figure and it is ironic that the life of the "cobbler poet" was to prove, briefly, a greater success than Shenstone's own. However, much of his fame was born of curiosity and unlike the latter he was not multi-talented, but an attractive firebrand which as quickly fizzled out.

Shenstone encouraged Amos Green and he helped Woodhouse: but his concern was also with the poor and the sick. For although, on occasion, one might be forgiven for thinking otherwise, he was a kindly man who took his responsibilities as a local landowner seriously. He allowed the tubercular Mary Rice, a young mother with several children, unlimited access to his park so that she might take advantage of its tranquil walks and beneficial silences away from the clamour and poverty of her home. The Reverend Alexander Carlyle, on a visit to The Leasowes in 1758, was to see the poet's concern at first-hand and takes up the story:

> *At the end of a high walk...I met with what struck me most – that was an emaciated pale young woman...Shenstone went up, and stood for some time conversing with her.⁴*

Shenstone was also to care for her family: and in 1761 he was to use his influence to obtain free hospital treatment for her equally ill young son by recommending him to Lord Foley's Hospital at Old Swinford. The same solicitude was to be shown by the poet on other occasions. Some years later when he and some friends, including the painter "Ned" Alcock, witnessed the plundering of a Leasowes' fishpond, the poet refused to bring charges against the culprit on the grounds that he had a wife and three children to support and "not a doit to procure them a meal". He makes a distinction between a robber and a pilferer and finds it inconceivable to give "the former appellation to a poor wretch who, in his hunger, has taken two or three fishes and as many loaves".⁵

A further incident concerning a robber at The Leasowes was published in the *Birmingham Mirror* in 1823. Shenstone, so the story goes, was walking with a lady-friend along one of his walks when he was challenged by a man brandishing a pistol, who demanded money. Without any sign of fear the poet parted with his purse, at the same time pointing out that there was little money in it and that the intruder must be "an unhappy man" to take such dramatic action. There was more. As the man fled, Shenstone had the presence of mind to call a servant and have him followed home where he was seen to throw the purse on the ground and lament to his wife "the dear bought price" of what he had done. Then he gathered up his children and burst into tears as he bemoaned the "ruination of his soul" to which his poverty had led. All this is supposed to have been viewed through a letter box! And, apocryphal or not, it gives a fair enough impression of what a man like Shenstone with undeniably progressive views might well have done. It is a story which ends with the poet offering him work as an odd job man around The Leasowes.

Shenstone's concern for ordinary people was genuine and for a number of years he had taken an active part in local affairs. In 1751, he had become a Justice of the Peace,[6] a privilege of which, as one has come to expect, he makes light:

> *I have been bestowing alteration upon an old House which it does not deserve; exhibiting my walks to persons of no taste; and making concerts in my neighbourhood for people that have no ear...and for all these Gallant Exploits they are going to make me a right worshipful Justice of the Peace.*[7]

And he points out with customary humour, that he intends to be inactive in the post and so make fewer mistakes! Other duties were quick to follow. In 1753, he was elected a governor, or feoffee, of Halesowen Grammar School and later in that same year was involved in lobbying for a turnpike Bill to facilitate travel by improving the road between Birmingham, Hales and Hagley:

> *I drew up a rough draught of a Petition to Sir George Lyttelton in regarding our turn-pike, meaning if it was approved to correct and transcribe it – And lo! The people of our Parish have signed and sent the Echantillon...*[8]

It was an endeavour which shows that even in affairs of the parish, Shenstone's passion for correction and "improvement" remained constant.

It was at this time that Shenstone was also involved in raising money for new bells at Halesowen Parish Church. "We are going to add two new bells to our present six...and to emerge a little from our obscurity"[9] he writes at the time to Graves. To Lady Luxborough he is more forthcoming. "I have promoted and accomplished the addition of two new Bells to our present six; towards which however I give only two guineas".[10] It was an undertaking which is of interest when one considers his relationship with the incumbent there, which was poor. For it is clear that the poet's concern for the good of the parish took precedence over a private quarrel with the Reverend Pynson Wilmot, one of the few, possibly the only person in the neighbourhood, with whom he had a serious and ongoing disagreement.

The quarrel arose over a path which ran alongside The Leasowes' park and crossed a neighbour's coppice. The poet had permission to use it, which he did frequently, and was in discussion with the man to buy the land over which it ran. However, upon returning home one day from a visit, he was both surprised and offended to discover that the route had been blocked. Upon investigation he was to discover the culprit. That during his absence, Pynson Wilmot had prevailed upon the owner, "to stock up every inch (and cause) the wilful destruction (of) the finest opportunity of improvement that ever a person had".[11]

Whatever the reason, it would seem to have been an act contrived with malice – and one wonders why? Could it have had something to do with Shenstone's progressive views which led him to criticise the Church? It cannot be known, but the outcome was one of longstanding controversy which would "probably last for life"; ferocious words from a man who was usually reluctant to engage openly in a quarrel. Even so, Shenstone must have drawn some comfort from the fact that the parson was universally disliked. Wilmot had outraged many of his parishioners and was to continue to do so for the remainder of his life.

Pynson Wilmot had been appointed vicar of Halesowen Parish Church in 1732 and unfortunately was to remain there until his death in 1784. He was a petty tyrant who from his pulpit ranted with medieval fervour; on one occasion, breaking off from his sermon to accuse a member of his congregation with a head cold, of behaviour like "the beast that perisheth;…even…a hog". Another time he allowed himself the black humour of a pun, equating the little town of Halesowen with "Hell's Own". A fitting description, as he saw it, of the people who lived there and to whom he was supposed to minister.

Away from church, his behaviour was as bad. He frightened local children, some as young as four years old, with threats of Hell Fire and eternal damnation, because it was Sunday and instead of reading their Bible, they were outside playing games. As Sir Thomas Lyttelton maintained, the man was mad, "but not mad enough"; by which he presumably meant, not sufficiently mad for action to be taken. Nobody was exempt, for he quarrelled as easily with his own kind. As Shenstone relates with relish, he "had a sort of Brush in Hagley Lane last week with Parson Lea".

There is a footnote to all this. Local rumour maintained that his wife went mad which would not have been surprising and cannot be verified. But the fact that the couple had a son, can. He, too, was ordained and one wonders how like his father he turned out to be? Such is a brief overview of some of "the people of our parish". Flesh and blood people with likes and dislikes, virtues and vices - like ourselves.

Chapter 16

NEW HORIZONS
AND THE MISCELLANIES

Shenstone had a gift for seeking out those who were empathetic to him and for keeping their affection. So he had embarked upon his friendship with Henrietta Knight, as she then was, with purposeful determination. "I am favoured with a certain correspondence…" he writes somewhat mysteriously to Jago, "which I should be glad to cultivate; and I find it very entertaining".

"Favoured" he had turned out to be, and for the next decade or so she and Barrels were to be of the greatest consequence to him. Her death left an empty corner in his life, and he reacted to it in much the same way as he had earlier to the demise of his great friend, Anthony Whistler – by focusing upon the present. Then, in spite of his grief he had exhorted the remaining members of his circle: "(to) stand firm to support the fabric of our friendship". Now he voices similar thoughts to the Reverend Holyoake. "On the death of one's friends one ever finds a propensity to *think on those that remain*".[1]

And "think on those that remain", he did. Graves and Jago, always important to him, were now even more so – but there was also more room for new friendships forged from relationships that had previously been slight. His publisher, Dodsley; the Birmingham printer, Baskerville, and Thomas Percy were all were men with whom he had during the latter part of the Luxborough decade forged friendships and at the same time maintained important working relationships. During the early seventeen fifties and later he was to participate in two of the most important literary events of the eighteenth century; Dodsley's last three volumes of his Collection, *Poems by Several Hands;* and Percy's *Reliques of Ancient Poetry*. Later Thomas Hull, the great actor/manager, was to join these ranks and with him Shenstone was to collaborate in the writing of his play, *Rosamond.*

A glance back at Shenstone's letters to his friends, Jago and Graves during the Luxborough period is enlightening. For in them one sees, not only "snapshots" of the time, but glimpses of the skills that would enable him to take on challenges that lay ahead.

Wittily he introduces us to the vagaries of coach travel:

How my Lord Dudley is tumbled about the world: He was
Overturned in going to town, and now again in coming back.
Is not this falling up Stairs and down Stairs?[2]

And to the custom of ringing church bells to welcome home a local dignitary.

My Lord Dudley came home last Saturday as I am well assured by Intelligence from the Steeple and other con-current Intimations; for I have not yet seen him.[3]

He writes of what is likely to have been his acquisition of a camera obscura, the forerunner of the magic lantern and our present day overhead projector..: "I have got a machine to exhibit landscapes…to advantage. It cost fourteen shillings…" and the projected pictures "appear ravishingly".[4]

But it is the emphasis that he places upon the endorsement of his friends that is most relevant: "My soul now leans entirely upon the friendship of a few private acquaintance, and if they drop, I shall be a wretched misanthrope".[5] It was reciprocity in the exchange of poems and criticism passed around the group that enabled Shenstone, who was anxious to offer as well as obtain advice, to write to Jago of "Good lines (to which) I propose some alteration". Or later on to Graves of "One stanza that concerns cards (which) should I think be corrected". It was also to Graves that Shenstone was to write in 1750 of:

My reigning toy at present (which) is a pocket book; and I glory as much in furnishing it with verses of my acquaintance, as other would with bank bills.[6]

By this time he was already at work: editing, collecting and collating material which eventually and two hundred years later, would be further edited and published by Professor Ian Gordon, in 1952, as *Shenstone's Miscellany*. It is a work which demonstrates that the poet's later collaboration with Dodsley and Percy was but a natural progression.

In fact, 1750 was to be a watershed in Shenstone's life. That summer Dodsley was staying with the Baskervilles at Easy Row in Birmingham and the two men took a trip over to The Leasowes. It was the first time that the poet and the publisher had met within a purely social context and the occasion turned out to be a great success; for it heralded the beginning of a warm friendship that was to last, with some highs and lows it must be said, until the poet's death. It was also to prepare the ground for what was to become a successful professional partnership between the two men; one which was to provide the eighteenth century with the publication of Dodsley's last three volumes of *Miscellanies*.

All this, arguably, is surprising. Before 1750, Shenstone's association with the publisher had been uneasy. They had met when the latter had published the poet's *Schoolmistress* and when in 1748 Dodsley included this in the first volume of *The Miscellanies*, or *Poems by Several Hands*, Shenstone was displeased. This was because no permission had been requested, and presented with a fait accompli, he had been unable, to "spruce her up a little", before she again appeared in print.

The subsequent success of the anthology had done little to mollify him. Well may it have consisted, if not of "Palaces like Dryden's *Ode to St Cecilia's Day*, then of villages composed of some very pretty houses"[7] and been in modern terms a bestseller!

Well may his *Schoolmistress* have been received as "…excellent of its kind and masterly"; neither was sufficient to put the matter right. Only the offer of a new and "improved" version of his poem for a forthcoming second edition could do that. Except that it did not. For Dodsley's acceptance of the offer had stressed the need for a speedy response and never a man to be hurried, Shenstone was to find himself flustered and flurried as he hastened "to have the opinion of my friends, what alterations or additions it will be proper to insert".[8]

Matters were made worse when weeks dragged by before the second edition (which contained three odes by Thomas Gray) duly appeared; and even then, Shenstone who felt that he had been unnecessarily harassed, was kept waiting for months before he saw a copy. He had, he writes to Lady Luxborough, "…waited long for a second edition which Dodsley proposed in great haste", but had yet to see it advertised. Not until November, when Her Ladyship came to his rescue and lent him her own copy was he somewhat mollified. For in it he was to find "…many good things". Indeed, he enjoyed the contents so much that he longed to annotate in pencil in the same way he would a book of his own. Years later, in 1760, he was to explain to Bishop Percy how this worked. In his own books he would place a cross at the head of each poem and the better he judged the verses to be, the more lines would appear on the crosses. Out of a score of three, the best would obtain ⌗. Next would come # and last of all +.

The success of this second edition was followed at the end of 1748 by a third in which Shenstone played no part. It contained contributions from giants of the literary scene such as Alexander Pope and James Thomson and was to prepare the way for the final three volumes in the series. It was in the preparation of these, both as contributor and editor, that the poet was to play an important role.

Not until 1753 did Dodsley turn his attention, once more, to the compilation of a fourth volume of his *Miscellanies*, a task in which Shenstone's involvement is a story punctuated by delays, setbacks and misunderstandings - a story which shows us Shenstone both at his best and at his worst. From the beginning there were setbacks. The original plan was for the publisher to visit The Leasowes in the summer of 1753 when the two men would exchange views; but this, because of the publisher's other commitments, was postponed. Instead, and not until September, did Dodsley write suggesting to Shenstone that he favour him "…with anything which you shall think proper", a request which the poet interpreted as an invitation both to contribute and edit all work that he deemed suitable. Surprisingly Shenstone accepted the challenge even though there were a number of problems looming. First was the, by now, inevitable request that all contributions should "…arrive within a month (which) would be soon enough". An appeal sufficient to set alarm bells ringing. Second was the complication of Dodsley's "loitering" letter. For he had misdirected it to Warwickshire. It had arrived late and precious days were lost before the work had even begun.

Nevertheless Shenstone, at first, really did try. He writes to enquire of Graves: "Whether I shall send any copy of yours?". He lists his own contributions and points out to would-be contributors that all work is to be sent "immediately". As a result, he was soon to find that he had more work than he could cope with and is complaining that, "the late arrival of (Dodsley's) letter allows me no time for application". By November things have deteriorated further and proportionately Shenstone's complaints have intensified. Now, not only does he have, "nothing in my hands to correct", but he has not time, due to problems with the revision of his own *Pastoral Ballad*, "to get anything corrected anyway". There were other complications too. Doubts about the quality of his own submissions intensified and the more stressed he became the less able was he to make up his mind.

By December, things seem to have got so out of hand that Shenstone was beginning to have second thoughts about the whole business. "The truth is" he writes to Lady Luxborough, "My mind is somewhat altered". Upon reflection he has "proceeded unadvisedly and must extricate myself as I can". He dangles the prospect of having his "better" compositions made up into "a 1s pamphlet", presumably to be printed by a Birmingham bookseller, instead of sending them to Dodsley. Here one feels that he is behaving improperly and not a little out of character, for Shenstone was always so loyal to his friends – but the devil was driving him. Dodsley, he writes, is "expecting a large cargo of my verses – but my cargo will not yet set forwards, and when it does, will not be large…".[9]

Fortunately in this case, and as with all the poet's airy plans for publication, his "1s pamphlet" came to nothing, and it is arguable that he was never serious about it in the first place. For in spite of protestations, a packet *was* duly dispatched to the publisher whose gentlemanly response should surely have made Shenstone blush. "I received and read with great pleasure your little poetical packet and shall wait with much impatience for your second".[10] This was encouraging; but there is little doubt that Shenstone's eye would have fastened with a gimlet intensity upon the "impatience" with which his friend awaited a *second* parcel of contributions, for there were to be more complaints and more delays before the second contingent was duly despatched and acknowledged. When it was, Dodsley's response occasioned enormous relief; the publisher, had changed his mind and the book was not to go to press "this winter". Because of forthcoming elections he had decided that the time was not opportune.

Shenstone, a man reprieved, immediately set about his task with renewed vigour. Forgotten was his earlier vacillation, his flirtation with the "1s pamphlet". Indeed his former behaviour is given the lie in a more balanced account of events that he writes to Jago in January 1754. He had first meant to contribute, "pretty largely – but afterwards" and, presumably when pressed for time:

> *changed my mind and determined to send only little Pieces. I did send him several of my own, some of my Frd, Whist., Graves, and some accidental Pieces of others which lay in my Drawer. I meant to send something of yours, of my own accord if I was hurried, otherwise not…without consent.*[11]

Clearly, it was this obtaining of consent that had caused many of the problems, for other contributors were sometimes slow in responding for the same reasons as Shenstone, himself. They, too, would miss a deadline because of time spent in re-casting. Seen in this light, a month was not so long after all and one can sympathise with the poet who felt that he was being unnecessarily hurried.

By July, Shenstone was expecting Dodsley "every week" to discuss matters. But again fate intervened and there were to be more delays. The publisher's beloved wife, Alice, was taken ill and instead of The Leasowes, a restorative visit to the sea at Portsmouth was deemed necessary. The months passed and to his chagrin the poet was to hear in October from Dodsley's brother, James, that "none of the papers I sent him are yet sent to press". Worse; the couple were not expected home until November and so publication was to be put off until then. Understandably Shenstone felt aggrieved: but he continued nonetheless to make good use of the extra available time. He begs "another copy at your leisure" of a poem from Graves and is prepared, if necessary, to "take any pains about it that you should desire me". He requests his friend's opinion "as to the manner of placing" what is sent, as well as advice on some small pieces of his own. And he was positive that work passing through his hands should be grouped together at the end of the Collection – which in the event, it was. But the lull could not continue. By December Dodsley was back home pressing for more contributions. In consequence it was not long before Shenstone, again, under stress, was once more experiencing doubt about the quality of his own submissions. As always he calls in his friends and, "on the very brink of the press" beseeches Lady Luxborough to "...honour me with your opinion in regard to a song or two which I enclose for your perusal".[12]

There were also problems with Shenstone's *Pastoral Ballad*. For in spite of Dodsley's repeated requests, the former had been unable to complete to his satisfaction an "improved" version of the work promised earlier. The poem had been back and forth several times between Barrels and The Leasowes with the result that upon her Ladyship's advice, a considerable part of Canto III had been omitted and the remainder altered. Even so, the present version had yet to be approved and her assistance as, "a genius, a florist, (many lines contain references to flowers!) and a friend", was sought before it was too late.

On the other hand there was no such uncertainty concerning the quality of Her Ladyship's verses: *Hark to the Blackbird* and *The Sun his Gladsome Beams* are "extremely elegant". Indeed, the latter is "equal to any song in the language": strong praise indeed. Thus he pleads their cause and briefly one glimpses the merry-go-round of sifting, editing and collating which weighed heavily upon a man whose emotional stamina was never robust and resultant "nervous fevers" frequent. In January 1755, letters to Jago illustrate how he felt. "It has been my lot", he writes, "to study the delicacies of poetry when my brain was not sufficient to indite a piece of common prose".[13] Dodsley, he complains, is pressing him, "to send conclusions every post": and with indignation bordering upon outrage, he claims that proof-sheets received before the end of the week are to be corrected and sent back "by *the return post*".

Over the next few days, comes a final, despairing plea for a meeting with Jago which "may finally and jointly fix the reading of your pieces, of my own, and those of our common friends..".[14] It was a crie-de-coeur to which, unfortunately, Jago's reply via "young" Mr Hylton arrived too late to be of use. For by then Shenstone had corrected the proofs and was awaiting publications almost, "hourly".

Again, expectations were to be dashed. Hours became days which stretched into weeks and as time passed Shenstone's protestations grew. "It is now three weeks or a month since I corrected the proof-sheets, "he writes to Jago in February and then:

> *I was so hurried in doing of it that I scarce knew what I wrote; and yet, in spite of all this hurry, the book is hitherto unpublished.[15]*

By this time concern over the quality of his own submissions has grown. Now, he will be, "utterly disconsolate" if "four or five little matters" are "printed with my name" – which, of course, they were. A week later he fires his parting salvo:

> *Had he allowed me but one* half *of this time to deliberate, I would have adjusted the share we have in it much more to my satisfaction.[16]*

One's sympathies go out to Shenstone even though his version of events is not wholly true. For from Dodsley's perspective things looked very different. He had a business to run and deadlines to meet and his ever polite requests met with no response. He had an original copy of the *Pastoral Ballad* which Shenstone forbade him to use and the "improved" version was so long in materialising that many editors would simply have walked away. Shenstone felt that he needed more time and undeniably he was very rushed: but just as some will never have enough money, no matter what, so others are spendthrift with time. Shenstone, as far as his own work was concerned, found it difficult to make decisions and he was incapable of meeting deadlines. One suspects that no time on earth would ever have been deemed sufficient.

But things could only get better and by March 1755 they had begun to look decidedly rosy. For by then the eagerly awaited complimentary copy of volume IV of Dodsley's Collection had arrived and with it, a reprinted "sett" of the three earlier editions. Excitedly, the poet writes to his friend of the "pleasure" this brings and of the many "excellent pieces" to be found inside. One can imagine the relief with which he is able to write to Lady Luxborough of, "having at last brought this affair to a conclusion", a task which, as a glance at the anthology demonstrates, was considerable. For Shenstone had supplied all the poems between pages 293-337; a group which included thirteen of his own – and also work by Jago, Somervile, Graves, Whistler and Lady Luxborough. It was a task triumphantly accomplished, for the volume was "well received in town": and with favourable reviews in both the *Edinburgh Review* and the *Monthly Magazine,* Shenstone felt decidedly encouraged: even expansive enough to wish, "I have done my friend some service" and to hope, for Dodsley's sake, that the book would be a substantial, financial success.

It was not until April of the following year, 1756, that mention of a further two additions to the Collection is made when almost as an afterthought, and in the postscript of a letter to his friend Dodsley writes:

> *I certainly intend to publish two concluding Volumes to my Miscellany next winter if I can get materials sufficient, and such as are to my mind; in which I hope for your assistance.[17]*

So began a re-run of earlier problems experienced in the completion of volume IV: the requests, the delays, the missed deadlines and the stress. Again one is struck by Dodsley's quiet courtesy and humour as he attempts to prise material from an apparently unresponsive Shenstone; a Shenstone in retreat and unapproachable. At first Dodsley resorts to badinage. He will "induce Mrs Cutler, to join with me in robbing your bureau of every scrap of poetry in it"[18]. Then to humour of a more obvious kind:

> *Where is Mr Hylton's* "Indian Ecloque"? *Is he gone thither to learn their manners? If not, pray give my compliments…and bid him make haste or he will come too late.[19]*

In fact Mr Hylton's poem did not "come" at all and Shenstone's subsequent letter to him does not offer much encouragement. "I am daily making ineffectual efforts" he writes, "to further Mr Dodsley's publication – but alas…at times I do not love poetry, I hate it – almost as bad as business".[20]

Upon closer examination, Shenstone's behaviour at this time, if not excusable, is understandable. For he was also involved with Dodsley in re-casting the epilogue of *Cleone,* the latter's soon-to-be successful tragedy which was to play at Covent Garden to full houses and much applause. Shenstone it would seem, was finding difficulty in apportioning his attention upon two important literary projects at the same time.

Even so he struggled on. Packets were sent to Dodsley but arrived intermittently, and the latter had to work hard to obtain even this minimal co-operation. Finally, and in desperation he is forced to spell out his own, by now, almost untenable situation. He has:

> *between 6 and 7 hundred pounds burry'd in the Paper and print of this edition which I want to pay and cannot till I publish (sic).[21]*

By our standards, today, this was a great deal of money and shows how committed to a successful outcome the publisher had to be. Even so, there was a final hiccup concerning Shenstone's own contributions, which was to prove insurmountable. Among these was his *Elegy XXVI,* a poem entitled *Jessie[22],* a poem of which Dodsley thoroughly approved, both for its literary and didactic qualities.

The poem's concern is with seduction. A young man, "schooled into the science of Love's mazy ways", looks back as he grows older upon a youthful indiscretion which still colours his perception of things. "When will the morn's once pleasing scenes return?". The death of the unfortunate and pregnant girl by drowning, warns of the consequences of such behaviour and to eighteenth century eyes was an acceptable postscript.

Dodsley had first seen and approved the poem on one of his summer visits to The Leasowes; had automatically assumed that it would find its way to Pall Mall for inclusion at sometime in one of his *Miscellanies*. In view of Shenstone's past behaviour, that this did not happen was perhaps not so surprising. For having dithered for weeks and finally decided that *Jessie* was not yet fit for publication he makes "a last ditch" attempt to play for time and in a letter to Dodsley at the end of 1757 explains "that incapacity I feel for criticism" and pleads, if it is not inconvenient, which of course it is, "to stop the press a little…" for further improvement.

Dodsley was dumbfounded; Shenstone was adamant. Without more time the poem would not appear. In vain does the publisher plead that the poet "revoke her doom"; pray that by the next post he will hear, after all, "that she is to appear". In vain does he list the merits of the poem and the good that will be done to Shenstone's reputation by its publication. It was fruitless and the presses rolled. *Jessie* did not find her way to Pall Mall, and indeed, did not appear in print until after Shenstone's death when Dodsley, as a fitting compliment to his friend, published the first edition of Shenstone's *Works* in 1764.

But surprisingly, and in spite of the problems with *Jessie*, Shenstone *had* managed to complete the final reading of the proofs by the end of January. A feat for which Dodsley's letter of acknowledgement is masterly enough to stifle the most vociferous of protests.

> *If you have forgiven me all my teasing impertinences, what a fund of good nature you must have…a wife could not have been a greater plague to you than I have been in the past.*[23]

Then by the middle of March, 1758, "A compleat Sett of the poems", carriage paid, was on its way. No doubt to the heartfelt relief of all concerned.

But that was not the end of the matter. For pleased though he would have been with his gilt embossed "sett", Shenstone was unhappy with the quality of some of the work included in volumes V and VI of the series. He felt that it did not measure up to the high standard of earlier editions. "To speak the truth, there are many things appear there very contrary to my intentions"[24] he writes to Graves in May, but is quick to exonerate Dodsley from blame, attributing any fault to his own illness. Indeed, it would seem that sometime during the previous winter, of 1757-1758, Shenstone had been quite seriously ill; so ill, in fact, that for a few days there was doubt as to whether he would recover. It was a state of affairs that encouraged his unpleasant nephew, "young Dolman", to stop his long and ongoing legal proceedings against the poet in the hope, no doubt, of obtaining his portion of the contested inheritance without involvement in extra legal fees. The situation would not have facilitated Shenstone's work for Dodsley and provides another clue to his earlier behaviour and apparent inactivity.

Now, by May, things were different. Shenstone was recovered and his critical faculty again acute. Already he was looking ahead in the hope that Dodsley could be prevailed upon to omit some of the poems in a future edition which he felt discredited the present volume. And he was not alone. Thomas Gray was also concerned about the quality of a number of the contributions, adhering to the general view that mediocrity debased the coinage of poems of merit.

Fortunately, and much to his delight, Shenstone's own contributions were deemed to fit the latter category: "I surely have some friend amongst the writers of *The Monthly Review*" he writes excitedly to Graves, "for I have not only escaped a flogging, but am treated with great civility". A glance at what *The Monthly Review* of June 1758 has to say, proves his point:

> *Perhaps a more excellent Miscellany is not to be met with in any language... (and) we shall close the article with a transcript of two, of Mr Shenstone's elegant and truly poetical pieces; the first entitled,* "An Ode to Health"; *the second,* "An Irregular Ode after Sickness".

So ends the saga of Shenstone's involvement with Dodsley in the production of the last three volumes of his *Miscellanies*, the series being, as Byron was to write later, "the last decent thing of the kind". It certainly was the most successful, in part because of Dodsley's numerous contacts. He knew all the right people and his publicity campaign, as we would say today, was excellent. But that was not all; for the time was right for such an undertaking and although the quality of the work is not consistent, some of the contributions are very fine. In future, Shenstone's talents were to be employed elsewhere - but meantime the reviews must have appeared to him as deliciously as fine wine to the connoisseur.

Chapter 17

'CLEONE' AND DODSLEY'S 'SELECT FABLES'

Over the years Shenstone's friendship with Dodsley grew and problems concerning the Miscellanies were easily forgotten within the context of other shared interests. Every year from 1751 onwards, Robert Dodsley was to spend an enjoyable summer interlude at The Leasowes and it was during these visits that the men indulged themselves, not only with poetry, but in coffee-house "gossip" from the capital: the plays and pamphlets – the novels hot from the presses.

Both men loved walking and both the theatre; not least Dodsley whose social satire, *The Toy Shop* had launched him at the age of twenty-five upon his play writing career. It was therefore to be expected that Shenstone would be one of the first to see a complete draft of *Cleone*,[1] "Doddy's" new tragedy. That before bringing her with him for his summer visit of 1756, the latter should alert Shenstone as to what he might expect:

> *I bring in my hand according to your request, an unfortunate melancholy creature whom you will find so perverse in her Disposition, that she will take pleasure in nothing so much as causing you Tears. However, ...if we find her in the least disagreeable we'll lock her up and banish her from our walks.*[2]

In fact, far from finding her disagreeable Shenstone was enthralled by *Cleone*, and when requested for his assistance in the rewriting of the epilogue, was at first delighted to help. A few weeks later in July, he writes to Graves of Dodsley's visit, giving a glowing account of what has passed between them.

> *He (Dodsley) has made a few days extremely agreeable to me...; and has been showing me his new Tragedy which I wished you might also peruse.*[3]

He continues that Dodsley, "has done me the honour to ask for an epilogue;" that it is a task he still wishes but now fears to undertake and would appreciate any "lucky hint" that Graves might be able to provide: and he adds that "the extraordinary merit of the performance", by which he means the play, "is altogether unquestionable". So the lines of the epilogue, cast and recast as they journeyed back and forth between London, The Leasowes and Graves' rectory at Claverdon, set out upon their hazardous and extended road to completion.

The weeks passed; and by October, in an attempt to get things moving again, Dodsley writes to Shenstone of his hopes that "before this time to have seen an epilogue from you". He feels that a corrected version already received from Graves "does not close happily" and he "could have wished for your name as it is better known and would have done me more honour".[4] As one has come to expect, it elicited little response and by the following March there has still been no epilogue from the poet: a situation made worse by the fact that in the meantime Dodsley has undergone the embarrassment of having his play turned down by Garrick.

It is a very strange story. Rumours, if that is what they were, abounded and the truth is elusive. But fact it is that both Garrick and Dodsley were then at the height of their respective careers: that the two men were supposedly friends. It is also true that Garrick was not only a jealous man but an arch snob in a world where snobbery, to modern eyes, was a way of life. Then comes the conjecture. For it was alleged that Garrick had refused the play on the grounds of Dodsley's "lowly" origins. That the latter who had started out life as a footman and never denied it, was deemed unsuitable as the author of a play to be presented at the auspicious Garrick Theatre.

As a friend Shenstone, only too aware of his own culpability, was concerned enough to emphasise that his silence had nothing to do with Garrick but rather his own health and to Graves he points out that "a thousand motives may affect a manager that have little or nothing to do with the merits of the performance".[5] By April, 1757, he was sufficiently contrite and recovered enough to write for his friend a masterly critique of *Melpomené*, a tragic ode that the two men had previously discussed and one which Dodsley was still working upon – in spite of – and as well as – everything else. With it one assumes that the latest copy of the "improved" epilogue was also sent although a definitive version was not to be arrived at for a further six months!

Meanwhile in London worse was in store; for Dodsley was to be insulted by being refused admission to the Garrick Theatre. One evening in October he was turned away by the doorman who knew him perfectly well, but who insisted that the publisher's name was no longer on the list of those who were privileged to receive what today would be called a complimentary ticket.

The quarrel became the talk of London's coffee houses: "Garrick and Doddy have had a spat" alleged Dr Johnson, but it would seem to have been more than that – a deliberately orchestrated snub in fact. But at any rate by October the epilogue was at last complete; and in a witty postscript to Graves, Shenstone describes its erratic path to completion;

Dodsley first liked it, then disliked it, and lastly liked it again; only desiring me to soften the satire, shorten the whole – and add a complimentary close to the boxes...[6]

all of which and to everyone's satisfaction he had finally and, as usual, at the eleventh hour – endeavoured to do.

Cleone was eventually to find a home at Rich's Covent Garden Theatre and to celebrate her first night, opened on Saturday the second of September, 1758, to a full and enthusiastic house. But rehearsals had been fraught with difficulty for many of "Doddy's" friends turned up with support that was both contradictory and unhelpful. The play was a domestic tragedy and its success or failure was dependent upon the performance of its leading lady. Rich had engaged Clara Bellamy, a well-known tragedienne for the role – and his choice was a wise one. But there were those who did not agree; and Dr Johnson, from his seat in the stalls, was one of the most vociferous protestors. He persisted that Bellamy's voice was not sufficiently strong and upon one occasion when she ignored his advice concerning a rising inflection when she posed a question, strode up on to the stage and pinched her arm in an attempt to attract her attention. In her *Memoirs* Mrs Bellamy recounts that the resultant bruise, inflicted at a time when she was already feeling unwell, lasted for weeks!

There was worse. For even the sanguine Dodsley became infected with doubt and began to feel that Clara Bellamy's delivery left much to be desired; and what is more, he told her so: waylaid her on her way to the dressing room and pointed out how unsuitable he now considered her to be. It can hardly have been encouraging. But she refused to be deflected. Refused to make use of histrionics more suitable to classical tragedy and endeavoured by other more subtle means to breathe life into a wholly innocent Cleone whose downfall, at the hands of her jealous husband, was to tug at so many heartstrings.

There was more. The play was to start its run on a Saturday and the previous evening Garrick had already proclaimed its doom; at the Bedford Coffee House had intimated that "it was the very worst piece ever exhibited". So the omens were not good and as Mrs Bellamy made her entrance on that first night, wearing a simple dress without the expected prerequisite of a hoop, she must have had doubts about the validity of her own judgement.

If she did, they were soon to be dispersed; for it was not long before the audience was caught up in the play's magic and "alternately cheered and wept" in all the right places. At the end of the performance the applause was deafening and so far exceeded expectation that at first even Mrs Bellamy, herself, found it difficult to comprehend. But then she heard a familiar voice that was to take her back to the incident of that pinch. "I will write a couple of verses upon her myself" it roared and Clara Bellamy knew then and beyond all doubt, that the play and her performance in it were both an unmitigated success.

And as for Dodsley? He was so pleased that from then on, so the story has it, and for the entire three week run of the play, he would take up his position in the wings of the theatre and weep without inhibition every night as his heroine "died"! It is a remarkable story of one woman's courage in the face of such trenchant opposition from those who should have been right – but in the event – were not. A success story in which Shenstone's epilogue had an important role to play and one which demonstrated how fruitful literary collaboration could be. So it was that, from his home at The Leasowes, the poet was as delighted with Dodsley's triumph as if he had written the whole play himself and it is hardly surprising that not long after he was also to become involved in another of the playwright's projects - his Fables.

After the success of *Cleone* Dodsley, with two brief exceptions, was to publish no more verse. Instead, this charming man who by today's standards would be classed as a "workaholic", from 1758 onwards was to devote himself to collecting material for his *Select Fables*, the work along with his *Miscellanies* for which he is best remembered. It is in a letter to Shenstone, dated 11 October, 1758, that the first intimation of any such undertaking is given, for it is then that he lets the poet into "a secret".

> *I am at present writing from Aesop and others, a hundred select Fables in prose for the use of schools; we having no book of that kind to put into the hands of youth, from the wretched manner in which they are written.[7]*

As always Dodsley was anxious to enlist Shenstone's help; but initially the poet was reluctant as he held a "mean" opinion of the art of fable writing and this had first to be overcome. Shenstone's reluctance was centred around the way in which a fable might be seen to differ from an ordinary tale; and Dodsley addresses this problem with his own definition which he hopes will clarify the situation and persuade the poet that the art of the fabulist is a worthwhile one. For whereas a tale is:

> *a series of events without regard to any moral; ...a Fable is one single event contrived on purpose to illustrate and enforce some moral truth.[8]*

And for good measure he sends Shenstone a fable of his own: *The Halcyon and the Sparrow*, "as a specimen of what I intend".

Shenstone's response was to undertake some research on the matter. He obtained an edition of La Motte, the French fabulist, whose fables had recently been re-issued and it did not take long before he began to change his mind. In the summer of 1759 he writes to Percy of the experiment:

> *La Motte has recently afforded me not a little Entertainment: I read it on account of Dodsley who, you know is writing Fables and asked my thoughts upon the subject.[9]*

That Shenstone was agreeably surprised is not so strange. For the writing of fables had an exemplary history; one into which a significant number of seventeenth and eighteenth century writers had dipped their pens with up-dated versions of Aesop to include "modern" fables and a "moral" introductory essay. Apart from La Fontaine and others, there was also the English Henry Brooke whose *Fables for the Female Sex* would cause outrage among women of today, but were then widely read. Then there was Ogilvy's rhyming paraphrase of Aesop, Bishop Croxal and even the great Samuel Richardson who tried his hand at the art.

Warming to his task, Shenstone invited Dodsley, "now you are a mythologist", to come to The Leasowes where he might see "every created Animal...(and is)...the only residence for a person that is writing fables". He even offered to provide some fables of his own – including 'The Two Swans' which never materialised.

Eventually Dodsley did arrive at The Leasowes for his annual summer visit and the two men immersed themselves in the genre which by now had the poet's enthusiastic attention. In an incident with which some may empathise the two managed to mislay some of the items and the poet fires off a note to John Scott Hylton who has also been involved; "Did Mr Hylton steal any of Mr Dodsley's Fables? He misses his *Earthquake* and *Thunderstorm* and...some more besides.."[10]

It was during Dodsley's five week stay that Shenstone's final doubts were resolved. His enthusiasm was kindled and at last he felt able to "take great liberties" with the material that they discussed. It was during this vacation that the publisher again visited his friend, Baskerville, and provisionally arranged for his *Select Fables* to be printed at Easy Hill in a special edition. Then he left The Leasowes for a meeting with other contributors at Bath where amicable disagreement ensued; for one of them, rather sensibly one would have thought, maintained that those fables with children in mind "should turn upon the obvious qualities of common and familiar objects".

Meanwhile, from The Leasowes Shenstone proffered a counter view; one with which he would, no doubt, have already acquainted his publisher friend. "I wish him (Dodsley)" he writes to Graves, "to devise uncommon subjects to inculcate refined morals": a view that was eventually to lead to the inclusion of a handful of fables concerning rare and mythological animals in the final selection of work. He also suggests that Dodsley should allow himself more time "to abridge and polish" before the publication date and writes with customary insight of the "peculiar advantage" of the genre which gives speech to animals – a device that removes at a stroke "the offensiveness of the advice".

In a revealing passage Shenstone explains to his friend how during the summer he and the publisher had worked together, "correcting" the fables that Dodsley wrote:

I find my ear much more apt to take offence than most other people's and as his *is far less delicate than mine, he must...believe in many places, that I altered merely for alteration's sake.*[11]

He continues that he "cannot be easy without some certain proportion betwixt one sentence and another;" that he cannot be content "without a melody at the close of a paragraph" - surely the comment of a true writer.

Behind the scenes Shenstone continued to busy himself with relevant work. By October and in an attempt to demonstrate the skill of the early masters he has translated from Phaedrus *The Wolf and the Crane*. He has also translated La Motte's *Discourse on Fable*, "a most excellent performance", which he hopes his friend will be able to make good use of in an introductory essay of his own.

Helpful or not, in the end Dodsley was to prefer an approach of his own. By January 1760, his *Essay on Fable* and his *Preface* were complete and posted off to Richard Graves and then on to Shenstone for comment. Shenstone, especially, was desired to look at them "carefully and critically", and to supply his comments and corrections on the blank side of each page before returning them "as soon as possible". The poet was in his element. A series of fables now circulated among the friends; *The Raven and the Magpie, The Sunflower* and *The Tuba Rose* which he believed "somewhat inferior", and he was so busy commenting upon and correcting the work of others that he had no time for any thought of a contribution of his own.

By July of the same year Shenstone was again looking forward to Dodsley's summer visit and enthusiastically writes to Graves of the latter's plans to print "*one* Edition of his Fables by means of Baskerville's press". As always the publisher arrived later than anticipated, not until August, to correct the proofs with the poet's help; and by October at the end of a two month stay, "is gone" writes Shenstone wittily, "to spur Baskerville; (and) returns on Friday to spur me…".

But there was to be a further delay; for mistakes at Easy Hill incurred the loss of "four reams of paper". It brought work to a standstill until a fresh supply arrived which took another four days. Baskerville finally published Dodsley's *Select Fables* on 9th February, 1761, in a fine edition of three volumes which included material from the time of Aesop and "modern" contributions from the eighteenth century. But the illustrations disappointed Shenstone because they were proportionately much too small for the size of the pages on which they appeared. With the aid of "Ned" Alcock who at the time was painting the poet's portrait, Shenstone had attempted, by obtaining a copy of the book before it was complete, to substitute different designs of his own. Unfortunately these were to arrive at the printers too late to be included in the first edition but none the less they are well worth comment. For now Shenstone was to demonstrate his eye for line and proportion as he already had his "delicate ear" in tune with the running of the prose. Previously he had illustrated his own poems "with many ornaments of the pencil" and presented them to Mary Cutler. And as in the design of his garden which he filled with poetry; or in his songs that he sang at his harpsichord; so it was with the *Fables*. In all Shenstone was to demonstrate the important role that a combination of both eye and ear were to play. For not only were the *Select Fables* to point a moral in a way that sounded right, but they were also to be illustrated in a way that illuminated the page and unlocked the understanding.

In a letter to Thomas Percy early in 1761, Shenstone describes some of his illustrations and it is interesting to compare them with the ones that Dodsley used. For example, the poet's choice of illustration for *The Trees and the Bramble* shows three boys and a double-headed busto. One of the heads is that of a beautiful woman who represents the fable which must be exquisitely realised; the other is of an ancient philosopher who symbolises the moral and its truth. Grouped around the busto are three children. Two of them are gazing at the loveliness of the young lady while the third is pointing towards the philosopher. So is made clear that the art of fable is both to entertain and instruct. That to make philosophical truths palatable for children, they have first to be presented in the garb of an attractive story. By comparison, Dodsley's illustration offers a literal interpretation, a bramble bush encircled by trees; and although suitable for young readers it offers no challenge, no new dimension to a story which is intended to show that "the most worthless persons are generally the most presuming".

Incorporated in the *Select Fables* is the novel idea of an Index which links each title with its moral. The work is wholly Shenstone's who had employed a similar device in his *The Schoolmistress* and here it shows him as a most skilful writer of aphorisms. *The Trees and the Bramble* has already been mentioned, but others, as for example Fable IX in volume 1, *The Wolf and the Lamb:* "Those who do not feel the sentiments of humanity, will seldom listen to the pleas of reason": or Fable II, *The Boys and the Frog:* " 'Tis unjust and cruel to raise ourselves mirth, at the expense of another's peace or happiness" are quintessential Shenstone of the kind that is found in the best of his prose and mottoes.

Always Shenstone was concerned with quality. In spite of cheaper copies of the book, it was the Baskerville editions that were for him the prize and he was set upon a second edition which would make use of his alternate designs and incorporate other fables of "singular merit" left out of the earlier Collection. In May 1761, he writes to Percy of these aspirations:

> *I fancy Dodsley thinks of causing Baskerville very soon to print a new edition of his Fables; and to have the Designs I showed you engraved for it...*[12]

And he hints that such an edition would not necessarily be directed at children. But tantalisingly, and although a second edition was soon to be forthcoming and use was to be made of a number of Shenstone's illustrations, no more mention is made of the enterprise in Shenstone's correspondence.

So ends the poet's collaboration with his friend Dodsley. It was a partnership which had resulted in the successful completion of three literary enterprises: the *Miscellanies, Cleone* and the *Select Fables*, all three of critical importance to eighteenth century literature. All were recognised by the publisher as being in considerable part the progeny of William Shenstone, his firm friend and the most astute of critics. A man without whose help he knew perfectly well he would not have achieved the acclaim that he did.

Chapter 18

PERCY, THE "RELIQUES" AND THE MULBERRY TREE PLOT

It is in a letter to Graves, written in 1741 that Shenstone first mentions Shifnal, the home of his friend, Humphrey Pitt with whom he had been staying. To appear agreeable he had even "rode-a-hunting", an experience which was not one that he would like to repeat for his horse almost ran him "headlong into deep water" and gave him a severe fright. The incident is of interest, not on its own account, but because of the link that it provides with Percy.

For Thomas Percy, another of Shenstone's friends in his later years, and one with whom he shared an abiding passion for old songs and ballads, was also a friend of Humphrey Pitt's and it is likely to have been through the latter that the poet first met him. Even more importantly, it was while Percy was a guest at Shifnal that he came across an old folio of ballads, "laying dirty on the floor under a bureau in the parlour, being used by the maids to light the fire".[1] How fortunate that Thomas Percy arrived when he did! For these, with contributions from Shenstone, were to provide the nucleus of what was to become another important literary achievement of the eighteenth century – Percy's *Reliques of Ancient English Poetry*.

The *Reliques* were to be published in 1765 after Shenstone's death, but in the Preface Percy makes clear his debt to his friend:

The plan of the work was settled in concert with the late elegant Mr Shenstone who was to have borne a joint share in it had not death unhappily prevented him. Most of the modern pieces were of his selection and arrangement, and the editor hopes to be pardoned if he has retained something out of partiality to the judgement of his friend.

Work on the *Reliques* was important to Shenstone in his later years, right up until his death; but earlier, he had included two of Percy's songs: *O Nancy wilt thou go with me* and *Cynthia* in volume VI of Dodsley's Miscellany. This meant that the two men already knew each other and that their future collaboration was to be in many ways a continuation of what had taken place before.

It was around the beginning of 1758 that Shenstone first came to hear of Percy's find, and in spite of his work on Dodsley's behalf he cannot control his interest.

You pique my curiosity extremely by the mention of that antient manuscript as there is nothing gives me greater pleasure than the simplicity of style and sentiment that is observable in Old English Ballads.[2]

Correspondence between the two men quickened; and it was not long before Shenstone was to become as involved in work on the *Reliques* as he had been with Dodsley's *Miscellanies* and was at present with his *Fables*. But interestingly to Percy, his letters demonstrate none of the hysteria that his work for Dodsley provoked. Instead, the poems supplied by Percy for comment are received as: "The many favours you have confer'd upon me by the packets I have received from Eatson-Maudit".[3]

Later, in the summer of 1760 after Thomas Percy had spent a brief holiday at The Leasowes and together the two men had pored over his fortuitous find, Shenstone is even sufficiently enthusiastic to embrace some kind of rudimentary time-table. Not only will he "try to return your parcels within a post or two together with my judgement of acceptance or reprobation",[4] but he suggests that all the poems be included, "in a large paper book" which will enable him also to consider the contents as a whole.

Later he offers advice concerning the positioning of the poems, maintaining that shorter ones should be interspersed with longer to add variety. He proposes changes to the poems that later literary critics have so disparaged. "I have retouched and transcribed both *Edom of Gordon* and *The Gentle Heardsman*" he writes and explains his rationale. "As to alterations of a word or two, I do not esteem it a point of conscience to particularise…"[5] The alterations of a whole line, however, are viewed differently: and what is re-written is to be defined by means of "Italick" type so as to make the changes clear, a process which he likens to the addition of a "toe or finger" to a damaged antique statue; in other words, as restoration which he believes to be wholly acceptable.

By our standards of today such meddling is not seen in this light, but when viewed within the context of the eighteenth century things appear differently. For then, even Shakespeare was deemed ripe for "improvement" and Thomas Hull's "improved" version of *The Comedy of Errors* at London's Lyceum Theatre in 1782 was greeted with enthusiasm. And it must be remembered that Shenstone's concern was with the marketing of the *Reliques*. He believed, and he may have had a point, that the public would not wish to make continual use of a glossary: that obsolete Old English words in the text were best replaced by ones that were more familiar. It was the spirit of the verses rather than the letter that attracted the poet. It was an attitude of mind which allowed, not only for retouching but also for "modern" imitations of old songs and ballads, providing that, like their models, they were not devoid of poetic spark.

Titles give a taste of what to expect. *Robin Hood, Lord Thomas* and *Fair Eleanor*: and songs such as: *Slighted Nancy* or *Allen-a-Dale* which, set to music, survive to this day. Shenstone's concern is with planning. Is there to be a distinction between songs and ballads? And if so, is this to be found in the storyline or in the passage of time which he believes turns "serpents into dragons and (possibly) songs into ballads?"

By July 1761, Percy's proposed *Reliques* have become for Shenstone "an event I have wished so long"; one which, in an editorial capacity, he is most anxious to further. He is busy obtaining "new" material; and writing to a Mr MacGowan, late of Edinburgh, is "unfeignedly thankful" for an early copy of translated verse fragments that he has been sent. He points out that an adaptation which takes considerable liberties with the original text is acceptable if, by such means, otherwise neglected works are rendered "highly striking". He continues that Percy "has offered me a rejectery power of which I mean to make considerable use". It is a welcomed editorial role by means of which the poet is able to counter his friend's fondness for antiquity at all costs, and to the clergyman he iterates the problem clearly. "My only fear has been that mere antiquity should sometimes impose upon you in the garb of merit".[6] Already he sees himself as the instigator and prime mover of the whole project and writes to Jago:

> *I have occasioned a friend of mine to publish a fair collection of the best English and Scotch ballads, a work I have long had at heart.*[7]

Shenstone's concern is also with layout. Placing each new poem on a fresh page will leave "a large interval" between contributions and this should be filled with an elegant tail piece in the form of a wood-cut. Then there is the question of subject matter. He warns of the over exposure of ballads that tell the story of King Arthur and Champion Guy. Two, in particular, have, "not a single particle of poetical merit (and) an over-proportion of this kind of ballast will sink your vessel to the bottom of the sea".[8] Later he is busy transcribing an "improved" version of *The Boy and the Mantle* and is bored by the "infinite tautology" of a Welsh Ode which is greatly lacking in inspiration. The same titles pass and re-pass. Some, like *The Spanish Ballad* and *The Gentle Heardsman*, are held in high esteem but over others there is much discussion. Occasionally mistakes are made. Shenstone misunderstands a query or is late returning a packet. But the overall impression is of work enjoyed, not endured. It would seem that the "old heroic ballads, songs and other pieces of our earlier poets…together with some few of later date"[9] which provide the sources for the *Reliques*, were responsible for providing the poet with more pleasure in the reading than they did pain in their "improvement".

Shenstone is indefatigable. He makes long lists; marking the titles, as is his wont, in order of merit by means of his four, three and two lined crosses. He offers detailed criticism relating to "Pieces…that falsify history almost in the same degree that they discredit poetry". Or, concerning a glossary: "…if you admit very many of the Scotch Songs, you will find it necessary to compose one, or to deface your margin by numerous explanations"[10] and he prefers the former option.

Always the comments are clear, concise and to the point; for here he is a very different man from the one who vacillates and agonises over his own poetry. Released from the anxiety of his own name appearing on the title page, Shenstone was free to function at his best; with the result that *The Reliques*, like the *Miscellanies*, were also to prove extremely popular. Published in 1765, the first edition was quickly followed by

Robert Dodsley, by Edward Alcock.

Thomas Percy, by Dickinson after Reynolds.

Lord Dudley's residence The Grange, Halesowen.

John Scott Hylton, by Horace R. Wilson. *James Woodhouse, by Henry Cook.*

Lapal House, by Horace R. Wilson.

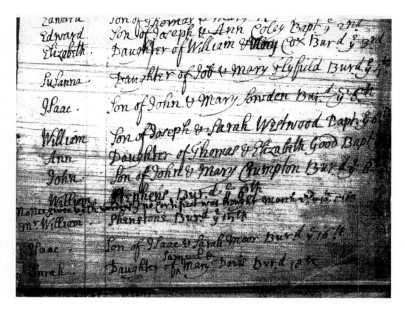

Record of Shenstone's burial, Halesowen Parish Register.

Memorial urn to William Shenstone in Halesowen Church.

Thomas Hull as Gloucester in Edward and Eleanora.

St John the Baptist Church, Halesowen, by David Parkes.

Busto of William Shenstone. The Collected Works.

THE
WORKS
IN
VERSE AND PROSE,
OF
WILLIAM SHENSTONE, Efq;

Moft of which were never before printed.
IN TWO VOLUMES,
WITH DECORATIONS.

——His ego longos
Cantando puerum memini me condere foles.   VIRG.

VOL. I.

LONDON:
Printed for R. and J. DODSLEY in Pall-mall.

M DCC LXIV.

Decorative page opposite frontispiece to volume one of Collected Works.

Decoration for Rural Elegance in volume one of The Collected Works.

I know that you will take a friendly part in any good that may befall me. Pray write, be it ever fo carelefsly; and believe me ever yours and Mrs. Jago's moft affectionate and faithful

W. S.

" The writer furvived the date of this letter but
" a fhort time, his death happening on the eleventh
" of the following month, to the inexpreffible grief
" of his more intimate friends, and the generous
" concern of thofe, who, too late acquainted with his
" merit, were indulging themfelves in the pleafing
" thought of having provided for his future eafe, and
" tranquil enjoyment of life."

Extract from William Shenstone's last letter as published by J Dodsley in 1769.

Shenstone's grave in Halesowen churchyard.

a second and a third and Percy, like Dodsley before him, was to reap the benefits. As has been seen, and in spite of the protestations of his friends who felt him ill done by, the poet's contribution was recognised; but only in the small print which was how he, himself, would have wanted it. How sad that he was not alive to share in the excitement and the acclaim with which the volumes were at first greeted.

* * * *

Important though the *Reliques* are for the place that they occupy in the history of eighteenth century literature, Shenstone's correspondence with Percy at this time that is also of interest for the light that it sheds upon the humour that both men shared. Take, for example, the case of Shenstone's boxes. The idea was to fool his friends with a "sett" of empty boxes, constructed to look like books, each with an amusing and provocative title on its "spine". Proportionately, the titles were to be as humorous as the "books" were empty and might: "Ridicule upon false science; or (be) grave and frivolous Disquisitions upon unimportant subjects...". So writes Shenstone to Percy for a few suggestions which should be "expressible in a few short words".

Percy responds with a ready wit. How about "Spiritual Spicery", or "Choice Comfits for Devotion?" Then there is the possibility of "A Cordial Dram for a Drooping Saint?" Or "A Mouse-trap for a Nibbling Sinner?" Two others: "Warburton on Humility" and "Pitt on Resignation", would not mean much today unless it were pointed out that Warburton was one of the most arrogant of bishops and Pitt the most adversarial and least likely to resign of politicians!

Having floated his idea of the boxes only to discard it, Shenstone then moved on from false science to the ridicule of false or "counter" taste, and his proposal for a ludicrous essay upon the subject resulted in the arrival of an amusing anecdote supplied by Percy. This concerned the antics of a certain Mr W. whose behaviour seemed to epitomise the way in which some people with money but without taste, sense or refinement, could behave.

According to Percy, this Mr W. had acquired an old mansion which commanded a pleasing view down the valley. It was an idyllic scene, but one which was to be ruined by the man's first venture into landscape gardening. For he planted two oblique rows of elms which approached a point at which he placed an "obelisk"; a device comprising a single and precariously up-ended board. This was painted by the local joiner and soon blown over by the wind – and there was worse to come. In a misplaced attempt at originality, this same "gentleman" caused a magnificently spreading ash tree in front of his parlour window to be painted white, leaves and all! The tree, not surprisingly, died; but, says Percy: "Its ghostly skeleton remained, as a monument to its owner's wisdom and ingenuity". And true or false, the tale caused much merriment between the two like-minded friends.

Unfortunately not all Shenstone's friends were visited with an equal degree of humour. John Scott Hylton was not, and a joke played upon him by the poet was to misfire. The story surfaces in a letter to Percy in which the poet is defensive: but first, a glance at what has gone before will help to set the scene for what is to come. The poet and Hylton had been good friends for a number of years and shared an interest in toys: small boxes, coins, buckles and what might loosely be termed "curiosities" which were to cause the problem. Under Shenstone's guidance Hylton had taken up painting and the poet writes to him of colouring. "The green is right" and he wishes that he who has "many times endeavoured to make it without success", could be as successful. Hylton also tried his hand, not very successfully, at writing poetry. He had thought, but got little further than that, of contributing an eclogue to Dodsley's *Miscellanies* and later we come across him collecting ballads for Percy's *Reliques*. "If Mr H. have done any more to his old ballad, I shall be glad to revise it",[11] writes Shenstone in 1759. But it was not forthcoming and one feels that the charming Mr Hylton – and from his letters there is little doubt that he was an engaging personality – possessed little of the intellectual rigour that would have made such a task within his grasp. However he did have a kind heart and helped nurse the poet back to health in 1758 when one of his attacks had been particularly severe. "I have not been six hours gone hence", he writes in a letter to Dodsley from the Leasowes in February 1758, "for he would not permit me to leave him; indeed I could not, it would have been cruel of me if I had".[12] Afterwards Shenstone continued to ask for his help. "I should be glad if Mr Hylton would send me a dose of rhubarb and cream of Tartar as before"[13] he writes in one of his later and frequent attempts to procure a satisfactory purge. And Hylton was also excellent and undemanding company; which makes it all the more unfortunate that Shenstone should have offended in the way he did.

It all began with the curiosities. For Hylton, in his quest for things unusual and extraordinary, was sometimes naïve; and this was certainly so in his search for memorabilia carved from the wood of "Shakespeare's" mulberry tree. In February 1759 Hylton writes to Shenstone that he has:

> ...*received the Tobacco Stopper which my friend Mr Percy bought at Moody's (in Birmingham) and also the letter to authenticate its being made of the tree he mentioned.*[14]

What he clearly did not realise was that a joke was being played upon him: that the letter of authenticity had been forged by the poet in order to determine how gullible his friend really was! For there was no wood from Shakespeare's mulberry tree any more than there had been, down the centuries, wood from the "true" cross of Christ. The "joke" continued and by November of the same year Shenstone had already enlisted Percy's help as more bogus antiquities were to find their way to Lapal House.

> *Could not Mr Percy procure for Mr Hylton one of those locks of Amazonian Hair by which the Amazonians are reported to have suckled children behind Their shoulders?*[15]

To Shenstone and Percy, no doubt, it seemed a harmless piece of fun; and neither appeared to have had much inkling of the eventual distress it would cause. But, in fact, the situation was one that is well summed up in the poet's own words: "One is many times led…to incur the blunders of the mole, and to fancy oneself *deep* when one is near the surface".[16] When Hylton found out what had been happening, he was upset and deeply offended.

However, the storm had yet to break and in the meantime the poet writes to Percy of the pool that their friend is constructing in the grounds of Lapal House. "Mr (Hylton) is making a Pool, which will add much lustre to his situation. 'Tis really a well-judged piece of work…". And he proposes a motto for a portrait that Alcock is painting of the young man.

> *J(ohn) S(cott) of (H......) heare stand I,*
> *Who built a new shit-house, and made the Pool bye.*[17]

No more of the ongoing "joke" is heard until the following midsummer, by which time Hylton has visited the toy maker, Moody, at his shop and pieced together the truth. He has also angrily confronted his friend. Here one feels that Shenstone is not seen at his best for he responds by attempting to justify his action. "The discovery regarding Moody and the Mulberry Tree was…imployed by (Hylton)…to account for much preceding impertinence", he later writes to Percy and grumbles that Hylton "cannot distinguish between solid censure and harmless raillery".[18]

The quarrel rumbled on until Percy, in response to a letter to Hylton, wrote to the poet, proposing that he attempt a reconciliation. The latter who was quick to point out that he "never once intended our bickerment should be perpetual", responded by inviting Hylton to dine at The Leasowes and talk over their differences. However, at the same time he made it clear that he would accept little of the blame, so it is not surprising that the invitation was declined!

Sadly the friendship never regained its earlier warmth although both men were civil in public and Hylton, at least, was to comment that he wished things could have remained as they used to be. After Shenstone's death it is clear that Hylton was helpful in providing any information that he could concerning The Leasowes' estate and also references in the elegies to people who might otherwise have remained unknown. It was an unfortunate end to a friendship which had endured well; and no doubt one in which blame was to be found on both sides.

Percy had done his best and so, in his way, had Shenstone although arguably it was not enough, and both in their shared concern for the *Reliques* quietly allowed the affair to rest. Up until the end of his life the poet was to continue his work with Percy upon these Old English songs and ballads and if he spared a thought for Hylton, it was a passing one which was not allowed to complicate matters or to deflect him from the task at hand.

Chapter 19

THOMAS HULL AND THE FINAL CURTAIN

Another of Shenstone's close friends during the last decade of his life was the dramatist and actor/manager Thomas Hull. Hull, who had taken over from Richard Yates, was the manager of Birmingham's King Street Theatre from 1759-1762. A site[1] later to be designated for a new, much grander building to be known, eventually, as the Theatre Royal in New Street.

From his earliest London days the poet had always loved the theatre: and although the production of plays in Birmingham must have seemed cruder and less ambitious than those staged in London he seems, when he visited the town, to have spent enjoyable evenings in the auditorium. Often on these occasions he would spend the night with friends such as the Meredith family at Aston; but it is worth remembering that he was also the owner of a little hostelry, the Cross Keys, situated near the Bull Ring end of New Street. One wonders whether he ever stayed there?

During Shenstone's day, performances at the King Street theatre took place on three nights a week only. The price of a ticket would cost between one and three shillings and the entertainment provided would have been varied enough to include Shakespeare and some of his contemporaries, opera and light musical entertainment.

Shenstone's head was full of ideas for improving the kind of productions that were frequently presented in Birmingham. In January, 1761, he writes to Hull with some suggestions concerning a discussion that they had had about a play to be based upon an old fragment, *The Spanish Lady*. Might it not be a good idea to introduce a little humour into some of the scenes? Especially those which featured a group of sailors? The image of the "Jolly Jack Tar" was an abiding and popular one – and a box office attraction. Somewhat ruefully, he points out that in order to become economically viable it is sometimes necessary to make compromises. "If Shakespeare cannot elicit a full house, Harlequin must extort it; but woe the while for the state of Letters and Genius!"[2] Some might echo his sentiments today. Not surprisingly, for it was usually the case, Shenstone's suggestions were well received and Hull's musical play, *The Spanish Lady*, complete with sailors and humour, was eventually to be produced in Birmingham at the King Street Theatre in 1765 and later still in London in 1769. How sad that by then the poet was dead and that he never was to see his ideas bear fruit.

In August 1761, Shenstone went to see another of Hull's productions in Birmingham, his *Rosamond*: the next day he writes to the dramatist to tell him how much he has enjoyed it, but also with suggestions which would enhance the play's dramatic impact:

I think the play has now so much good in it that it may be worth Mr Hull's while to give it a few more finishing touches.³

In fact, these "finishing touches" turned out to be a detailed re-evaluation of the plot and characters. They provide for character development; explain why the characters behave as they do and turn what Hull describes in his notes as "a hasty and imperfect compilation of scenes" into a coherent story with a clear moral. Soon after, Shenstone writes to Graves that he has:

... assisted my friend Hull the comedian in altering the Tragedy of Rosamond; had it brought upon the stage to a full house at Birmingham, where it was very well received; put Hull into a way of making an indirect compliment to the...King in the last ten lines of his Epilogue.⁴

He adds that this was followed by "God save great George" sung by a chorus of actors and audience "drawn out abreast upon the stage". No doubt an impressive finale enjoyed by all!

The story of *Rosamond* is another of Shenstone's successes. As Dodsley and Percy before him, Hull was to make good use of the poet's perceptive and judicious advice: and the play was produced with appropriate additions at London's Covent Garden Theatre in 1775. It was the actor's Benefit Night and in the programme Hull acknowledged "how fully the author has availed himself of the kind and judicious hints supplied by the late William Shenstone".⁵

But to return to the present. By now, Hull was also a member of the coterie of friends who were invited to supply material for Percy's *Reliques*. In October 1761 Shenstone writes to thank him for *The Bitter Fruits of Jealousy*, a ballad, "written in the audient style" and which included an image of young girls' tears which greatly appealed to him:

Appear they not as drizlinge Dewes
Freshninge some faded Floure?⁶

At Christmas he was to respond to two further poems and his comments reflect what he believes to be a prerequisite for all poetry of this kind. Songs and ballads, including his own, should express sublime sentiment in "a simple and unaffected manner". They should demonstrate a naivety, and by this he means freshness or innocence, in the way they are presented. All are attributes which he finds in *The Bells They Rang all the Morn*, a "truly beautiful" ballad which arrived too late to be included in Percy's first edition of the *Reliques*.

In Hull, Dodsley and Percy, Shenstone was blessed with friends who were not only extremely fond of him, but also vastly appreciative of his standing as a man of letters. His skills as a landscape gardener had brought him many influential friends, but now his literary aspirations, too, were fulfilled and his reputation in the field of letters established. It was a time in his life when, with the exception of his university days, Shenstone was happier than at any other; for he was a man who had finally earned the esteem he deserved – had arrived at where he wished to be – if not quite.

During the last few years of his life the poet even began again to think of publishing a collection of his own poems and what we have is a re-run of what happened before; except that this time he was greatly encouraged by his friends. For now it is Graves who urges upon him the necessity "of losing no time" and Dodsley who suggests, in 1762, a subscription edition of the poems and uses his considerable influence to facilitate matters. "Mr Shenstone", he writes in July 1762 to the important Elizabeth Cartwright, "is preparing to publish his works by subscription... (and) ...I fancy he will have a large number of subscribers".[7]

But of course it was not to be. In vain might Shenstone enter into the spirit of it all and write to Graves that "I mean to collect and publish what I have written". Or later, that "(both) you and Mr Dodsley would be mighty unanimous with regard to the propriety of setting my subscription on foot".[8] In vain because although he appreciated their encouragement which boosted confidence, he was still incapable of taking that final step involved in the presenting of his work to the wider world. He wanted to but he could not for the pendulum of his mood was forever swinging back and forth. "When I am low spirited", he explains:

> *I almost shudder at the tremendous contract with the public; when my spirits are elevated, I see the necessity that you do, of not losing a moment's time...*[9]

This was a very human predicament and one which he dealt with as before – by procrastinating. He turned his attention to other matters, to a social calendar of visits to people of quality who continued to clamour for his advice and help in the re-design of their estates. It cheered him and it boosted his confidence for he was much more at ease when considering the problems of other people. To Graves, in November 1762, he writes of Dodsley's usual summer visit and the way in which they filled their time. "...we paid our devoirs to a good deal of genteel company" and there follows a list of sixty or more of these important people including, rather surprisingly, Baron Plesson, Gentleman of the Bed-Chamber to the King of Denmark and Lord Mansfield, the Lord Chief Justice of the Court of Common Pleas, "a man of wit rather than a man of taste". So long, indeed, is the list that even Shenstone is surprised: "I did not imagine my list would have engrossed so much of my paper!".

Enthusiastically he describes a visit in November to Lord Foley of Witley Court in Worcestershire. "His Table...is the most magnificent of any I ever saw: eighteen or twenty elegant dishes...". He extols the park: "...capable of being rendered fine, if he would fell some Oaks...and some Hawthorns".[10] But it is the Foley chapel that really excites: not only is the exterior "very superb and elegant" but inside:

His Pew is a Room with an handsome Fire-place; the Ceiling carved, painted in Compartments, and the Remainder enriched with guilt Stucco-Ornaments; the walls enriched in the same Manner: (and) the best painted Windows I ever saw...[11]

Clearly it was a chapel in which one might be encouraged to dwell upon the wealth and status of the Foley family, rather than the worship a wise and omnipotent God.

At around this time much had happened to raise Shenstone's spirits. Dr Johnson had found time to send him a copy of William Vernon's *Parish Clerk*, a poem which turned a pretty compliment on *The Schoolmistress*. He was much in demand by the gentry who clamoured for his advice concerning their country estates:

I have three or four more of these superb visits to make... to Lord Plymouth, next week; Lord Stamford the week after; then to Lord Lyttelton,...and then to Lord Foley.[12]

In high spirits, he writes to Graves of the merry-go-round that was his social life. He was busy at home and still making improvements at The Leasowes. He has knocked down a front wall and extended his path "and made a handsome ring". But even so and in spite of activity at home and the advice that he dispensed elsewhere, Shenstone's influence was to extend even further that he could have imagined. For as Alice Gaussen points out, when years later Thomas Percy was inducted as Bishop of Dromore, one of the first things that he organised was to have his palace grounds planted:

In imitation of those of his early friend Shenstone at The Leasowes. He clothed the surrounding hills and woods and planted a glen in view of the drawing room window. The Landscape was further improved by the addition of artificial water, the value of which was fully recognised in the eighteenth century.[13]

Another of Shenstone's diversions was to have his portrait painted. For just as everybody of fashion was having his "busto" sculpted so was portrait painting popular. Shenstone exchanged portraits with both Graves and Dodsley. Dodsley was painted by Reynolds – a very ambitious affair and one with which Shenstone could not compete. Instead the latter was painted by the Birmingham painter, Edward Alcock, a portrait which now hangs in the National Portrait Gallery. Before the sitting began, Shenstone was concerned about the pose he should adopt and sends sketches to Graves for his advice. "Tell me what you think of some of the attitudes I enclose?" he asks, and points his own preference, marked AA, which is intended "to lesson my dimension" by means of a "kind of nightgown". Later, when plans are more advanced, he sends a sketch of the chosen design which is to include not only the emblems of a water nymph and of the God Pan, but his "faithful hound Lucy". The picture is to measure from four feet eleven inches in height by two feet three and three quarter inches in width and the central figure is to be three feet three and a half inches tall. But what of Alcock, himself? He is "good-natured and slovenly but would improve much by application", is Shenstone's conclusion couched in the language of a school report.

In fact, Alcock had been busy on behalf of the poet and his acquaintance for some time. In the early months of 1760, The Leasowes had played "open house" as, with Shenstone by his side, the artist had worked on various portraits of local residents who all were keen to sit for him. The experience was new and interesting and all progressed smoothly until Shenstone's own turn when work upon *his* portrait ran into difficulties. The poet believed the painter to be progressing too slowly which is ironic in view of the delays which he, himself was causing Dodsley in the publishing of his *Fables*! "Alcock shou'd by promise have come yesterday – but he regards neither promises, nor politeness..." he complains to John Scott Hylton: and the following week, even when he has managed to cajole the painter into the house, it is with little result because "Alcock", he complains, "has (all morning) scarce done any stroke to my face".

But come the new year of 1761, things appeared more hopeful. "Alcock is now here and proceeding on my Picture with a promise to finish it before he leaves"[14]: and one is reminded of similar assurances that come, as this one did – to nothing. A fortnight later the portrait was still unfinished and Shenstone is obliged to indulge in a little wishful thinking.

> *My picture now draws to a conclusion and will be finished when I can get a good day to sit three or four hours together.*[15]

But finding a "good" day proved difficult and the weeks rolled by. By the end of February, however, the portrait is "in a manner finished" and to Shenstone's "tolerable pleasure" was hanging up in his study for all to see. And suddenly! Alcock has become "one of the best young fellows in the World": a young man who Shenstone had grown both to like and admire; enough to invite him to dinner and seek his help in the execution of illustrations for Dodsley's Fables.

The experience had a part to play in the improvement of Shenstone's mental health. For a while it took him away from the consideration of poetry – whether his own or of others and enabled him, if not to relax, at least to view things from a different perspective. Indeed, the perspective was constantly changing. For it was not long before a second portrait was planned to send to Graves. Then, by September began a re-run of the earlier saga. Alcock has "promised to come every week for the past three months" Shenstone complains and his estimation of the man correspondingly dips.

If portrait painting proved a diversion, other circumstances too, conspired to make life easier over the final years of the poet's life. Litigation that had engaged him over his nephew, "young Dolman", which had sapped his energy and destroyed his peace of mind, was finally settled in 1760. The dispute had lasted nearly a decade and an unsuccessful outcome would have meant that Shenstone's income would have been halved. Also, he would have forfeited Harborough Hall and a lifelong love affair with the old mansion house would have been over.

It was small wonder that he had been worried; that it had been a situation which had made him, "rude to my superiors and deaf to all inviting offers; and neglectful at once to my old friends and new".[16] But now, due to Lord Stanford's "generous intervention" it was all over and upon the eve of resolution Shenstone writes to Graves of what has been the irony of his predicament.

During the former part of life, I languished for an acquaintance somewhat more extensive, and when the company that flocked to see my place removed all grounds of that complaint, this accursed dispute arose, and mixed with every enjoyment that was offered me.[17]

Now the future was brighter. He was busier and more fulfilled than at any other time of his life and yet...there was always to be the problem of his health. For the "Drowsihed and Lentor" of which he was still complaining to Percy in June, 1759, and which seems to have taken the form of an extreme lethargy which made concentration difficult, was never, now, to leave him for long. Then there were his fevers. In March, 1761, he writes to Percy of "an attack of my old fever" and because he has been unable to work has, "such a multitude of things to say and enquire after that I know not where to begin".[18] It was a predicament which will, no doubt, have resonances for many.

But with the coming of summer his health improved and his spirits rose; and he can write gaily of being "distracted by concerts and horse racing" instead. He finds time to read Mary Wheatley's *Original Poems on Several Occasions* which are "written in an excellent and truly classical style" and refers to the advice he has given her, " in what kind of manner she might improve many of the Pieces". On her behalf he writes to a Mrs Bennet and a Mr Bridgens of Pater Noster Row to thank them for the "pains you took at my request to revise poor Mrs Wheatly's poetry", and generally uses his influence to help in any way he can. He is busy promoting the work of James Woodhouse whose "*Ode to Benevolence*" is "within my drawer" and concerning which he is going to propose "Some little alterations". He encourages the young man to move house which he believes would "furnish his friends a better opportunity of doing him service" and writes to Dodsley in an attempt to promote a scheme which would result in the poet obtaining a financial settlement that would be to his advantage.

It was not until January 1763, that Shenstone was first to mention in a letter to Jago, the possibility of a proposed pension for his services to literature. "I have heard nothing since I wrote last in regard to my affair" he writes and adds with characteristic wit that he has little doubt but that the favour, should it materialise, will bestow "mortification in one place (in order to) preclude mortification in another". Even so he set out by appointment and in high spirits to see Lord Stamford at Enville to discuss the matter and upon his return was optimistic, for his Lordship had promised to do everything that he could to promote a successful outcome. And to Jago, Shenstone is confident that "You will take a friendly part in any good that may befall me".

How tragically ironic that it was not to be. That upon reaching the calmer uphills of contentment Shenstone's life was to be cut short at the very moment when it seemed that the benefit of a pension, the rightful fruits of his labours, was within his grasp. But that is what happened and seemingly with very little warning. On 16th January 1763, he was back home at The Leasowes; and surprisingly, because the winter months always depressed him, in an ebullient mood. There was a severe frost and he was unable to get out but, no matter, a parcel of books from the Percys was keeping him occupied. His larder was also well stocked with snipe and "fieldfare" that friends and neighbours had sent. He describes himself as "quite pampered" and one gets the impression that there was much to live for. There was a "possible" edition of his poems to be published by Dodsley; an event to be savoured and dangled. There was the near certainty of an annual pension which would have enabled him to live more comfortably: and more importantly, would have brought with it enormous psychological benefit – the knowledge that he was at last appreciated. His final letter ends with the bravura of one of Shenstone's most delightful aphorisms. "I profess", he writes, "no party but moderation", a reflection which is worthy of considerable thought today.

Shenstone died on 11 February 1763, at 5.00 in the morning after contracting a severe and feverish cold of the kind that, today, we would probably diagnose as influenza: and no doubt he would have had his devoted Mary Arnold and Mary Cutler at his bedside. He was buried on 15 February and even in death were the priorities of class, preserved. For the parish register records the burial of *Mr* William Shenstone on a page where no other name is dignified by such a title. Shenstone, the 'prince' of letter writers and master of aphorisms, was dead. For who could have voiced so succinctly his views on religion? "There is no trifling with any *part* of orthodoxy with impunity". Or his opinions of those who set too much store upon material possessions? "With whom 'tis vain that your mind is furnished if your walls are naked…". On all subjects: from princes and politics to friendship and flattery: "A friendly ear…is very near as partial as a flatterer's tongue", they tumble from his pen to raise both his letters and his prose works into the realms of literature.

Shenstone's death both shocked and deeply saddened. He had died, writes Dodsley, not only "…to the inexpressible grief of his more intimate friends" but at a time when:

The generous concern of those, who, too late acquainted with his merit, were indulging themselves in the pleasing thought of having provided for his future ease, and tranquil enjoyment of life.[19]

These are wise words, pointing as they do the inescapable fact that Shenstone's merit, both as a writer and as an editor, was recognised too late to benefit him in any material way. And it is vain to iterate, yet again, that this was in most part the poet's own fault. That is how it was. In the final analysis, his fear of adverse criticism outweighed his undoubted desire for fame and recognition: a fear which manifested itself with pathological intensity – in his repeated and continual efforts at improvement.

In *Aris' Gazette* on 14 February 1763, there appeared Shenstone's obituary notice written by James Woodhouse:

On Friday, the 11th of February 1763, after a short but violent fever which he bore with philosophic fortitude and a Christian resignation, dy'd aged 48, William Shenstone Esq. Of The Leasowes: the pride of his country, the favourite of the muses, and what still redounds to his praise, the enemy of vice and the friend of virtue; but to delineate the utmost of his inestimable worth would swell a folio, and no surviving genius is equal to the task. Ask his foes his character: but where shall they be found? Ask his acquaintances: they would talk down the sun in his praise. Ask his friends: Sorrow will choke their utterance. And the poor will reply – alas – but with tears. But the voice of the world will then pronounce: He liv'd – universally belo'd, and dy'd – universally lamented.

This might have been the end but it was not. For Dodsley was determined that Shenstone's works should be published and was to spend the last few years of his life furthering this. It would have been a gargantuan task: for which, of all the "definitive" versions of each poem, was to be preferred? The letters and the prose works would also have been problematic for there were several versions of these too. But Dodsley persevered and triumphantly a Collection of the poems appeared in 1764 to be followed by the prose works later in the same year. Finally the letters were published by J. Dodsley, Robert's brother, in 1769. Some of the longer and overtly didactic poems are not read today for they are a world away from our modern perception of things. But there are many delightful songs and ballads which have lost none of their freshness and can still be enjoyed for what they are: for their melody and simplicity of structure. And the *Letters*? Some have and many should continue to appreciate them: not only for their humour and wisdom but for the glimpses they proffer of life in rural Warwickshire and Worcestershire in the eighteenth century when brutality and bigotry were commonplace and the enlightened perceptions of Shenstone and his friends shone, by contrast, all the more brightly.

Chapter 20

THE WILL

William Shenstone's will which is a complicated and unsatisfactory affair, was signed on 5 February 1763, a few days before the poet's death. In it, and apart from other bequests, he left Miss Cutler an annuity of thirty pounds a year as well as an extra twelve pounds to be paid half yearly for care of the, by now, elderly Mary Arnold. This all seems straightforward, but it was not; for also contained in the will was an agreement to pay Mary Cutler all monies owing to her "over and besides". In other words, he was to pay off past debts – pay back to her all the money that he had borrowed from her over the years.

There was less of a problem with the annuity and with the additional twelve pounds for the care of Mary Arnold. But as the months passed and it became clear that little else was likely to be forthcoming, Miss Cutler came to feel that she was defrauded of the rightful money owing to her and in consequence and after much legal wrangling, was obliged to bring a Chancery suit against Graves in his role as one of the three of the will's executors.

Much of the problem would seem to have been due to interpretation of the words "over and besides": and clearly, Graves did not accept Mary Cutler's version of what these words meant. For the latter alleged that, in fact, she was owed an additional five hundred pounds and her story is a plausible one. She argued that the sum included one hundred and sixty pounds in unpaid wages; an unpaid bond of one hundred and fifty pounds; a further bond of one hundred pounds and a twenty pound note. Most importantly of all, Miss Cutler further alleged that in an earlier will, made in the autumn of 1758, Shenstone had bequeathed to her Ivey Farm, and although it is not possible to know the precise truth of this matter, it is likely that she was telling the truth; that Shenstone's friends were unwilling to believe her because they could not understand how the latter could have withheld payment from an employee for so long and in such a manner.

Upon Shenstone's death it would seem that the two women went first to live at the old priory where mercifully their stay was to be brief; for John Hodgetts, the new owner of The Leasowes, proved to be a negligent landlord and the building, which was in a bad state of repair, had a leaking roof which according to Hylton "let damp into every room". Both Hylton and Dodsley did their best to help. In a letter to Baskerville, in the early part of 1764 the former points out that:

> *Hodgetts pays no regard to Mr Dodsley's letter on Mrs Cutler's behalf, who is in a very deplorable condition, and I fear will soon be worse off, unless she will throw her complaint into Chancery; and that to my sad experience, is a desperate remedy!*[1]

It was a remedy which, as has been seen, Miss Cutler was driven to take, and one in which contrary to all expectation, she was successful. For when Catherine Hutton visited her in 1768, it was to take tea at Ivey Farm and a glance at Miss Cutler's will reveals that she was eventually to bequeath the property to her sister, Mrs Tupper. As for the money: it would seem that in the end, Mary Cutler was obliged to settle for less, a state of affairs which could not have been the poet's intention for it was not within the nature of the man to have been so capricious. As Marjorie Williams points out:

> *It was entirely like Shenstone to be so indefinite in formulating the terms of this Will that there could be difficulties in carrying out the details.*[2]

So the story can here be ended. Miss Cutler lived on happily at Ivey Farm surrounded by Shenstone memorabilia and memories of the old days at The Leasowes. Except that there was an added twist. It did not concern Mary Cutler that is true, but it did have repercussions for Richard Graves. As a close friend, Graves was anxious that the poet should be remembered in a way that was both proper and fitting and so it was that he wished to raise a memorial urn, eloquently inscribed with the appropriate sentiments. This he intended should be placed upon the grave and elegantly fenced around with railings.

However, because he lived near Bath, he left what he thought to be the implementation of his scheme to Hodgetts, the only one of the three executors who lived within the vicinity and who could therefore see to it that the plans were carried out as prescribed. Having paid the bill, he returned home to await news that the work had, indeed, been accomplished. One can imagine how he must have felt when he discovered the truth. For Hodgetts did see to it that a graceful urn was raised and that it was properly inscribed with the words provided by Graves. Then came the alterations; for instead of Richard Graves' name he had his own inscribed; and rather than place the urn upon Shenstone's grave, he had it installed inside the church where it remains to this day. So Hodgetts took the credit and Graves provided the money in a situation only partly rectified by the eventual addition of the initials R.G. at the bottom left hand corner of the inscription which now bears the name of both men.

So that really is the end of the story. One which would have distressed Shenstone both on account of Miss Cutler and on account of his friend. He could not have envisaged either the Chancery suit, or the behaviour of Hodgetts; but it is as unfortunate as it is true, that even honest and well intentioned people can make mistakes, difficult enough in life to put right – and in death, impossible.

Chapter 21

CONCLUSION

Shenstone was a multi-talented, well-educated and cultured man. Critics point out that in his poetry is to be found influences of James Thomson, the melancholy of Milton's *Il Penseroso* and the philosophy of Pope and Bolingbroke. But this is the stuff of literary criticism and does not explain Shenstone's fascination as a writer and as a man; for the two are interdependent. Shenstone believed in the didactic role of poetry, but this does not demonstrate why, although he was not a great poet, he did on occasion write magnificent verse. Why *The Schoolmistress*, *The Pastoral Ballad* and *Lines Written at an Inn*, have stood so triumphantly the test of time. Why it is that in these poems he is able to transcend the limited confines of eighteenth century convention – leave behind the Chloes and Damons of classical tradition, and speak direct from the heart?

For Shenstone was a man with considerable heart and therein lies the answer to his fascination. In his letters and his prose works he frequently demonstrates this as we are treated to his forward looking and humanitarian views. What he has to say regarding religion:

> *It is a common argument amongst divines...that a contrary behaviour has... consequences when we come to die...Is it not a stronger persuasive, that virtue makes us happy daily, and removes the fear of death from our lives antecedently, than it smoothes the pillow of the death bed?*[1]

And he has this to say about war:

> *If national reflections are unjust, because there are good men in all nations, are not national wars upon much the same footing?*[2]

In his private life the poet could be pernickety and awkward. His horror of commitment meant that he had difficulty in making decisions or keeping to deadlines and in arranging dates. His dependence upon his friends for moral support could at times become emotional blackmail. He took umbrage where there was none to be taken and frequently his poor health meant that he had time to brood upon imaginary shortcomings of others.

But all this is to make him human; and it was these very qualities which also enabled him to empathise with others. For empathise he did. He was supportive of his friends in times of need; and a highly developed social conscience made him a considerate employer and a caring landlord. It was these qualities that enabled him to pen such an accurate portrait of the times in which he lived. Of the small things: the petty jealousies as well as the pleasantries of his day; of old Emma, the local post lady's fear that she was about to lose her job, and the "wickedness" of his neighbour who blocked up one of the paths on his estate. From London he writes of Lord Bath's coachman who "got drunk and tumbled from his box" and of "the apprehension of...whores and the suffocation of four in the round-house", a building subsequently demolished by the mob and constantly in the process of being rebuilt.

He writes of books and plays; and poetry and art; and he says what he thinks and not what is expected. For who would have dared as he did, to criticise Handel for not marrying his music with the words! Shenstone's style is polished. In it is coupled the lustre of cut glass with the precision of a watchmaker's art. It is high time that his *Essays on Men and Manners,* written within the tradition of the great French pensée writers, are again read and appreciated. The poetry, too, deserves to be remembered. Especially the shorter pieces to which he frequently gives the appellation of "song". For these have a musicality which lingers in the mind long after they have been read.

Shenstone once gave some light-hearted advice to his close friend, Richard Jago:

> *I would have you cultivate your garden; plant flowers, have a bird or two in the hall (they will at least amuse your children); write now and then a song; buy now and then a book; write now and then a letter.*[3]

They are words which reflect his own life and illustrate the manner in which he felt best able to make use of his own talents. Simply and charmingly he incorporates his craft as poet, gardener and letter writer in a manner which intimates how rewarding all three pastimes can be – not only for Shenstone – but, one might add, for his readers too.

BIBLIOGRAPHY

Anderson, (ed.) *The Life of Shenstone. Poets of Great Britain Vol.9 (1785)*

Bennett, William, *John Baskerville the Birmingham Printer, his Press, Relations and Friends,* 2 vols. (City of Birmingham School of Printing, 1937).

Burnham, John, *Old Warwickshire Families and Houses* (Birmingham 1934).

" " *Warwickshire People and Places* (Birmingham 1936).

" " *In the Forest of Arden* (Birmingham 1948).

" " *Solihull and its School* (Solihull 1949).

Burritt, Elihu, *Walks in the Black Country and its Green Borderland* (Kineton 1976).

Carden, Arthur, E, (compiled). *The Knights of Barrels* A scrap book of documents and information; a limited edition (Falmouth 1993).

Carlisle, Alexander, *The Autobiography of the Revd. Dr Alexander Carlyle* (Edinburgh 1860).

H. Chalmers ED. *The Works of the English Poets* (London 1810) vols XVII & XVII

Cooper, William, *Henley in Arden* (Buckingham 1946).

Courtney, W.P., *Dodsley's Collection of Poetry. Its Contents and Contributors.* A Chapter in the History of English Literature in the Eighteenth Century, 2 vols. (1910).

Crumpton, William, *Treatise of Decimals and Mensuration* (Birmingham 1776?)

D'Israeli, Isaac, *Curiosities of Literature* (New York, London 1832).

Dodsley, Robert, ed. *Select Fables of Esop* and Other Fabulists (London 1761).

Duggan, Audrey, *Catherine Hutton. A Lady of Letters* (Studley 2000).

Gaussen, Alice.C.C, *Percy: Prelate and Poet* (London 1908).

Graves, Richard. *Recollections of some Particulars in the Life of the Late William Shenstone Esq* (London 1788).

" " *Columella* or *The Distress'd Anchoret* 2 vols. (London 1799).

Grazebrook, H Sidney, *The Family of Shenstone the Poet* (Birmingham 1890).

Heeley, Joseph, *A Description of Hagley, Enville and The Leasowes* (Birmingham 1890).

Hey, G Colin, *The Warwickshire Coterie* (Stratford upon Avon 1991).

Hill, Charles, Jarvis, *The Literary Career of Richard Graves* (Northampton, Mass 1930).

Houdart de La Motte, *Antoine, Dissertations in verse...accompanied by a discourse on poetry 1709, Fables 1719* (Paris, c.1720).

Humphreys, A.R., *William Shenstone, An Eighteenth Century Portrait* (Cambridge, 1937).

Hutton-Beale, Catherine, ed. *Catherine Hutton and her Friends* (Birmingham, 1895).

Johnson, Samuel, *Lives of the Most Eminent English Poets* (London, 1779-81).

La Fontaine, Jean De, *The Fables of La Fontaine*, trans. By Elizur Wright (New York, 1892).

Miller, Hugh, *First Impressions of England and its People* (Edinburgh, 1861).

Pococke, Bishop Richard, *Travels Through England...*Vol.1 (Camden Society N.S. 42, 1888).

Purkiss E.M., *William Shenstone, Poet and Landscape Gardener* (Wolverhampton, 1931).

Sichel, Walter, *Bolingbroke and his Times* (London, 1902).

Somers, Fand K.M., *Halas, Hales, Halesowen,* (Worcestershire, 1967).

Strauss, Ralph and Dent R.K., *John Baskerville, a Memoir* (Cambridge, 1907).

" "   *Robert Dodsley, Poet, Publisher and Playwright* (London, 1910).

Wain, John, *Samuel Johnson* (New York, 1975).

Whitelaw, Jeffrey, *Follies* (Princess Risborough, 1997).

Williams, I.A., *Seven Eighteenth Century Bibliographies* (1924).

Williams, Marjorie, *Lady Luxborough goes to Bath* (Oxford, 1946).

" "   *William Shenstone: A Chapter in Eighteenth Century Taste* (Birmingham, 1935).

GENERAL REFERENCE

A Collection of: *The Portraits etc of Shakespearian Actors & Actresses 1750 - 1915*

Alumni Oxoniensis (Lichtenstein, 1968).

Aris' Gazette

Austin, Jane, *Emma* Penguin Classics (Vol.1) (London, 1966).

Burke's Peerage.

Colville, F.L., *Worthies of Warwickshire* (Warwick, 1869).

Curnock, Nehemiah, (ed.) *The Journal of the Rev. John Wesley* (vol. 6) (London, 1915).

Dictionary of Actors, Actresses...and Other Stage Personnel (Illinois University Press, 1982).

Dictionary of National Biography

Fleming, John; Honour, Hugh and Pevsner, Nickolaus., (eds.) *The Penguin Dictionary of Architecture and Landscape Architecture* (London, 1998, 5th Edition).

The Gentleman's Magazine, Vols. 62, 63, 65, 68, 73, 74, 81, 87.

Handford, Margaret, *"Sounds Unlikely"* (Birmingham and Midland Institute, 1992).

Harvey, Paul and Heseltine J.E., (eds). *Oxford Companion to French Literature* (Oxford, 1959).

Hill, Joseph, *The Bookmakers of Old Birmingham* (Birmingham, 1907).

Huxley, Anthony, (ed), *The New Horticultural Society Dictionary of Gardening* (London, 1992).

Johnson, Samuel, *Dictionary of the English Language* (London, 1755).

Langford, J.A., *A Century of Birmingham Life* (Vol.1) (Birmingham, 1820).

Lewis, Samuel, *A Topographical Dictionary of England* (London, 1835).

Nash, T.R., *Collections for the History of Worcestershire* (London; Oxford: Worcester 1781).

Parton-Williams, Sara, *The Art of Dining* (National Trust 1993-95).

Pemberton John, *Solihull and its Church* (Birmingham 1905)

Sadie, Stanley, (ed.), *The New Grove Dictionary of Music and Musicians* (Vols. 1, 7, 8) (London, 1981).

Schwarz Hans and Lena, *The Halesowen Story* (Halesowen 1955).

Waterhouse, Ellis, *The Dictionary of British Eighteenth Century Painters* (Woodbridge, Suffolk, 1981).
Wyndham, Maud, *Chronicles of the Eighteenth Century* (2 Vols.)(London, 1924).

MANUSCRIPTS AND MAGAZINES

Edge, Bernice, *Lady Luxborough and her Circle* (Birmingham, May 1930).
Hutton, Catherine, Journal in private collection.
Hylton, John Scott, Letter to Bishop Percy 1778. Ms.286893. Birmingham Central Library Archive.
McKe, Robert, Andrew, *A Commentary on the Life and Works of William Shenstone* (Birmingham April 1976).
Birmingham City Archives MS 931/1: *Letters from Shenstone to Mrs Bennet,* (30/10/1761).
Birmingham City Archives MS 931/2: *Letters from Shenstone to R. Dodsley 1762,* (14/3/1762).
William Salt Library Stafford: *Letters from Shenstone to Lady Luxborough,* (SMS 582)

* * * *

Andrews, Bryan, (ed.), *The Torrington Diaries* (Eyre and Spottiswode 1934 Vol.1).
Burns, Dr Francis, *William Shenstone's "Priory" at The Leasowes, Halesowen,* (The Black Countryman No.4 Autumn 1998).
Burns Dr. Francis Notes & Queries, Vol 243 No. 4, William Shenstone's years at Oxford.
Burt, Phyllis, *Exile in Arden* (*The Lady* 27 February 1975).
Dunphy, Angus, *The Leasowes* illustrated by P.A. Barnet, N.R. Wilson and D Parkes (The East High School and Dudley Teachers' Centre) 1982.
Ellis, Havelock, *William Shenstone* (The Dial Vol. 82).
Foorde, Lynn, *The Leasowes Restored 1997-2001* (Halesowen 1999).
Lambert, David, *William Shenstone and the Fairy Landscape* (The Gregorian Group Journal 1986).
McKillop, Alan D, *Thomson's Visit to Shenstone* (Philological Quarterly, 23 July 1944).
Smith, Betty, *Remembering Past Glories* (*The Lady* 27 February 1975).

LETTERS

Dodsley, James, ed. *Letters written by the Right Honourable Lady Luxborough to William Shenstone.* (London, 1775).
Hull, Thomas, ed. *Select Letters Between The Late Duchess of Somerset,...William Shenstone and Others. Vols. 1 and 2* (London, 1778).

Mallam, Duncan, ed, *The Letters of William Shenstone* (Minneapolis, 1939).
Tierney, James E, *The Correspondence of Robert Dodsley 1733-64* (Cambridge, 1988).
Williams, Marjorie, ed, *The Letters of William Shenstone* (Oxford, 1939).

SHENSTONE'S COLLECTED WORKS AND ANTHOLOGIES

Dodsley, Robert, (ed.) *Elegies written on many different occasions* Vol.1 (London, 1764).
" " *Essays on Men and Manners and Things* Vol.2 (London, 1764).
" " *Containing Letters to Particular Friends, from the year 1739* Vol.3 (London, 1769)
" " *The Schoolmistress* (London, 1742).
" " *The Labours of Hercules* (London, 1741.
Ellis, Havelock (ed.), *Shenstone's Works,* Selected (with) introduction; Golden Cockerill Press,1927.
" " *Men and Manners.* ?1928.
" " *William Shenstone's Poems upon Various Occasions* (Oxford, 1937).
Gilfillan, Rev. George *William Shenstone's Poetical Works* (Edinburgh, 1854).
Gordon, I.A. (ed.) *Shenstone's Miscellany 1759-1763* (London, 1952).

WILLS

Copy of will of William Shenstone. MS 3066, *Birmingham City Archives.*
Will of Mary Cutler [microfilm]. *Worcester Records Office.*

PERSONALIA

Alcock, Edward (Ned) (fl.1757-78). Miniaturist and portrait painter. Best known for his portrait of Shenstone who sat for him at The Leasowes during 1759/60. Now hangs in the National Portrait Gallery.

Arne, Thomas (1710-78). Leading British composer. Composed the masque *Alfred* which includes the well known song *Rule Britannia*. Set Shenstone's *Pastoral Ode* to music.

Arnold, Mary (dates unknown). Shenstone's loyal retainer at The Leasowes from 1739 onwards.

Baskerville, John (1706-75. Printer and typographer of Easy Row, Birmingham. Friend of Shenstone. Invented Baskerville type and published an edition of *Virgil*, and Dodsley's *Select Fables* (1761) for which the poet contributed illustrations.

Boulton, Matthew (1728-1809). Industrialist, entrepreneur and philanthropist. Friend of Shenstone. Built and lived at Soho House next door to his works in Birmingham. Employed both Amos Green and Frankie Holyoake, son of Lady Luxborough's chaplain who operated a private postal service from the Soho premises.

Cibber, Colley (1671-1757). Actor and playwright. Best known for his play *The Careless Husband* 1705. Satirised by Pope in *The Dunciad*. Created Poet Laureate in 1730. Published a best selling autobiography 1740.

Cutler, Mary (-d. 1781). A highly regarded employee. Became Shenstone's housekeeper in 1745 until his death.

Dalton, John (1709-63). Tutor to Lord Beauchamp (son of the Duchess of Somerset). Best known for his adaptation of Milton's *Comus*. Provided the excuse for Lady Luxborough's banishment to Barrels.

Dibdin, Charles (1745-1814). English composer, impresario, and singer. Remembered for his songs, *The Bells of Aberdovey, Tom Bowling* and a setting of Shenstone's *The Western Sky was Purpled O'er.*

Dodsley, Robert (1703-64). Publisher, writer and bookseller. Footman who rose to fame with *Servitude*, a poem (1729) followed by *The Toy Shop*, a satirical play. Published works by Pope, Goldsmith and Johnson. Best known for his six volumes of *Miscellanies*, to which Shenstone both contributed and helped to edit in part. Also his *Select Fables* illustrated by the poet.

Dolman, Maria (1733-54). Shenstone's cousin and daughter of the Reverend Thomas Dolman. Spent her short life at the vicarage in Broome. A great favourite of Shenstone who erected a gilt painted urn to her memory in Lover's Walk at The Leasowes.

Dolman, Rev. Thomas (-d. 1745). Vicar of Broome in Staffordshire. Married Mary Penn, Shenstone's aunt. Provided a home for the poet and his brother upon their mother's death.

Dudley, Lord Ferdinando Dudley Lea, 5th Baron (-d. 1759). Of the Grange, Lapal, Halesowen. Shenstone's friend and neighbour. Died unmarried.

Fielding, Henry (1707-54). Educated Eton and the Bar. Foremost playwright and novelist of his day. Published *Shamela* in 1742 a parody of Richardson's *Pamela*. Other works include *Tom Jones* and *Joseph Andrews*.

Foley, Lord Thomas 2nd Baron (-d. 1766). Entertained Shenstone at his seat Witley Court in Worcestershire. Died unmarried.

Garrick, David (1717-79). Actor, playwright and theatre manager. Pupil of Samuel Johnson. Licensee of Drury Lane Theatre. Initiated concealed lighting. Prohibited seating of spectators on stage. Wrote with Coleman *The Clandestine Marriage* 1766.

Graves, Morgan (1707-70). Elder brother of Richard and heir to Mickleton Manor. Influenced by Phillip Southcote. Introduced Shenstone to "new" concepts in garden design. Bencher of the Middle Temple.

Graves, Rev. Richard (1715-1804). Poet, novelist and first biographer of Shenstone met at Oxford. Ordained 1740. Rector of Claverton near Bath. Novels include *Columella* and *The Spiritual Quixote*.

Gray, Thomas (1716-1771). Foremost poet of his day. Friends include: Walpole, Middleton and Christopher Smart. Best known for his *Elegy Written in a Country Churchyard* 1751. Also his *Ode on the Death of a Favourite Cat*. Contributed to Dodsley's *Miscellany* volume IV.

Green, Amos (1753-1807). Painter employed by Boulton at his Soho premises. Illuminated trays and boxes. Later specialities flowers, fruit pieces and birds. Neighbour and friend of Shenstone.

Gunn, Barnabus (- d. 1753). Birmingham composer, postmaster and organist of St Philip's and St Martin's in the Bull Ring. Presented summer concerts at Duddeston Gardens and elsewhere.

Handel, George Frederick (1685-1759). Foremost German composer and organist. Resident in England from 1711. Composed operas and dramatic oratorios, including *Messiah* (1742). Awarded an annual pension of £600 by George II.

Hodgetts, John (dates unknown). Shenstone's cousin to whom he left The Leasowes. Proved a poor landlord and miserly heir. Took credit for a memorial to the poet in Halesowen parish church paid for by Graves.

Holyoake, Rev. William (1694-1768). Rector of Oldberrow from 1725. Lady Luxborough's chaplain and friend. Informed Shenstone of her death in 1756.

Howard, Samuel (1710-82). Composer and organist at St Clement Danes and St Bride's Fleet Street. Set Shenstone's *Florellio* and *Daphne* to music in his *The Musical Companion*(?) 1775.

Hull, Thomas (1728-1808). Playwright, actor and manager of Birmingham's King's Street Theatre 1759-75. His two musical plays: *The Spanish Lady* and *Rosamond*, both largely Shenstone's work. His *Select Letters*, published in two volumes 1778, contain letters of Shenstone, Whistler, Dodsley and others.

Hutton, Catherine (1756-1845). Daughter of William Hutton, Birmingham's first historian. Her *Journal* describes a visit to tea with Mary Cutler in 1789, after Shenstone's death.

Hylton, John Scott (1725-1784). Of Lapal House, Halesowen. Friend and neighbour of Shenstone. Editor of a selection of Richard Jago's poems. Contributor to The *Gentleman's Magazine*. Buried at Halesowen Church.

Jago, Rev. Richard (1715-1781). Son of rector of Beaudesert in Henley-in-Arden. Educated Solihull School and Oxford. Lifelong friend and correspondent of Shenstone. Minor poet. Published 1759, *Edgehill*, an autobiographical poem in four parts. Contributor to Dodsley's *Miscellany*. Rector of Harbury in Warwickshire.

Johnson, Samuel, (1709-1784). Known as Dr Johnson. English lexographer, author and critic. Brilliant conversationalist. Dominant figure of London literary scene. Published his *Dictionary* 1755 and *Rasselas* 1759. Met Boswell in 1763 whose classic *Life of Samuel Johnson* records his wit and breadth of vision.

Knight, Henrietta, née St John. (Lady Luxborough). (1699-1756). Half sister to Henry St. John Viscount Bolingbroke, Tory politician and foreign secretary, 1710-14, to Queen Anne. Married Robert Knight. Estranged 1734. Banished to Barrels Hall, Ullenhall. Minor poet. Contributor Dodsley's *Miscellany*. Author *Luxborough Letters*. Friend and confidant of Shenstone.

Knight, Robert, Baron Luxborough, Earl of Catherlough (1702-1772). Estranged husband of Henrietta. Son of Cashier of South Sea Bubble Company. After a second marriage (unconsummated) to Lady de Quesne 1756, took as his common law wife Jane Davies, daughter of a tenant. By her fathered five children.

Lyttelton, Lord George, 1st Baron (1709-1773). Son of Sir Thomas Lyttelton. Born at Hagley. Educated at Eton and Oxford. Entered Parliament 1735. Minor poet and generous patron. Friend of Pope, Thomson, Fielding and Shenstone. Publications include *Monody* 1747 and *Dialogues of the Dead* 1760. His *History of the Life of Henry II* published in four volumes 1767-71.

Miller, Sanderson (1717-80). Amateur architect of Radway in Warwickshire. Designer of sham castles including Hagley Hall's "Gothic" folly. At first disliked by Shenstone. Lived at Radway in Warwickshire.

Parkes, David (1763-1833). Artist and teacher. Born Halesowen the year of Shenstone's death. Sketched Shenstone's ruinated priory and many scenes from The Leasowes.

Percy, Bishop Thomas (1729-1811). Son of a Shropshire grocer. Educated Bridgnorth Grammar School and Christ Church, Oxford. Vicar of Easton Maudit in Northamptonshire and later Bishop of Dromore, Ireland. Published *The Pleasing History*, 1761 a translation from the Chinese. With Shenstone co-edited *Reliques of Ancient English Poetry*. Published 1765 after latter's death.

Pitt, William (The elder) First Earl of Chatham (1708-1778). "The great commoner". British Whig politician. Entered Parliament 1735. Prime Minister in coalition governments 1756-61. Friend of Sir George Lyttelton. Visited Shenstone at The Leasowes in 1739.

Plymouth, Earl of, Uther Lewis Windsor. 10th Lord Windsor (1731-1790). Of Hewel Grange. Shenstone's advice sought concerning landscaping his estate.

Pococke, Bishop Richard (1704-65). Son of Rev. Richard Pococke, Rector of Colmer, Hampshire. Educated Highclere Rectory and Oxford. Travel writer. Recorded a visit to The Leasowes. See his *The Travels Through England of Dr R Pococke.*

Pope, Alexander (1688-1744). Son of a London linen merchant. Principally self educated. Published his poems, *An Essay on Criticism* 1711 and *The Rape Lock* 1712. Established as poet of the first rank. Translated Homer's *Iliad* 1715. Much sought after figure.

Richardson, Samuel (1689-1761). Son of a Derbyshire joiner. At seventeen a stationer's apprentice in London. Formed own printing and stationery company. Married twice. First to Martha Wilde his employer's daughter. Then to Elizabeth Leake whose brother owned a book shop in Bath. Printed periodical *The True Briton* and newspapers, *The Daily Journal* and *Daily Gazette*. Published novels: *Pamela or Virtue Rewarded* 1740. *Clarissa* in five volumes between 1747 and 1748.

Shenstone, John (d. 1745). Distant relative of William. Tenanted The Leasowes until his death.

Shenstone, Joseph (1722-51). Younger brother of William. Trained as attorney in Bridgnorth but never practiced. Repeatedly ill. Lived with William at The Leasowes. Well thought of by Lady Luxborough.

Smith, Utrecia (c.1726-1746). Daughter of Rev. Smith of Mickleton. Friend of Shenstone and close friend of Richard Graves from whom no offer of marriage was forthcoming. Died, allegedly, of a broken heart. Subject of Shenstone's Elegy IV, *Ophelia's Urn*. Remembered Mickleton Church by Graves' commemorative urn.

Somerset, Duchess of (Lady Hertford). Née Frances Thynne. Married 1713. Duchess of Somerset 1748. Mother of Lord Beauchamp. Patroness of James Thomson. Celebrated letter writer, see Hull's *Select Letters*. Friend of Lady Luxborough and acquaintance of Shenstone whose poem, *Rural Elegance*, was dedicated to her.

Somervile, William Sir (1675-1742). Warwickshire poet and country gentleman of Edstone near Henley in Arden. Educated Winchester and New College Oxford. Published, 1735, *The Chase*, a poem in blank verse and four books concerned with hunting. *Hobbinol*, 1740, a mock heroic account of rustic May Games in the Vale of Evesham. *Field Sports*, 1742. Friend of Lady Luxborough and Shenstone. Early member of the Warwickshire coterie.

Southcote, Philip (c.1700-1750). Distant relative of Morgan Graves. Gentleman farmer and innovative gardener. Embraced Roman concepts of antiquity. Turned his farm at Woburn into a ferme ornée. Influenced Shenstone.

Stamford, 4th Earl of, (Harry Grey) (1715-17??). Landscape gardening enthusiast and friend of Shenstone. Involved in negotiating the poet's pension. At The Leasowes a root house was dedicated to him.

Walpole, Horace (1717-97). 4th Earl of Oxford. English novelist and politician. Whig Member of Parliament. Converted his home at Twickenham into "Gothic" castle. Published 1764 *The Castle of Otranto*. Established genre of the "Gothic" novel.

Warburton, Bishop William (1693-1761). Bishop of Gloucester. Friend of Richard Graves.

Whistler, Anthony (1714-54). Born Whitchurch, Berkshire. Educated Eton and Oxford University. Lifelong friend and correspondent of Shenstone. Author of *The Shuttlecock* 1742, a mock heroic poem which pleased Lady Luxborough. Contributor to volume IV of Dodsley's *Miscellany*. Member of the Warwickshire Coterie.

Wilmot, Rev. Pynson (1706-1789). Vicar of Halesowen Church c.1736-1789. Disliked by numerous parishioners. Quarrelled with Shenstone over land rights. Conducted the poet's funeral service.

Woodhouse, James (1735-1820). Born Rowley Regis. Known as the cobbler poet. Befriended by Shenstone 1759. Published *Poems on Sundry Occasions* 1764 with dedication to the poet. Land steward to Edward and Elizabeth Montague 1765. By 1788 an Establishment figure.

REFERENCES

Introduction
1   In Shenstone's day The Leasowes was in Shropshire.
2   Johnson, Dr Samuel, *Lives of the Poets*, p.322

Chapter 1: School Days and Early Influences
1   Pemberton, *Solihull and its Church, p.153*
2   Jago, *Edgehill,* iii, p.101
3   Ibid, p.104

Chapter 2: Oxford and Friendship
1   Certainly
2   In the memory of W.G.. Parish Clerke at Broome. This verse from a previously
     unpolished poem written by Shenstone c.1739, re-surfaced in Gentleman's
     Magazine, May 1798.
3   Chambers, The Works of the English Poets, xvii, p.313
4   Graves, *Recollections*, p.15
5   Dodsley, Miscellany, iv, p.329
6   Gilfillan (ed.), *Shenstone's Poetical Works, Ode to Memory*, p.117
7   Ibid, Elegy viii, p.15

Chapter 3: Early Poetry
1   Gilfillan (ed.), *Shenstone's Poetical Works, Colimira: A Culinary Eclogue*, p.71
2   Ibid, *Love and Music,* p.144

Chapter 4: Harborough and Mickleton
1   Graves, *Recollections, p.7*
2   Williams, *William Shenstone*, p.13
3   Gilfillan (ed.), *Shenstone's Poetical Works* p.97
4   Ibid, p.98
5   Graves, *Recollections*, p.115
6   Gilfillan (ed.), *Shenstone's Poetical Works*, p.8
7   Hull, *Select Letters*, p.18

Chapter 5: Settling In: 1736-1740
1   Wyndham, *Chronicles of the Eighteenth Century,* pp.40-41
2   Ibid, p.41
3   Dodsley (ed) *Luxborough Letters*, p.2

4   Williams (ed), *Letters of William Shenstone,* p.92
5   Ibid, p.86
6   Ibid, p.81

Chapter 6: Man About Town
1   Williams (ed.), *Letters of William Shenstone,* p.15
2   *Gentleman's Magazine,* April 1739
3   Williams (ed.), *Letters of William Shenstone,* p.19

Chapter 7: The Schoolmistress
1   Williams (ed.), *Letters of William Shenstone,* p.34
2   Gilfillan (ed.), *Shenstone's Poetical Works,* p.269
3   Ibid, p.267
4   Ibid, p.270
5   Williams (ed.), *Letters of William Shenstone,* p.40
6   Shenstone, *Poems on Several Occasions*
7   Ibid, p.48
8   Gilfillan (ed.), *Shenstone's Poetical Works,* pp.266-267
9   Clarendon Press, Reprint 1742 Edition of *The Schoolmistress*
10   Williams (ed.), *Letters of William Shenstone,* p.42
11   Williams (ed.), *Letters of William Shenstone,* p.44
12   Composed by Henry Carey
13   Williams (ed.), *Letters of William Shenstone,* p.56
14   Ibid, p.57
15   Ibid, p.105

Chapter 8: Mary Arnold and Mary Cutler
1   Williams (ed.), *Letters of William Shenstone,* p.61
2   Ibid, p.75
3   Ibid, p.79
4   Ibid, p.284
5   Ibid, p.73
6   Graves, *Columella* ii
7   Williams (ed.), *Letters of William Shenstone,* p.95
8   Ibid, p.69
9   Catherine Hutton's Journal, p.17
10   Duggan, *A Lady of Letters,* p.14

Chapter 9: Cheltenham and The Pastoral Ballad – A Chapter Ends: 1743-1745
1   Williams (ed.), *The Letters of William Shenstone,* p.76
2   Ibid, p.45
3   Gilfillan, *Shenstone's Poetical Works,* p.154

4   Williams (ed.), *Letters of William Shenstone*, p.90
5   Ibid, p.91
6   Ibid, p.97
7   Hull, *Select Letters*, i, p.24

Chapter 10: The Luxborough Letters
1   Williams (ed.), *Letters of William Shenstone*, p.109
2   Ibid, p.184
3   Dodsley (ed.), Luxborough Letters, p.10
4   Ibid, p.106
5   Dodsley (ed.), Shenstone's Works, iii, p.vi
6   Williams (ed.), *Letters of William Shenstone*, p.158
7   Ibid, p.140
8   Ibid, p.169
9   Ibid, p.159
10   Dodsley (ed.), *Luxborough Letters*, p.111
11   Williams (ed.), *Letters of William Shenstone*, p.155
12   Ibid, p.282
13   Ibid, p.168
14   Ibid, p.260
15   Ibid, p.331
16   Dodsley (ed.), *Luxborough Letters,* p.303
17   Williams (ed.), *Letters of William Shenstone*, p.369
18   Ibid, p.283
19   Dodsley (ed.), *Luxborough Letters*, p.370
20   Ibid, p.277
21   Ibid, p.144
22   Williams (ed.), *Letters of William Shenstone*, p.264
23   Ibid, p.198
24   Ibid, p.140
25   Ibid, p.167
26   *Dictionary of National Biography*
27   Williams (ed.), *Letters of William Shenstone*, p.249
28   Dodsley (ed.), *Luxborough Letters*, p.295
29   Williams (ed.), *Letters of William Shenstone*, p.329
30   Dodsley (ed.), *Luxborough Letters*, p.296
31   Williams (ed.), *Letters of William Shenstone*, p.330
32   Ibid, p.448
33   Gilfillan (ed.), Shenstone's Poetical Works, Song xi p.177
34   Dodsley (ed.), *Luxborough Letters*, p.211
35   Williams (ed.), *Letters of William Shenstone* p.452
36   Dodsley (ed.), *Shenstone's Works* ii p.373

Chapter 11: A Garden of Poetry and Emblem

1   Gilfillan (ed.), *Shenstone's Poetical Works*, p.202
2   Williams (ed.), *Letters of William Shenstone*, p.88
3   Ibid, p.93
4   Gilfillan (ed.), *Shenstone's Poetical Works*, p.134
5   Williams (ed.), *Letters of William Shenstone*, p.223
6   Ibid, p.280
7   Dodsley (ed.), Shenstone's Works ii, p.141
8   Williams (ed.), *Letters of William Shenstone*, p.410
9   Ibid, p.109
10   Ibid, p.197
11   Ibid, p.202
12   Gilfillan (ed.), *Shenstone's Poetical Works*, p.273
13   Williams (ed.), *Letters of William Shenstone*, p.204
14   Ibid, p.254
15   Ibid, p.150
16   Ibid, p.148
17   Ibid, p.149
18   Gilfillan (ed.), *Shenstone's Poetical Works*, p.274
19   McKillop, *Thompson's Visit to Shenstone*, Philological Quarterly, 23 July 1944
20   Gilfillan, (ed.), *Shenstone's Poetical Works*, p.348
21   Dodsley (ed.), *Shenstone's Works*, ii, p.348
22   Williams (ed.), *Letters of William Shenstone*, p.253
23   Ibid, p.207
24   Gilfillan (ed.), *Shenstone's Poetical Works*, p.277
25   Williams (ed.), *Letters of William Shenstone*, p.532
26   Ibid, p.147
27   Ibid, p.157
28   Ibid, p.282
29   Fairclough, (trans.), Virgil's *Aeneid*, Loeb Classical Library, 1947-9
30   Williams (ed.), *Letters of William Shenstone*, p.44
31   Williams (ed.), *Letters of William Shenstone*, p.384
32   *Shenstone's Works*, ii, p.128
33   Williams (ed.), *Letters of William Shenstone*, p.384

Chapter 12: Songs: Ballads and Elegies

1   Dosley (ed.), *Luxborough Letters*, p.1
2   Gilfillan (ed.), *Shenstone's Poetical Works*, p.173
3   Organist at St Philip's Church and St Martin's in the Bull Ring, Birmingham
4   Williams (ed.), *Letters of William Shenstone*, p.6
5   Ibid, p.494
6   Gilfillan (ed.), *Shenstone's Poetical Works*, p.141

7	Ibid, p.184
8	Ibid, p.179
9	Ibid, p.77
10	Ibid, p.77
11	Williams (ed.), *Letters of William Shenstone*, p.144
12	Chalmers (ed.), *The Works of the English Poets*, xvii, p.316
13	Williams (ed.), *Letters of William Shenstone*, p.358
14	Ibid, p.151
15	Dodsley (ed.), *Luxborough Letters*, p.68
16	Williams (ed.), *Letters of William Shenstone*, p.181
17	Gilfillan (ed.), *Shenstone's Poetical Works*, p.26
18	Dodsley (ed.), *Luxborough Letters*, p.80
19	Gilfillan (ed.), *Shenstone's Poetical Works*, p.64
21	Williams (ed.), *Letters of William Shenstone*, p.161
22	Dodsley (ed.), *Luxborough Letters*, p.353
23	Gilfillan (ed.), *Shenstone's Poetical Works*, p.21
24	Ibid, p.14
25	Ibid, p.136
26	Ibid, p.105

Chapter 13: The Pensées

1	Dodsley (ed.), Shenstone's *Essays on Men, Manners and Things*, p.212
2	Ibid, p.228
3	Ibid, p.4
4	Ibid, p.230
5	Ibid, p.279
6	Ibid, p.76
7	Ibid, p.297
8	Ibid, p.236
9	Ibid, p.232
10	Ibid, p.234
11	Ibid, p.153
12	Ibid, p.148
13	Dodsley (ed.), *Shenstone's Works*, ii, p.154
14	Ibid, p.157
15	Ibid, p.170
16	Ibid, p.266
17	Ibid, p.219
18	Ibids, p.258

Chapter 14: Friends and Family: 1745-1755

1   Williams (ed.), *Letters of William Shenstone*, p.385
2   Hull (ed.), *Select Letters*, I, p.104
3   Williams (ed), *Letters of William Shenstone* p.386
4   Hull (ed.), *Select Letters*, I, p.104
5   Williams (ed.), *Letters of William Shenstone*, p.319
6   Ibid, p.344
7   Hull (ed.), *Select Letters, I, p.138*
8   Gilfillan (ed.), *Poetical Works of William Shenstone*, p.84
9   Williams (ed.), *Letters of William Shenstone*, p.396
10   Ibid, p.398
11   Ibid, p.404
12   Williams (ed.), *Letters of William Shenstone*, p.327
13   Ibid, p.328
14   Dodsley (ed.), *Luxborough Letters*, p.294
15   Williams (ed.), *Letters of William Shenstone*, p.333
16   Gilfillan (ed.), *Poetical Works of William Shenstone*, p.119
17   Shenstone's scullery maid
18   Williams (ed.), *Letters of William Shenstone*, p.396
19   Gilfillan (ed.), *Poetical of Works of William Shenstone*, p.125

Chapter 15: "People in our Parish".

1   Williams (ed.), *Letters of William Shenstone* p.474
2   Woodhouse, *Poems on Sundry Occasions,* p.7
3   Ibid, Introduction iv
4   Carlyle, *Autobiography, p.387*
5   Williams (ed.), *Letters of William Shenstone*, p.605
6   Whereas Quarter Sessions are well document, Petty Sessions are not and so we remain ignorant of the sentences that Shenstone passed
7   Williams (ed.), *Letters of William Shenstone*, p.322
8   Ibid, p.358
9   Ibid, p.356
10   Ibid, p.358
11   Ibid, p.219

Chapter 16: New Horizons and the Miscellanies

1   Williams (ed.), *Letters of William Shenstone*, p.453
2   Ibid, p.109
3   Ibid, p.287
4   Ibid, p.177
5   Ibid, p.150
6   Ibid, p.294

7   Strauss, *Robert Dodsley, Poet, Publisher and Playwright*, p.108
8   Williams (ed.), *Letters of William Shenstone*, p.134
9   Ibid, p.387
10   Strauss, *Robert Dodsley, Poet, Publisher and Playwright*, p.119
11   Williams (ed.), *Letters of William Shenstone*, p.393
12   Ibid, p.418
13   Ibid, p.423
14   Ibid, p.425
15   Ibid, p.426
16   Ibid, p.429
17   Tierney (ed.), *The Correspondence of Robert Dodsley,*p.223
18   Strauss, *Robert Dodsley, Poet, Publisher and Playwright*, p.137
19   Ibid, p.138
20   Williams (ed.), *Letters of William Shenstone*, p.473
21   Tierney (ed), *The Correspondence of Robert Dodsley*, p.334
22   Gilfillan (ed.), *Shenstone's Poetical Works*, p.64
23   Tierney (ed.), *The Correspondence of Robert Dodsley*, pp.334-335
24   Williams (ed.), *Letters of William Shenstone*, p.482

Chapter 17: Cleone and Dodsley's Fables

1   Dodsley's *Cleone* makes use of the same theme as Shakespeare's *Othello*; but in this play dramatic interest focuses instead upon the wronged wife
2   Tierney (ed.), *The Correspondence of Robert Dodsley*, p.230
3   Williams (ed.), *Letters of William Shenstone*, p.455
4   Strauss, *Robert Dodsley, Poet, Publisher and Playwright* p.207
5   Williams (ed.), *Letters of William Shenstone*, p.463
6   Ibid, p.410
7   Tierney (ed.), *The Correspondence of Robert Dodsley*, p.375
8   Ibid, p.410
9   Williams (ed.), *Letters of William Shenstone*, p.514
10   Ibid, p.519
11   Ibid, p.534
12   Ibid, p.603

Chapter 18: Percy, The Reliques and the Mulberry Tree Plot

1   Williams (ed.), *Letters of William Shenstone,* p.33
2   Ibid, p.478
3   Ibid, p.517
4   Ibid, p.561
5   Ibid, p.562
6   Ibid, p.600
7   Ibid, p.597

8   Ibid, p.642
9   Ibid, p.480
10   Ibid, p.660
11   Ibid, p.537
12   Tierney (ed.), *The Correspondence of Robert Dodsley,* p.339
13   Williams (ed.), *Letters of William Shenstone,* p.526
14   Tierney (ed.), *The Correspondence of Robert Dodsley,* p.339
15   Williams (ed.) *Letters of William Shenstone,* p.545
16   Dodsley (ed.), *Shenstone's Works,* ii, p.171
17   Williams (ed.), *Letters of William Shenstone,* p.553
18   Ibid, p.558

Chapter 19: Thomas Hull and The Final Curtain
1   The site is approximate
2   Williams (ed.), *Letters of William Shenstone,* p.566
3   Ibid, p.584
4   Ibid, p.588
5   Ibid, p.585
6   Hull (ed.), *Select Letters, ii, p.125*
7   Tierney (ed.), *The Correspondence of Robert Dodsley,* p.462
8   Williams (ed.), *Letters of William Shenstone,* p.639
9   Ibid, p.639
10   Ibid, p.634
11   Ibid, p.643
12   Ibid, p.528
13   Gaussen, *Percy: Prelate and Poet,* p.204
14   Williams (ed.), *Letters of William Shenstone,* p.539
15   Ibid, p.545
16   Ibid, p.452
17   Ibid, p.527
18   Ibid, p.574
19   Williams, *William Shenstone,* p.98

Chapter 20: The Will
1   Birmingham Central Library, Archive M.S. 286893
2   Williams, *William Shenstone,* p.145

Conclusion
1   Dodsley (ed.), Shenstone's Work, ii p.300
2   Ibid, p.148
3   Williams (ed.), *Letters of William Shenstone,* p.129

LIST OF ILLUSTRATIONS

Frontispiece:
William Shenstone by Edward Alcock (By courtesy of the National Portrait Gallery, London).

Gallery One:
The Leasowes; birthplace of William Shenstone by W.J. Child. (In possession of the author).

The Leasowes by William Shenstone. Gentleman's Magazine. (Courtesy of the Birmingham Library Services).

Shenstone's dame school. (Courtesy of Shropshire Archives).

Malvern House, Solihull, where Shenstone went to school. (Courtesy of Solihull MBC, Heritage and Local Studies Service Solihull Central Library).

Brome church and bell. Gentleman's Magazine (Courtesy of Birmingham Library Services).

The haunted churchyard, All Saints, Harbury. (Photograph by Geoffrey Duggan).

William Shenstone as a young man, by Thomas Ross. (Courtesy of the National Portrait Gallery, London).

Harborough Hall, the home of the Penn family. (By kind permission of Clifford Whittaker).

William Somervile. Artist unknown. (Courtesy of the National Portrait Gallery, London).

Richard Graves, by Samuel William Reynolds: engraving by James Northcote. (Courtesy of the National Portrait Gallery, London).

Mickleton Manor today: a rear view. (By kind permission of Mr and Mrs Paul Johnson. Photograph by Geoffrey Duggan).

Entrance to Mickleton Manor. (By kind permission of Mr and Mrs Paul Johnson. Photograph by Geoffrey Duggan).

St Lawrence's Church, Mickleton. (Photograph by Geoffrey Duggan).

Memorial urn to Utrecia Smith in St Lawrence Church, Mickleton. (By kind permission of the Churchwardens. (Photograph by Geoffrey Duggan).

The first Lord Lyttelton, by Benjamin West. (By kind permission of Lord Cobham).

Hagley Hall. (By kind permission of Lord Cobham).

Shenstone's illustration of his dame school for *The Schoolmistress* 1742. (In possession of the author).

Thomas Arne's setting for *The Pastoral Ballad*. (Courtesy of the Birmingham Library Services).

Gallery Two:

Lady Luxborough and autograph. *Bolingbroke and his Times*. (Courtesy of the
   Birmingham Library Services).

The Old Chapel, Ullenhall. (Photograph by Audrey Duggan).

The Luxborough coat of arms in Old Chapel, Ullenhall. (Photograph by Geoffrey
   Duggan).

Illustrated letter from Lady Luxborough to William Shenstone. (Courtesy of the
   Shakespeare Birthplace Trust).

Page of a letter from William Shenstone to Lady Luxborough, 6 June 1752. (By kind
   permission of the trustees of the William Salt Library, Stafford).

Virgil's Grove from an engraving by Thomas Smith. (In possession of the author).

The Leasowes and Priory Seat, by D. Jenkins. (Courtesy of Shropshire Archives).

The Old Priory in 1761. (Courtesy of Shropshire Archives).

A Gothic Alcove at the Leasowes. (Courtesy of Shropshire Archives).

Gothic Seat in the High Wood, by David Parkes. (Courtesy of Shropshire Archives).
   [SA 6001/154]

The Temple of Pan, by David Parkes. (Courtesy of Shropshire Archives).

All friends round the Wrekin, by David Parkes. (Courtesy of Shropshire Archives).

Memorial urn to Maria Dolman, by David Parkes. (Courtesy of Shropshire Archives).

View of Leasowes, by David Parkes. (Courtesy of Shropshire Archives).

Memorial urn to William Somervile. (Gentleman's Magazine, September 1807.
   Courtesy of Birmingham Library Services).

Memorial urn as reproduced in volume one of *The Works*. (In possession of the
   author).

Sanderson Miller's folly at Radway. (Now part of the Castle Inn. Photograph by
   Geoffrey Duggan).

James Thomson, artist unknown. (Courtesy of the National Portrait Gallery, London).

The "Castle" at Hagley Hall. (By kind permission of Lord Cobham).

Gallery Three

Robert Dodsley, by Edward Alcock. (Courtesy of Birmingham Library Services).

Thomas Percy, by Dickinson after Reynolds. (Courtesy of the National Portrait
   Gallery, London).

Lord Dudley's residence The Grange, Halesowen. (By kind permission of Peter
   Russell).

James Woodhouse, by Henry Cook. (Courtesy of Birmingham Library Services).

John Scott Hylton, by Horace R. Wilson.

Lapal House, by Horace R. Wilson.

Record of Shenstone's burial, Halesowen Parish Register. (Courtesy of Worcester
   Records Office).

Memorial urn to William Shenstone in Halesowen Church. (Photograph by Geoffrey
   Duggan).

Gallery Three (cont.)

Thomas Hull as Gloucester in *Edward and Eleanora*. (Courtesy of Birmingham Library Services).

St John the Baptist Church, Halesowen, by David Parkes. (Courtesy of Dudley Archives and Local History).

Busto of William Shenstone. *The Collected Works*. (In possession of the author).

Decorative page opposite frontispiece to volume one of *Collected Works*. (In possession of the author).

Decoration for Rural Elegance in volume one of *The Collected Works*. (In possession of the author).

Shenstone's grave in Halesowen churchyard. (Photograph by Geoffrey Duggan).

A SELECTION OF POEMS

LINES WRITTEN AT AN INN

To thee, fair Freedom! I retire
From flattery, cards, and dice, and din;
Nor art thou found in mansions higher
Than the low cot or humble Inn.

'Tis here with boundless power I reign;
And every health which I begin,
Converts dull port to bright champagne;
Such freedom crowns it, at an Inn.

I fly from pomp, I fly from plate!
I fly from Falsehood's specious grin!
Freedom I love, and form I hate,
And choose my lodgings at an Inn.

Here, Waiter! Take my sordid ore,
Which lackeys else might hope to win;
It buys what courts have not in store
It buys me freedom at an Inn.

Whoe'er has travell'd life's dull round,
Where'er his stages may have been,
May sigh to think he still has found
The warmest welcome at an Inn.

SONG XI. 1744

Perhaps it is not love, said I,
That melts my soul when Flavia's nigh;
Where wit and sense like hers agree,
One may be pleased, and yet be free.

The beauties of her polish'd mind
It needs no lover's eye to find;
The hermit freezing in his cell
Might wish the gentle Flavia well.

It is not love – averse to bear
The servile chain that lovers wear;
Let, let me all my fears remove,
My doubts dispel – it is not love.

Oh! When did wit so brightly shine
In any form less fair than thine?
It is – it is love's subtle fire,
And under friendship lurks desire.

HERE, IN COOL GROT

HERE, in cool grot and mossy cell,
We rural fays and fairies dwell;
Though rarely seen by mortal eye,
When the pale moon, ascending high,
Darts through yon lines her quivering beams,
We frisk it near these crystal streams.

Her beams, reflected from the wave,
Afford the light our revels crave;
The turf, with daisies broider'd o'er,
Exceeds, we wot, the Parian floor;
Nor yet for artful strains we call,
But listen to the water's fall.

Would you then taste our tranquil scene,
Be sure your bosoms be serene;
Devoid of hate, devoid of strife,
Devoid of all that poisons life:
And much it 'vails you in their place,
To graft the love of human race.

And tread with awe these favoured bowers,
Nor wound the shrubs, nor bruise the flowers;
So may your path with sweets abound;
So may your couch with rest be crown'd!
But betide the wayward swain,
Who dares our hallow'd haunts profane!

SONG II. THE LANDSCAPE

How pleased within my native bowers
Erewhile I pass'd the day!
Was ever scene so deck'd with flowers?
Were ever flowers so gay?

How sweetly smiled the hill, the vale,
And all the landscape round!
The river gliding down the dale,
The hill with beeches crown'd!

But now, when urged by tender woes,
I speed to meet my dear,
That hill and stream my zeal oppose,
And check my fond career.

No more, since Daphne was my theme,
Their wonted charms I see;
That verdant hill, and silver stream,
Divide my love and me.

IMPROMPTU TO MISS UTRECIA SMITH

ON HER NOT DANCING. 1748.

Whilst round in wild rotations hurl'd,
These glittering forms I view,
Methinks the busy restless world
Is pictured in a few.

So may the busy world advance,
Since thus the Fates decree:
It still may have its busy dance,
Whilst I retire with thee.

SLENDER'S GHOST

VIDE SHAKESPEARE

Beneath a churchyard yew,
Decay'd and worn with age,
At dusk of eve methought I spied
Poor Slender's Ghost, that whimpering cried,
"O sweet! O sweet Anne Page!"

Ye gentle Bards! Give ear,
Who talk of amorous rage,
Who spoil the lily, rob the rose,
Come learn of me to weep your woes:
"O sweet! O sweet Anne Page!"

Why should such labour'd strains
Your formal Muse engage?
I never dreamt of flame or dart,
That fired my breast or pierced my heart,
But sigh'd, "O sweet Anne Page!"

And you! Whose lovesick minds
No med'cine can assuage,
Accuse the leech's art no more,
But learn of Slender to deplore;
"O sweet! O sweet Anne Page!"

contin...

And ye! Whose souls are held,
Like linnets in a cage;
Who talk of fetters, links, and chains,
Attend and imitate my strains,
"O sweet! O sweet Anne Page!"

And you! Who boast or grieve,
What horrid wars ye wage,
Of wounds received from many an eye,
Yet mean as I do, when I sigh,
"O sweet! O sweet Anne Page!"

Hence every fond conceit
Of shepherd or of sage;
'Tis Slender's voice, 'tis Slender's way,
Expresses all you have to say,
"O sweet! O sweet Anne Page!"

EPILOGUE: TO THE TRAGEDY OF *CLEONE*

Well Ladies – so much for the tragic style –
And now the custom is to make you smile.
To make us smile! – methinks I hear you say –
Why, who can help it, at so strange a play?
The captain gone three years! – and then to blame
The faultless conduct of his virtuous dame!
My stars! What gentle belle would think it treason,
When thus provoked, to give the brute some reason?
Out of my house! – this night, forsooth, depart!
A modern wife had said – "With all my heart –
But think not, haughty Sir, I'll go alone;
Order your coach – conduct me safe to Town –
Give me my jewels, wardrobe, and my maid –
And pray take care my pin-money be paid."
　　　Such is the language of each modish fair;
Yet memoirs, not of modern growth, declare
The time has been, when modesty and truth
Were deem'd additions to the charms of youth;
When women hid their necks, and veil'd their faces,
Nor romp'd, nor raked, nor stared at public places,
Nor took the airs of Amazons for graces:
Then plain domestic virtues were the mode,
And wives ne'er dreamt of happiness abroad;
They loved their children, learnt no flaunting airs,
But with the joys of wedlock mix'd the cares.

Those times are past – yet sure they merit praise,

For marriage triumph'd in those golden days;

By chaste decorum they affection gain'd;

By faith and fondness, what they won, maintain'd.

      'Tis yours, Ye Fair! To bring those days again,

And form anew the hearts of thoughtless men;

Make beauty's lustre amiable as bright,

And give the soul, as well as sense, delight;

Reclaim from folly a fantastic age,

That scorns the press, the pulpit, and the stage.

Let truth and tenderness your breasts adorn,

The marriage chain with transport shall be worn;

Each blooming virgin, raised into a bride,

Shall double all their joys, their cares divide;

Alleviate grief, compose the jars of strife,

And pour the balm that sweetens human life.

THE SHORTER PENSÉES

Shenstone's *Pensées* are notable for their wit. They also demonstrate the poet's compassion, the breadth of his understanding and ability to get to the nub of the problem.

EGOTISMS.

There are a sort of people to whom one would allot good wishes and perform good offices; but they are sometimes those, with whom one would by no means share one's time.

I am obliged to the person that speaks fair to my face. I am only more obliged to the man who speaks well of me in my absence also.

Not Hebrew, Arabic, Syriac, Coptic, nor even the Chinese language, seems half so difficult to me as the language of refusal.

ON WRITING AND BOOKS.

Superficial writers, like the mole, often fancy themselves deep when they are exceedingly near the surface.

The world may be divided into people that read, people that write, people that think, and fox-hunters.

A poet, that fails in writing, becomes often a morose critic. The weak and insipid white wine makes at length a figure in vinegar.

The words "no more" have a singular pathos; reminding us at once of past pleasure, and the future exclusion of it.

OF MEN AND MANNERS.

I am afraid humility to genius is as an extinguisher to a candle.

Zealous men are ever displaying to you the strength of their belief, while judicious men are shewing you the grounds of it.

A miser grows rich by seeming poor; an extravagant man grows poor by seeming rich.

There is nothing more universally commended than a fine day; the reason is that people can commend it without envy.

Jealousy is the fear or apprehension of superiority. Envy our uneasiness under it.

Hope is a flatterer; but the most upright of all parasites, for she frequents the poor man's hut, as well as the palace of his superior.

If anyone's curse can effect damnation, it is not that of the pope, but that of the poor.

POLITICS.

Laws are generally found to be nets of such a texture, as the little creep through, the great break through, and the middle-sized are alone entangled.

INDEX

Index Note:

Locators printed in capitalised roman numerals refer to illustration pages.

WS = William Shenstone;
LL = Lady Luxborough.

A

Alcock, Edward, 97, 114, 125–6
Aldsworth, 8
Allen, Parson of Spernal, 50
Allen-a-Dale (song), 117
Aris' Gazette, 129
Arne, Thomas, his setting for *The Pastoral Ballad, VIII*
Arnold, Mary (WS's housekeeper), 33–5, 36, 37, 93, 130
Austen, Jane, *Emma,* 23

B

ballads and songs, 75–7, 82, 116–19, 123
Ballamy, Clara, 111
Ballard, I. A., 16
Banks, Miss, 87
Barrels Hall, Ullenhall, 20, 44, 45: gardens, 53–4; LL's lingering presence, 22-3; running of, revealed in Luxborough Letters, 51–2, 53, 58; visitors to, 94–5
Baskerville, Perry, 55–6, 100, 101, 113, 114
Bath, 57
Bedford Coffee House, 111
Belchoir, Mr, (clergyman), 50

Bells They Rang all the Morn, The (ballad), 123
Birmingham, King Street Theatre, 122–3
Birmingham Mirror, 98
Bitter Fruits of Jealousy (ballad), 123
Boughton, Sir Edward, 49
Boy and the Mantle, The (ballad), 118
Boys and the Frog, The, WS's index to, 115
Brooke, Henry, *Fables for the Female Sex,* 112
Broom, 5: WS visits (1745), 42-3; church and bell, *III*
busto of WS, 55, *XXI*
Byron, Lord, 108

C

Cambridge "fizzers," 6
Carlyle, Reverend Alexander, 97
Cartwright, Elizabeth, 124
Chandler, Matthew and Richard, 37
Cheltenham Spa, 22, 38–9
Cheyne, Dr George, 8: *Essay on Health and Long Life,* 7
Cibber, Colley, 23
clergymen of the eighteenth century, 48–50
Comus (play), 23, 44
Cotton, Charles, *Virgil Travestie,* 9
Covent Garden Theatre, 110–11, 123
Cross Keys hostelry, Birmingham, 122
Crumpton, Reverend William, 2
Cutler, Mary, 35–7, 93, 114: brings Chancery suit against Graves, 130–1

D

D'Israeli, Isaac, *Curiosities of Literature*, 29
Dalton, John, 44, 45
dame school attended by WS as a child, *III, VII*, 1
Derby, Elizabeth, 37
Dibdin, Charles, *Tom Bowling*, 76
Dodsley, Alice, 104
Dodsley, James, 97, 104, 129
Dodsley, Robert, *XVII*, 24, 29, 31, 66, 72, 90: encourages WS to publish collection of poems, 124; Mary Cutler and, 36, 106; on death of WS, 128; on Virgil Grove, Leasowes, 65; publishes collection of WS's poems (1764), 129; **works:** *Cleone*, WS's writes epilogue, relationship with Garrick, 106, 109–11, 161-2; *Description of the Leasowes*, 65; *Essay on Fable*, 113; *Halcyon and the Sparrow*, 112; *Miscellanies*, works with WS on, 100, 101–8, 116; *Selected Fables*, writes to and works with WS on, 112–15; *Toy Shop, The*, 109
doggerel verses, 23–4
Dolman, Maria (WS's cousin), 5, 42, 43
Dolman, Maria (WS's niece), 67, 95: memorial urn at Leasowes, *XIV*
Dolman, Reverend Thomas (WS's uncle), 5
Dolman, Thomas (WS's cousin), 5, 42, 43: legal proceedings against WS, 57–8, 107, 126–7
Dragon of Wantley, The (burlesque opera), 29
Dudley, Lord, 41, 50, 86–7
Dudley Castle, 33
Dudley Grammar School, 2

E

Eckhard, Johannes, *Causes of the Contempt of the Clergy* 3, 9
Edinburgh Review, 105
Edom of Gordon (poem), 117
Edstone Hall, Henley-in-Arden, 3
Egerton, Lady Caroline, 74
elegies of WS, and *Preface* to, 78–80, 81–2
Ellis, Havelock, 83, 85
English Landscape School of gardening, 61

F

Fair Eleanor (song), 117
Fane, Lady, 41
Fieldhouse, Mrs, 36
Fielding, Henry, 13; *Tom Jones,* 56
Fletcher, Fanny, 18
Fletcher, Winnie, 42–3
Fletcher family, 42
Foley, Lord, 124
follies, 69–73, *XVI*
Fondlewife (play), 23

G

Garrick, David, 110
Gentle Heardsman, The (poem), 117, 118
Gentleman's Magazine, 23–5, 35
George's Coffee House, 25
Gordon, Ian, 101
Gothic Seat in the High Woods at Leasowes, *XIV*
"Gothick" Alcove at Leasowes, *XIII*, 69–70
Grange, The, Halesowen, *XVII*, 51, 52–3, 86
grave stone of WS, *XXIV*

Graves, Lucy, 8–9
Graves, Mary, 16, 18, 39
Graves, Morgan, 15–16, 18, 38
Graves, Richard, *VII*, 33, 42, 55: family
    background, career and marriage,
    8–9, 16, 18; John Hodgetts and
    WS's memorial urn, 131; Lady
    Luxborough on, 47; love of
    Utrecia Smith, 17–18; Mary
    Cutler sues over WS's Will, 130;
    offends WS, 15; working
    breakfasts with WS at Oxford, 9;
    WS visits at Mickleton, 15–17;
    WS writes to, 21, 26, 28, 30-1,
    32, 61, 95, 102–3, 104, 113, 114,
    123, 125, 127; WS's relationship
    with Mary Cutler and, 35; WS's
    reworkings of *The Schoolmistress*
    and, 30–1; WS's work on
    Cleone epilogue and, 109–10;
    works: *Columella*, 8, 35;
    Parting, The, 9;
Gray, Thomas, 19, 102, 107
Green, Amos, 96

H

Hagley Hall, *VII*, 19, 47, 65: follies
    constructed at, *XVI*, 71–2; WS
    reads at table, 80–1
Halesowen; dame school, 1; local choir,
    76; postmistress, 21
Halesowen Grammar School, 98
Halesowen Parish Church, *XX*, 98–9:
    WS's grave stone, *XXIV*
Hall, Parson Thomas, 48, 49, 53
Hannah (WS's scullery maid), 51, 94
Harborough, 49
Harborough Hall, *IV*, 12, 15, 58, 126
Harbury, 6–7
Harbury churchyard, *V*
Hazlett, William, 30

Hearn, Thomas, 16
Hervey, John, Baron of Ickworth, 19–20
Hewell Grange, 74
Hey, Colin, 23
Hodgetts, John, 130, 131
Hoitt, John, 3–4
Holyoake, Reverend, 48–9, 50, 59, 100
Howard, Samuel, 76
Hull, Thomas, *XIX*, 12–13, 71, 117,
    122–3
Hutton, Catherine, on Mary Cutler, 36,
    131
Hylton, John Scott, *XVIII*, 52, 71, 87–8,
    95, 106, 126: falls out with WS
    over practical joke, 120–1; Mary
    Cutler after WS's death and,
    130–1

I

Ivey Farm, 36–7, 130, 131

J

Jackson, Tom (WS's gardener), 51–2
Jago, Reverend Robert, 6, 20
Jago, Richard (friend of WS), 1, 2–3,
    20–1, 33, 44, 75: education and
    supernaturalism, 6–7; pastiche on
    Hamlet, 78; WS writes to, 45,
    60–1, 63–4, 65, 71, 103, 104–5,
    118, 133; *works*: *Peto's Ghost*, 6;
    Edgehill, 2-3
Johnson, Samuel, 1, 5, 6, 19, 125:
    Dodsley's *Cleone* and its
    production, 110, 111; *Lines
    Written at an Inn at Henley* and,
    90; on James Woodhouse, 97; on
    pastoral literary form, 40; on *The
    Schoolmistress*, 27; on WS, *x*;
    works: *Lives of the Poets*, *x*, 7

K

King Street Theatre, Birmingham, 122–3
Knight, Henrietta *see* Luxborough, Lady
   Henrietta
Knight, Robert, 44–5, 58
Knight, Sir Thomas, 42

L

La Motte, 112: *Discourse on Fable*, 113
Lane, Mrs (LL's housekeeper), 52
Lapal House, *XVIII*, 121
Lea, Miss (sister of Lord Dudley), 52, 87
Leasowes, The, *I*, 7, 8, 41, 49, 88, 128:
      after WS's death, 130; Edward
      Alcock works at, 126;
      housekeeper, Mary Arnold, 33–5;
      Lord Dudley visits, 87; maid,
      Mary Cutler, 35–7; Parkes' View
      Of, *XV*; refurbishment, 73–4;
      robbery at, 98; Robert Dodsley's
      visits to, 109, 113, 124; running
      of, revealed in Luxborough
      letters, 51–2, 53–4; scullery maid,
      Hannah, 51, 94; WS inherits, 12;
      WS moves into, 19, 20–1
Leasowes garden, 52, 54: Gothic Seat in
   the High Woods, *XIV*; hermitage
   (Temple of Pan) and "Gothick"
   alcove, *XIII, XIV*, 69-70; LL's verse
   on, 59; Parkes' *All friends round the
   Wrekin*, *XIV*; ruinated priory, 70–1,
   XII, XIII; statues and memorial
   urns, *XIV, XV*, 66–8, 95;
   Thomson's sexual imagery and, 67;
   Virgil's Grove and visitors to, *XII*,
   63–6, 86, 93; WS's vision, 60–3, 72
Letters of William Shenstone, 71
Lichfield Cathedral, 42
Lloyd, Sarah (WS's childhood
   schoolmistress), 1

Lloyd, Thomas, 1
London: Pantin craze, 54–5; WS's visits
      to (1740) 22-3; (1741) 26; (1742)
      29-30; (1744) 41-2
London Magazine, 30, 66
Lord Thomas, 117
Lowe, Mrs (LL's housekeeper), 94
Lucy (WS's greyhound), 54, 125
Luxborough coat of arms, *IX*
Luxborough, Lady Henrietta, 9, 34, 78,
      IX: as subject in WS's poems,
      76–7, 80; death of, 59, 100;
      encouraging WS in his work, 79;
      essence lingering at Barrels Hall,
      22–3; friendship with WS, 44, 45,
      58–9, 81; John Scott Hylton and,
      88; letters from WS, 62, 63, 102,
      103, (*see also* Luxborough
      Letters); on receiving WS's
      verses, 75, 20; on WS's "Gothick"
      alcove, 70; separation from
      husband, 44–5; supports WS at
      death of his brother, 57, 93;
      works: *Hark to the Blackbird*,
      104; *Sun his Gladsome Beams,
      The*, 104; verses on Leasowes, 59
Luxborough Letters: artistry and tailoring
      of, *X*, 45–6; as primary source
      material on country clergymen,
      48–50; crazes and trends of the
      time mentioned, 54–6; Dolman
      litigation mentioned, 57–8; during
      time of WS's bereavement, 56–7;
      examples of modesty, flattery and
      WS's style, 47–8; page of letter
      from WS, *XII* running of
      Leasowes, Barrels and Grange
      revealed in, 51–4; *Tom Jones* and
      Clarissa discussed in, 56; written
      in instalments, 58–9; *see also*
      Luxborough, Lady Henrietta;
      Shenstone, William (letters)

Lyttelton, Dean, 81
Lyttelton, George, 1st Lord, *VI*, 19, 67, 70
Lyttelton, Sir Thomas, 74
Lyttelton, Sir William, 68

M

MacGowan, Mr, 118
Malvern House, Solihull, *II*
Mansfield, Lord, 124
memorial urn to WS, *XIX*, 131
memorial urns and statues at Leasowes,
    XIV, XV, 66–8, 95
Meredith, Patty, 55
Mickleton Church, *VI*, 18
Mickleton Manor, *V, VI*, 15–18, 32, 38
Miller, Sanderson, 68–9, 70, 71
Miss "C," 39, 40
Montague, Edward and Elizabeth, 97
Monthly Magazine, 105
Monthly Review, 108
Moody's curiosity shop, Birmingham,
    120–1
Moore, Hannah, 37
Mynde, James, 29

N

Newstead Park, 65
Night Thoughts (Young), 41

O

O Nancy wilt thou go with me (song), 116
Outing, Mr. (LL's xecretary), 26, 29
Oxford, WS and friends' time there:
    5–11, 12

P

Palgrave's *Golden Treasury,* 90
Pantin craze, 54–5

papier-mâché craze, 56
Parish Clerk (poem), 125
pastoral literary form, 40
Penn, Ann *see* Shenstone, Ann
Penn family, 1, 43
Percy, Thomas, *XVII*, 84, 100, 102, 112,
    115, 121: sharing sense of
    humour with WS, 119; works
    with WS on *Reliques of Ancient
    Poetry,* 116–19; **works**: *Cynthia,*
    116; *O Nancy wilt thou go with
    me,* 116
Perry, Reverend John, 49, 50
Phaedrus, *Wolf and the Crane, The,* 113
Piping Faunus statue at Leasowes, 66
Pitt, Humphrey, 116
Pitt, William, 19
Pixal, Reverend, 48
Pixell, Reverend John, 86
Plesson, Baron, 124
Plymouth, Lord and Lady, 74
Pococke, Bishop, 71
Poems by Several Hands, 31, 101
Pope, Alexander, 42: *Rape of the Lock,
    The,* 9-10, 12, 13
Preface to WS's Elegies, 79–80
Priory at Leasowes, *XII, XIII,* 70-1

R

Radcliff, Dr John, 25
Radway 68: "Gothick" tower, *XVI*, 69, 71
Rape of the Lock, The (Pope), 9–10, 12, 13
Reynold, Jackie, 20
Rice, Mary, 97
Rich, John, 110–11
Richardson, Samuel, 112: *Clarissa,* 56
riddle writing, 23–4
Robin Hood (song), 117
Rock, Sally (Dudley's housekeeper), 52
Rosamond (play), 13, 122–3
Ruskin, John, 80

S

Scott, Sir Walter, 30
Shakespeare, William; *All's Well That
    Ends Well,* 29; *Comedy of Errors,*
    117; *Merry Wives of Windsor,* WS
    on, 23
Shenstone, Ann (WS's mother), 1, 5, 33
Shenstone, John, 12, 20
Shenstone, Joseph (WS's brother), 1, 33,
    67: illness and death, 52, 92–4,
    95; WS's inscription to, 67
Shenstone, Thomas (WS's father), 1, 5,
    33
Shenstone, William:
  character: compassion towards under
      privileged, 84, 85, 97–8; fear
      of adverse criticism and need
      of friends' approval, 78–9, 104;
      humanitarian and progressive
      views, 132–3; illnesses, 33,
      107, 120, 127; insecurity in
      affairs of the heart, 39–40; lack
      of skill at card playing, 84, 89;
      loneliness and importance of
      letter writing, 21, 23, 32, 83,
      100–1; melancholy and inertia,
      22, 26; mood changes and
      procrastination, 15, 42, 62,
      124; passion for simplicity, 7,
      10, 16–17; physical
      appearance, *IV*, 7, 64; political
      moderation, 84; religious
      views, 5–6, 42, 84, 132; sense
      of humour, 21, 85, 119;
  gardening: constructs hermitage and
      "Gothick" alcove, 69–70;
      constructs ruinated priory,
      70–1; creates Virgil's Grove,
      meets artist Thomas Smith,
      63–6; inscriptions, 66-7, 70,
      72-1; placing of statues and
      memorial urns, 66–8, 95;
      vision of, 60–3, 72
  letters, extracts from: exchanging
      criticism and on everyday
      events, 32; on Dodsley, 113; on
      Edmund Spencer, 28; on effect
      of grief, 93; on effect of
      cousin's litigation, 127; on
      Lord Dudley, 100–1; on folly
      erected at Hagley Park, 71; on
      garden at Leasowes, 60–1, 62,
      63–4; on index to *The
      Schoolmistress,* 28; on La
      Motte, 112; on London
      entertainments (1742), 29; on
      love and his maid, 36; on own
      mental state, 26, 42; on plans
      for Leasowe park, 72; on
      reworkings of *The
      Schoolmistress,* 31; on Richard
      Graves' father, 16; on role as
      Justice of the Peace, 98; on
      Somervile's death, 30; on
      songs and on Handel, 76; on
      the art of writing letters, 45–6;
      on Thomas Smith, 65; on
      transcription of elegies, 78–9;
      the last letter, *XXIII*; to Miss
      "C," 39; to Thomas Gray on
      critical acceptance, 108; *see
      also* Luxborough Letters
  literary career: concern with process
      of writing, 85; early poetry,
      12–14; early unpublished
      poems, 5; edits Dodsley's
      Miscellanies, indecision over,
      101–8; elegies and
      prevarication over publication,
      78–80; illustrates dame school
      for *The Schoolmistress, VII*;
      inscription to housekeeper,
      Mary Arnold, 35; literary

passions, 9, 10; poems set to song, 75–7; publication and reception of *The Judgement of Hercules,* 24–5; reads at table at Hagley Hall and awaits Duchess of Somerset's response to poems sent, 80–1; riddle writing controversy, 23–4; seeks pension for services to literature, 127–8; thinks of publishing a collection of poems, 124; works on Dodsley's *Selected Fables,* doubts over, illustrates and writes index, 112-15; works with Percy on *Reliques,* 116–19, 123; writes epilogue to Dodsley's *Cleone,* 109–10, 111, 161–2; writes *Lines Written at an Inn at Henley,* 90–1; writes, revises and publishes *The Schoolmistress,* 27-31, 101-2

private and family life: at Leasowes, 32–3, 41, 73–4, 94; attends Pembroke College, Oxford, 5–6; childhood, early education and influences, 1–4, 14; comes down from Oxford, inherits Leasowes, 12; death of WS, 128-9; death of brother, 56–7, 92–4, 95; death of niece, 95; death of parents, 5; falls in love with Miss "C," 39; finances, 11, 17, 30; funeral and grave stone in Halesowen churchyard, *XXIV*, 55; has portrait painted, 125–6; memorial urn to, *XIX*, 131; moves to Leasowes, takes up country life, 19, 20–1; obituary notice, 129; portrait by Thomas Ross, *IV*; record of burial, *XIX*; relationship with Mary Arnold, his housekeeper, 33–5; relationship with Mary Cutler, his maid, 35–7; relationship with Mary Graves, 16, 18; Thomas Dolman's legal challenge to inheritance, 57–8, 107, 126–7; visits Dolman cousins (1745), 42–3; WS's Will and its consequences, 130–1

public life and friendships: death of LL, 100; death of Utrecia Smith, 18; death of Whistler and loss of letters to, 91–2, 100; death of William Somervile, 30; disagreement with Graves, 15; falls out with Hylton over practical joke, 120–1; falls out with Whistler, 88–90; friendship with Amos Green and James Woodhouse, 96–7; friendship with Anthony Whistler and Richard Graves, 8–11; friendship with James Thomson, 67–8; friendship with John Pixell and Lord Dudley, 86–7; friendship with John Scott Hylton, 87–8; friendship with LL, 20, 44, 45, 58–9, 75, 81; friendship with Richard Jago, 6; friendship with Thomas Hull and interest in theatre productions, 122–3; friendship with Thomas Percy and Humphrey Pitt, 116; friendship with Winnie Fletcher, 42–3; meets Sir George Lyttelton and William Pitt, 19; memorials after death, *XIX*, 13, 116, 123, 131; raises money for new church bells and quarrels with incumbent, 98–9; role as Justice of the Peace, 98; social life in last months of his life, 124–5, 127; visits Cheltenham Spa (1743), 38–9; visits Graves' household at Mickleton, 16–18, 32; visits London (1740) 22-3; (1741) 26; (1742) 29-30; (1744) 41-2; visits Lord Foley at Witley Court, 124–5; visits Radway, 69; visits Worcester (1740), 22

works: *Blackbirds, The*, 2; *Colimira*, 13; *Diamond, The*, 12–13; *Dying Kid, The*, 77; *Eighteenth Elegy*, 66; *Elegies*, 78–80, 81–2; *Elegy upon Autumn*, 94; *Elegy VIII*, 10, 82; *Elegy XI*, 81–2; *Elegy XV*, 12; *Elegy XXVI*, 80, 106–7; *Epilogue: to the Tragedy of Cleone*, 161-2; *Here, In Cool Grot*, 63–4, 156; *Impromptu to Miss Utrecia Smith*, 158; *Jemmy Dawson*, 77; *Judgement of Hercules, The*, 24–5; *Lines Written at an Inn at Henley*, 90–1, 154–5; *Love and Music*, 14; *Melpomené*, 110; *Ode to a Young Lady*, 82; *Ode to Memory*, 10; *On Taste*, 88; *Ophelia's Urn*, 18; *Pastoral Ballad, VIII*, 39–40, 77, 103, 104, 105; *Pastoral Ode, A*, 80– 1; *Pensees* (or *Men and Manners*), 6, 45–6, 75, 83–5, 163–4; *Poems on Several Occasions*, 12; *Progress of Taste, The*, 60; *Rural Elegance*, 14, 58, 61, 80, 95; *Schoolmistress, The*,

VII, 1, 9, 12, 21, 27–31, 101–2; *Slender's Ghost*, 77–8, 159–60; *Snuff Box, The*, 12–13; *Song XI*, 58; *Unconnected Thoughts on Gardening*, 62, 68, 69; *Upon a Visit to a Lady of Quality*, 77; *Verses to a Lady*, 13; *Verses Written Towards The Close of the Year 1748*, 20, 47, 68, 80; *Western Sky is Purpled O'er, The*, 76; *"When Bright Ophelia Treads the Green"*, 75;

collected works: *Collected Works*, *XXI*, 55; *Letters of William Shenstone*, 71; *Shenstone's Miscellany*, 101; *Works of William Shenstone*, *XV*, 75

Shuckborough, Ernest, 29

Slighted Nancy (song), 117

Smith, Admiral, 74

Smith, Thomas, 65

Smith, Utrecia, 17–18: memorial urn, *VI*: WS's poem dedicated to, 158

Solihull School, 1–4

Somerset, Duchess of, 58, 81

Somervile, William, *IV*, 3–4, 20, 44, 45: LL's memorial inscription to, 53–4; memorial urn to, *XV*; WS on, 30; works: *Chase, The*, 3

songs and ballads, 75–7, 82, 116–19, 123

Southcote, Philip, 61

spa towns, 7

Spanish Ballad, The, 118

Spanish Lady, The (musical play), 122

Spencer, Edmund, 2, 9, 28

Stanford, Lord, 127

statues and memorial urns at Leasowes, *XIV*, *XV*, 66–8, 95

Sun Rising Inn, Edgehill, 90

T

Temple of Pan at Leasowes, *XIII, XIV,*
69-70
Temple, Lord, 81, 87
Thomson, James, *XVI,* 20, 54, 67–8
Tom Bowling (song), 76
Trees and the Bramble (fable), 114

U

Ullenhall's Old Chapel, *IX*

V

Venus de Medici statue and inscription,
66
Vernon, William, *Parish Clerk,* 125
Virgil, *Aeneid,* 72
Virgil Travestie (burlesque), 9
Virgil's Grove, Leasowes, and visitors to,
XII, 63–6, 86, 93
Voltaire, *Mahomet,* 42

W

Walpole, Horace, 19: *Castle of Otranto,*
The, ix
Warwick Company of Comedians, 38
Warwickshire Coterie, 9–10, 47
Wheatley, Mary, *Original Poems on*
Several Occasions, 127
Whistler, Anthony, 29: death of, 91–2,
100; falls out with WS, 88–90;
friendship with WS, 8, 12, 42;
working breakfasts with WS,
9–10; WS introduces to Lady
Luxborough, 47; *works*:
Shuttlecock, The, 47
Whitchurch, 8, 89
Whitfield, George, 6
Williams, Dr Marjorie, 77, 131

Wilmot, Reverend Pynson, 55, 99
Wintle, Mr (perfumer), 22–3
Wolf and the Lamb, The, WS's index to,
115
Woodhouse, James, *XVIII,* 96–7, 129:
Poems on Sundry Occasions, 97
Wootton Wawn, 3–4
Worcester, 22, 42
Works of William Shenstone, XV, XXII, 75

Y

Young, Edward, *Night Thoughts,* 41

BY THE SAME AUTHOR

Rhyme on the Spray – Collected Verse

A Sense of Occasion – Mendelssohn in Birmingham

A Lady of Letters – A Biography of Catherine Hutton